PRAISE FOR
12 Steps of Self-Leadership

The *12 Steps of Self-Leadership* has all the elements that can help any motivated individual become a real Difference Maker in every aspect of life. The authors clearly map out the 12 steps necessary for doing the inner work that leads to genuine transformation. They incorporate the spiritual element without resorting to religion or dogma. There's a gentle encouragement in the writing that invites you to go deeper than you've probably gone before in exploring and identifying what's held you back in the past. The book appeals to different styles of readers by providing a succinct overview at the beginning of each chapter, with excellent questions and "stepping stones" (next actions) included at the end. In between is a wealth of information, stories and quotes to guide you about the particulars of each step. This is a comprehensive work that you don't read once and put on the shelf. It's a manual that you refer to often as you learn to step into your own greatness and live a life filled with purpose.

—*Meredith Bell, President, Performance Support Systems, Inc., Hayes, VA USA*

This was an exciting read! I can imagine leaders from many facets of life moving out of stagnation into the refreshing breeze, and even winds of change, as they engage with this material. I know that this is fruit produced out of the well tilled soil of your own lives and as such it has a clear ring of truth and authenticity.

I love the fact that you have taken the "old, old, story" of the 12 Step Process and recast it into a modern day process and understanding of the stages of vibrant growth. I have worked with hundreds of individuals in the recovery process over the past 30 years and I would have no hesitation in recommending this book to those now at the stage of moving beyond abstinence to embrace their true human potential.

—*Larry Larson, Certified Professional Counsellor/Psychotherapist, Recovery Centre for Addictions, Trauma and Families, Winnipeg, MB Canada*

12 STEPS OF SELF-LEADERSHIP

The Difference Maker's Guide to Living and Leading on Purpose

Doug Lester

with Cheryl Lester

 FriesenPress

Suite 300 - 990 Fort St
Victoria, BC, Canada, V8V 3K2
www.friesenpress.com

ISBN
978-1-4602-6893-3 (Hardcover)
978-1-4602-6894-0 (Paperback)
978-1-4602-6895-7 (eBook)

1. *Business & Economics, Leadership*
2. *Personal Growth, Success*
3. *Body, Mind & Spirit, Inspiration & Personal Growth*

Distributed to the trade by The Ingram Book Company

This book is dedicated to my wife Cheryl—my partner, friend, and muse.
Without her this book would never have come to life.

Contents

EXPLORATION   69

Step 4 - Discovering Treasures Within

Step 5 - Impact Assessment

PREPARATION   111

Step 6 - Divided No More

Step 7 - Integral Pause

APPLICATION   145

Step 8 - Call to Conscious Leadership

Step 9 - Purposeful Leading

Step 10 - Putting it all Together

Step 11 - Transformational Leadership

Step 12 - Keeping It Fresh

The Journey Continues...

Appreciation

Our Self-leadership journey over the last twenty-seven years has been influenced by many people, places, and opportunities. The dream of shaping our learning into a book began during our year-end visioning process two years ago. Thank you to all of those who encouraged and dialogued with us as the process took shape. We are forever grateful to all the authors and teachers whose wisdom is quoted as part of our book. Special thanks to the poets and agents who have granted permission to include their inspirational writing at the start of each chapter. Also thanks to those who have read portions of the manuscript and given us honest and helpful suggestions.

We are deeply grateful for all who have served, formally or informally, as our teachers and mentors along the journey of life and leadership. You, along with members of our family—particularly our four children (Stephanie, Jason, Heather, and James), their partners, and our grandkids already here and those yet to be born—have been, and no doubt will continue to be, important influencers for us, personally and professionally.

Special appreciation to our FriesenPress team—Daemon, Heather, Mary, Colin, and James—for the encouragement, advice, wisdom, and support during our first publishing experience.

To all the Difference Makers who have shaped and inspired us, and to other people around the globe willing to take steps toward becoming more effective Self-leaders in service to Self, others and the greater good, thank you!

Doug & Cheryl

INTRODUCTION

Open Your Eyes
By D.H. Lester

Open your eyes little one
There's so much more for you to see
Open your life little one
There's so much more for you to be
The Universe is calling you
To play a larger part
To live and lead intentionally
With body, mind and heart
The path you've travelled
Up to now has given you a key
Interpret well the treasure map
And find your destiny.[1]

Leading From Within

Welcome to *12 Steps of Self-Leadership.*

- Are you seeking a journey of Self-discovery and Self-development?

- Are you ready to break free?

- Do you feel you are capable of being and doing more?

- Are you tired of status quo living?

- Are you seeking a compelling purpose?

- Are you intrigued by the idea of being a Difference Maker?

If you answered 'yes' to one or more of these questions, then join us as we guide you on an exciting adventure toward realizing your true potential and being a Difference Maker.

We have written *12 Steps of Self-Leadership* to provide a map for courageous people like you who are ready to live and lead at new levels of engagement. Each Step of the *12 Steps* contains a concept that if fully embraced will change your life and your Difference Making Quotient™ (DMQ™) in life, work, and relationships. However, the sum of the parts of the *12 Steps* when integrated and practiced on a regular basis will be much more powerful than any one of the concepts on its own.

We realize there are many reasons why people come to Self-leadership programs. Some of you are reading this book because you are already on a journey of Self-discovery and Self-development and you are seeking to enhance your skills and add some new levels of understanding. Some of you have moments of discomfort and a sense that you are capable of more than you are asking of yourself. Others are comfortable in your present routines, but are intrigued by the idea of being a Difference Maker.

For many of you the need for change is crying out. You are drowning in a sea of boredom and drudgery. You need changes now in order to survive. You are struggling at work, at home, and in all aspects of life. You are angry, scared, confused, and desperate. You may look good on the outside, but you know that your inner life is out of control. You are at a point in your life when you have begun to question the path you have been on, your work, and your relationships. Just getting through the day is depleting you. You face real life issues and you need real life answers now. You are searching for a new way of being and doing that will give you a renewed sense of purpose.

Whatever brings you to this opportunity we invite you to explore what is possible if you commit to Self-leadership and an increased Difference Making Quotient. We have written this book with a Fast Track section for a quick overview of the Step. These executive summaries will serve as a quick read of the key elements, leadership value, and guiding principle of the Step, and give you a Foothold to anchor the concept, and act as a touchpoint in the future as you revisit the *12 Steps,* or focus in on one of the concepts as you continue to use the *12 Steps* as your Self-leadership handbook.

The questions and exercises at the end of the chapters are written in a way that allows you to use the Stepping Stones as a pathway to deepen your learning. We also offer light and lively Travel Tips statements that will encourage and guide you along the way.

As leaders, learners, and life and business partners, Cheryl and I have been 'writing' this book experientially for a combined total of 130 years and as leadership coaches for the last 20 years. Although I have done much of the actual writing, Cheryl has been a thought and writing partner every step of the way. Both of us experienced losses in childhood. Both of us have been through divorce. Both of us have been deeply involved in faith-based communities and spiritual study. We have lived and coached every concept we write about. Both of us have been involved in senior leadership positions in large organizations. We have coached and mentored leaders in Canada and over 55 other countries around the world. Through our work we've also created development programs and curriculum for management and board members within the not-for-profit sector, and led a number of workshops/retreats designed to help leaders develop inner awareness that increases outer effectiveness. Through early morning debates and midnight solitudes, through personal crises and relationship disasters, through leadership successes and business failures, we have traveled the Self-leadership path we are guiding you on. Through writing, coaching, mentoring and consulting, nationally and internationally, our ideas have been tested and enhanced in the crucible of reality.

For those of you who need immediate shifts in inner awareness and outer effectiveness, we have created a Fast Track section proceeding each of the Steps. These executive summaries will serve as a quick understanding of the key elements, leadership value, and guiding principle of the Step, and give you a Foothold to anchor the concept. These are by no means a replacement for doing the work of the Leadership Quest. As soon as you complete a quick overview we encourage you to circle back to the beginning and work the 12 Steps over the coming year.

As you interact with the concepts and use the 12 Steps as your Self-leadership handbook, the questions and exercises at the end of the chapters are written in a way that allows you to use the Stepping Stones as a pathway to deepen your learning. We also offer light and lively Travel Tips statements that will encourage and guide you along the way.

This book is designed to help you systematically build a set of skills and attitudes that will increase your DMQ in all aspects of your inner and outer life. Drawing from many of the greatest teachers and thought leaders of our time, our book will provide you with principles, concepts and practical Steps that will serve as a handbook for further learning and a reference for years to come.

We need to point out from the start that we are choosing to capitalize 'Self.' We believe each of you at your core is creative, resourceful, and whole. Your best Self is capable of much more than the small "s" social self that often flits through your life. Your current state of affairs and your DMQ directly correlate with how effectively you are Self-leading your FISC™— your own 'royal treasury' of Facts, Influences, SoulDNA™, and Characters that makes you 'you'. As you work with the Steps, increased Self-awareness will give you access to new levels of potential and transform your life from the inside out.

The *12 Steps of Self-Leadership* is a process, not just another book to be read and placed on your shelf. Learning to live from within while being fully engaged in the outer life is not a simple task. The noises and demands of the outer world and the frantic pace of living often push our best hopes and inner wisdom to the margins of our awareness. Yet the answer is not in escape from the outer world but in synergy. Self-awareness is best served through the interplay of the inner and outer worlds. Effective Self-leadership integrates and synergizes inner awareness with outer effectiveness.

Disrupting the Status Quo

Our home library is filled with leadership books from the best and brightest from the last forty years. Many, like *The 7 Habits of Highly Effective People*, have helped millions of leaders be more proactive and effective in life, work, and relationships. Yet in our own lives and in our work with leaders around the world we continue to find even some of the most thoughtful leaders are struggling to manage their inner lives and the complex outer demands. Much of the leadership development in the past has tended to focus on plans and solutions that are externally applied and measured.

Too much of current leadership thinking is action oriented and thought dominated. In order to be an effective Difference Maker you will need to go beneath the surface. We believe that the path to meaningful change and success as a leader demands much more of you and begins deep within. As Otto Scharmer puts it, "This blind spot concerns not the what and how—not what leaders do and how they do it—but the who: who are we and the inner place or source from which we operate, both individually and collectively."[2]

Otto's inner exploration has been inspired in part by an interview with Bill O'Brien, the late CEO of Hanover Insurance who stated, "The success of an intervention depends on the interior condition of the intervener."[3] In other words, as a leader your primary source of success will not be what you do or how you do it, but the inner place from which you lead.

It has been said, "If you always do what you've always done you'll always get what you've always got." For too long change catalysts have presented great workshops, and provided outstanding consulting, but it hasn't changed the core assumptions and daily practices of the individuals and the systems they are a part of. Real life is disruptive. To be fully alive and actively engaged it is necessary to embrace complexity and let go of the illusion of an external stability. True joy and meaningful engagement comes from accepting change as a given and welcoming complexity.

The basic premise of this book is that each of you is a product of genetics, environment, life experiences, attitudes, and beliefs creating a unique blend of resources and potential. The leader's quest is to truly know, understand, and manage your 'Self' with courage, spirituality, and wisdom through intentional coordination of the inner parts. With clear intention and mindful discipline, you will have the clarity to train the body, heart, and mind so that as a Self-leader you become more than the sum of the parts. A coordinated voice will emerge that will facilitate your nimbleness to live and lead in flow with purpose and effectiveness.

This book is not about surviving. It is about thriving. It is not about maintaining the status quo. Instead it is an invitation and a road map for a journey far beyond ordinary. Self-leadership is a quest to be fully present in life, work, and relationships through intentional practices and courageous decisions that increase awareness, authenticity, fulfillment, and effectiveness.

What makes this leadership quest unique is that in our *12 Steps of Self-Leadership* we will include psychology, spirituality, science, and business practice in an integrated journey that offers leaders, and those who aspire to lead, a practical, pragmatic road map that prepares each of you to lead with calm confidence, intuitive creativity, and meaningful practices that are efficient and effective.

For pragmatic realists this is a challenging path since routines and rugged individualism are built on the solid footing of the past. You will need to explore new ways of being so that you can move intuitively into the emerging future, which is dreamed into reality as you move forward. Seeing Self-leadership as an ongoing quest means leaving old views and trusted processes behind and venturing into an uncertain tomorrow. This book and the processes in it are designed to positively disrupt your status quo.

This is not a self-help book with a few new tools to help you manage the challenges and pressures of responsibility. Quite the contrary. This is a Self-liberation book that will awaken and equip you with the best you have to offer. True Self-leadership is about being a change-maker and catalyst in life, work, and relationships. This is your call to transformative leadership and conscious living. This is a leadership book inviting you to become a courageous champion of the 'both—and' life where both inner awareness and outer effectiveness weave a dynamic new fabric of life and leadership for the evolving world.

You do not have to choose between the inner and outer life. When you take charge of your unique blend of energies, beliefs, facts, influences, parts, and traits that make you

'You' and become a Self-leader you can live in a seamless flow—being aware of and benefitting from inner wisdom while leading effectively in the midst of real time demands. To do this will require a level of introspection and honesty that is rare in the competitive world of business and organizational leadership. The *12 Steps* is an invitation to leave the crowd, do the work to examine your life, and proactively and intentionally take charge of the only one you can truly lead—yourself.

We invite you to take the next steps in your emotional-social growth and become a change agent for yourself and others. We invite you to follow a path of learning and transformation. Let go of the shoulds and if-onlys. Open your heart, mind and essential core to becoming all that you know—or don't yet know—that you can be.

It's Not a One-Time Journey

The practices of the hero's journey of Self-leadership are not a one-time solution to the challenge of authentic living and integral awareness. Poet and novelist E.E. Cummings, whose life and writing often went against the flow wrote, "To be nobody but yourself in a world which is doing its best day and night to make you like everybody else means to fight the hardest battle which any human being can fight and never stop fighting."[4]

There will be defining moments in your life just as there were in the lives of Moses, Buddha, Jesus, Mohammed, Tama Kieves, Parker J. Palmer, Cheryl Strayed, Buckminster Fuller, Scott Peck or any other leader, but the real impact of choosing the "road less traveled" is that you will be living fully with purpose and passion. Each new day will be an invitation to transformative living. It takes courage to answer the call—especially on the days when your energy is low and the road is rough. The world is waiting anxiously for people like you to accept the challenge to do the personal work so that you can help lead us forward with integrity and strength.

For some of you this will be a process that you can integrate with your present work; the *12 Steps* will enhance and enrich the work you are already doing. For others this work will be more disruptive. Working your way through the Steps will cause you to realize that, in order to respect the dignity and sanctity of your authentic Self and the people you care most about, radical changes will be required.

It takes great courage to step away from what others may see as success to recalibrate and integrate all the parts of your Inner Treasury. It will require you to accept the lonely yet rewarding call to a hero's journey in order to do the work we will set out for you in *12 Steps of Self-Leadership*.

Why the 12 Steps?

Our goal with *12 Steps* is to take the wisdom of great teachers and thought leaders, and share experience-proven concepts with you in ways that will support and enhance the effectiveness of veteran leaders while serving as a life map and guide for those who are just starting on the transformative journey of Self-discovery and personal growth.

Joseph Campbell's *12 Step Hero's Journey* and AA's twelve steps have both helped shape our thinking.

To embark on the inner journey of becoming a courageous Self-leader involves a quest to explore who you are and what your work really is. As we studied the elements of leadership, Joseph Campbell's summary of the hero's journey became a model for our program of leadership exploration and courageous manifestation of new ways of being and doing.

For heroes to begin their journeys, they must be called away from the ordinary into an adventure of challenge and discovery. Success on the hero's quest is life-changing—for them and often for many others. By undertaking the quest and being transformed, the hero returns bringing new insights and new skills. The hero returns having grown in spirit and strength. They have proved themselves worthy of even bigger things and often become important leaders in bringing change and making a difference in their community. This is what we envision for you.

The *12 Steps of Self-Leadership* is a set of principles and practices that invites you to explore what is possible in your life. These principles and practices are based on years of working with leaders in many different settings. We also draw inspiration and wisdom from many great philosophers, coaches, and teachers who have shared their wisdom with the world. We are not watching from the sidelines. We have traveled the transformative path individually and as a leadership team. We are still on the journey of learning and transformation as well. We are not just shaping a process, the process is shaping us. Each day, as we read and learn, lead, explore and discuss, we continue on our own purposeful quest to live and lead effectively with dignity and respect for Self, others, and this precious planet we call home.

Our starting point is a belief that in spite of unlimited inner potential most of us lose contact with many aspects of who we truly are through traumas and disappointments during early childhood or in the chaotic formative years as we struggle for acceptance and material success. We also believe that each person is a complex mix of inner and outer skills and preferences. We believe Self-leadership begins with a thorough knowledge and mastery of the inner life informed by the honest appraisals of the effectiveness of our work and our relationships with Self and others. Our Self-leadership Program provides a process of discovery and inner transformation that will empower all those who want to be Difference Makers through living empowered lives with purpose and meaning.

Henry David Thoreau, in the 1840's stated, "The mass of people lead lives of quiet desperation."[5] We believe it doesn't have to be that way. Pioneers like Joseph Campbell, Carl Jung, William Glasser, Robert Quinn, Martha Beck, Stephen R. Covey, and a host of more recent leadership and relationship experts have opened up exciting new possibilities for inner awareness and outer effectiveness in all aspects of life, work, and relationships.

We want to help you take the steps that will allow you to benefit from our years of study, living, counseling, and coaching. We believe there is a universal organizing energetic intelligence, or life force, that co-creates with each individual. This life force is both within each of us and in every atom in the universe. It is both a part of us and beyond us. For the purposes of this book we will refer to this life force as the Energy of Life. We invite you to let us be your mentor-coaches or guides as you embark on new levels of co-creation, surrender, practicality, and possibility. We believe a connection with a Power Beyond Ourselves is essential in connecting with our full potential. We don't see this Energy of Life as an entity but more as a profound mystery that opens our hearts and minds, and fills us with awe and gratitude. For some of you, your belief in a Divine Entity or God gives your life meaning and purpose. For some of you, embracing Infinite Mystery, Energy of Life, or the concept of a power beyond yourself may be a challenging new experience.

When we speak of Self-leadership we are talking about weaving a fabric of life that has strong vertical and horizontal elements that create balance and strength. The vertical energy comes from a calm contented mind, a growing awareness of an integrated Self that is creative, resourceful, and whole, with a vibrant continuous connection with the Energy of Life. The horizontal energy comes from a well-nourished body, the support of friends and family through meaningful relationships, important work, and a continuous co-creative connection with community.

As you work the *12 Steps of Self-Leadership* you will develop new principles and practices and strengthen and refine others that have served you well. You will begin to connect more powerfully with the Energy of Life, yourself, and others. You will take ownership and responsibility as CEO of Self Inc.™, your own unique contribution to the world. You will experience greater aliveness and an increased willingness and effectiveness in contributing to the larger community.

Although the comments and concepts in *12 Steps of Self-Leadership* will be helpful, the real benefits will be in the doing. You may read through the book quickly and smile and nod. You might even have an 'aha moment' or a tear, but flying over a country at high altitude is not the same as backpacking across the country for thirty days in an experience like the pilgrims on the El Camino de Santiago. Real awareness involves sweat and blisters, unexpected encounters, struggles and insights along the path. As a runner, I have read hundreds of running magazines and the articles have been very inspiring and informative, but it wasn't until I bought the recommended shoes and ran the recommended miles that I developed the strength, skill, and stamina to run my first marathon.

We are inviting you to live large. Not in a selfish 'me first' kind of way, but in a seize the moment, laugh out loud, cry when you're sad, dance every day, be the change, shine your light, embrace life, love your neighbour and yourself, authentic way.

William Hutchison Murray, a Scottish mountaineer and writer who wrote an entire book on rough toilet paper while in a German prisoner of war camp wrote,

Until one is committed, there is hesitancy, the chance to draw back, always ineffectiveness. Concerning all acts of initiative (and creation), there is one elementary truth, the ignorance of which kills countless ideas and splendid plans: that the moment one definitely commits oneself, then Providence moves too. All sorts of things occur to help one that would never otherwise have occurred. A whole stream of events issues from the decision, raising in one's favour all manner of unforeseen incidents and meetings and material assistance, which no man could have dreamt would have come his way.[6]

Our *12 Step* process is not a lock step, climb up a mountain, program. It is a guided process with proven Steps to increase your awareness and your effectiveness. Empowered living involves all aspects of human development—heart, mind, body, and spirit. As you work through the *12 Steps* it is important to develop daily practices to increase your awareness and capacity in each of these areas.

Just like people working the 12 Steps of Alcoholics Anonymous, most of you will be able to work more than one step at a time. Even though you may be struggling to connect with the mystery of life in Step 2 you may already be helping others live more fulfilled and integrated lives through Step 11. As you know from your leadership experiences of the past, we learn best through doing and by failing. As Dr. David Burns, the author of *The Feeling Good Handbook,* teaches in his workshops, the secret to success is to try many things, fail often, fail quickly, and keep trying new approaches until you find what works. This ability to prototype and learn in real time will make the processes and practices grounded and real all along the path. The *12 Steps* is not about perfection. It is about dancing in the moment with reality as your mentor.

12 Steps of Self-Leadership is a process of waking up and experiencing your best life. It is both a daily process of awareness and gratitude and a lifelong quest made up of small consistent transformational steps that shake up your world and enlarge your perspective. Along the path you may have the occasional epiphany that changes your worldview in an instant, but for the most part it will be a continual disciplined process of working the Steps and repeating the process again and again until new attitudes and behaviours become comfortable and rewarding.

Awareness has its own special set of metaphysical muscles that improve with exercise. Each time you shift your state of awareness you build capacity to move to a new stage of development. As you reach new stages of consciousness each one is like a plateau on a mountain path. As your vista enlarges you will be able to see new possibilities for increased awareness and increased effectiveness in your relationships and activities. In these moments of pause and reflection you will realize how far you have come and realize that the path still rises ahead into the mist and invites you to continue to advance.

As you travel with us, keep in mind the principles of sowing and reaping. The soil may need preparation. Seeds don't thrive on hot pavement or busy paths. It is not wise to keep digging up the seeds to see how they are doing. There is mystery in the process of germination and sprouting. When you prepare the soil, plant good seeds, and care for the field you will harvest more than you sow. You are a field of infinite possibility.

The ideas and exercises in this book are like seeds. Some of the concepts we share will seem very simple, perhaps even repetitive. Don't be fooled by impatience. It's OK if you choose to run ahead or look off the path if you're curious or bored, but be aware that shifts in consciousness and energy happen over time. Deep insights and true transformation occur when you walk slowly and listen carefully allowing the new life to sprout deep within your being. As you awaken to new levels of spirit and understanding you will begin to notice that in both thought and action you are growing stronger and wiser.

The 12 Step Path

The *12 Steps of Self-Leadership* — and the concepts upon which the steps are built — is organized into four sections:

Steps 1–3:   Invitation

Steps 4–5:   Exploration

Steps 6–7:   Preparation

Steps 8–12:   Application

Here are the *12 Steps* Sections and Concepts:

INVITATION

- Step 1 — The Birth of Awareness: As a leader I sense the need to lead from a place of greater awareness, integrity, effectiveness, and purpose.

- Step 2 — Doorway to Possibility: I open myself to my full potential by seeking to live an integrated, vibrant, Self-authored life.

- Step 3 — Crossing the Threshold: I commit to trusting both Self and other wisdom as I embark on the journey of exploring, discovering, and integrating my inner and outer life.

EXPLORATION

- Step 4 — Discovering Treasures Within: I acknowledge the Facts, and Influences, SoulDNA, and Characters that have shaped me and continue to affect my Difference Making Quotient.

- Step 5 — Impact Assessment: I conduct an honest and transparent review of who I've been, what I've done, what I've not done, what I have ignored, and what I have hidden away.

PREPARATION

- Step 6 — Divided No More: I take restorative action to address attitudes, behaviours, wounds, or barriers that diminish my DMQ.

- Step 7 — Integral Pause: I regularly engage in times of pause, retreat, and reflection.

APPLICATION

- Step 8 — Call to Conscious Leadership: I accept the call to effectively manage, develop, and employ the elements of my FISC in conscious service to Self, others, and the greater good.

- Step 9 — Purposeful Leading: I clarify my purpose in order to effectively contribute to the well-being of Self and the systems that I am part of.

- Step 10 — Putting it all Together: I actively engage in regular planning and review to manage and monitor my ability to make a difference.

- Step 11 — Transformational Leadership: As a leader, I inspire, engage, empower, and facilitate transformational change in the world—individually and collectively.

- Step 12 — Keeping It Fresh: I intentionally Self-lead in ways that inspire, engage, and transform my evolving effectiveness as a Difference Maker.

We look forward to sharing this journey of inspiration, engagement, and transformation with you.

FOUNDATIONS

How to Climb a Mountain
By Maya Stein

Make no mistake. This will be an exercise in staying vertical.
Yes, there will be a view, later, a wide swath of open sky,
but in the meantime: tree and stone. If you're lucky, a hawk will
coast overhead, scanning the forest floor. If you're lucky,
a set of wildflowers will keep you cheerful. Mostly, though,
a steady sweat, your heart fluttering indelicately, a solid ache
perforating your calves. This is called work, what you will come to know,
eventually and simply, as movement, as all the evidence you need to make
your way. Forget where you were. That story is no longer true.
Level your gaze to the trail you're on, and even the dark won't stop you.[7]

Preparation for the Journey

Although there will be learning and training all along the way, there are some foundational Self-leadership attitudes and beliefs that will be helpful as you start the work. Although we speak of Steps, the central metaphor for this work is really a winding pathway through a challenging and at times unfamiliar terrain—the inner space of emotional, spiritual, and metaphysical beliefs, attitudes, and experiences, and the outer spaces of the facts and influences, challenges and opportunities of your life. Venturing beyond the familiar into new ways of seeing and experiencing life and leadership will take you on a challenging path that will at times cause you to stumble and lose your footing; at other times it will open up new vistas that will inspire and strengthen you. Take heart, Cheryl and I, and the leaders we will introduce you to in this book have benefitted from traveling a similar route.

We live in an exciting time of change and renewal as global consciousness is increasing and our planet's ability to sustain life is stretched and strained. To benefit from the rapid shifts that are occurring and be a student of the possible, it will be necessary for you to learn how to hold a space for transforming conversations, both inner and outer, from debate to dialogue, from isolation to collaboration. This sounds much easier than it is. We mention it now to stimulate your internal dialogue. You will be challenged again and again on the Self-leadership quest, by your own biases and habits, to move from recycling old thoughts and responses to living creatively in the moment and leaning into the emerging future.

In *Leading from the Emerging Future*, Otto Scharmer writes,

> Modern society emerges from the interplay of two powerful social fields: presencing and absencing. The field of presencing works through the opening of the mind, heart, and the will. We know there are many inspiring stories of this across the planet. But everyone who works in institutions and systems also knows there is another field out there. That field is characterized by getting stuck with the idea that there is only One Truth rather than operating with an open mind, by getting stuck in Us versus Them rather than operating with an open heart, and by being frozen inside one rigid identity rather than operating with an open will. What do we call social systems that have these three characteristics? Fundamentalist. Fundamentalism is the result of closing down and freezing our mind, heart, and will—as opposed to opening, warming, and illuminating them.[8]

Most leaders realize that fundamentalist beliefs and warring factions can only lead to pain and destruction, yet many of us are still developing our ability to engage fully as global citizens interested in a larger conversation. As you examine your foundational beliefs and attitudes we ask you to open yourself to possibilities of other views. Begin to sort through your baggage. Be curious. Hold your present perspectives lightly. Live the questions as you grow into the answers.

Steve Jobs said,

> Your time is limited, so don't waste it living someone else's life. Don't be trapped by dogma—which is living with the results of other people's thinking. Don't let the noise of other's opinions drown out your own inner voice. And most important, have the courage to follow your heart and intuition. They somehow already know what you truly want to become. Everything else is secondary.[9]

Difference Making Quotient (DMQ) Quiz

The Difference Making Quotient™ Quiz is a simple tool we've developed that is designed to help you assess and reflect on your DMQ™. Your results help you identify those areas of your performance as CEO of Self, Inc. where you are strong as well as those that calling for your attention and action. There is no limit on the number of times that you can use the DMQ Quiz link, so we encourage you to complete the online quiz at the beginning of your Self-leadership journey, and again (and again if you like) as you move along the path. You can find the DMQ Quiz at www.eagletreeleadership.ca/DMQQuiz/.

Travel Jargon

- Difference Making Quotient™ — The level of your effectiveness in using *12 Steps of Self-Leadership* to manage, develop and employ the elements of your FISC™ and provide conscious and transformational leadership in service to Self, others, and the greater good.

- DMQ™ = (Facts + Influences + SoulDNA™ + Characters) x Self-leadership — This is not meant to be a formula as much as a concept that your Difference Making Quotient is directly correlated to the level of your Self-Leadership awareness, ownership, and management of your Facts, Influences, SoulDNA™, and Characters.

- Emerging Future — The well-being potential of our Selves, our global community and the planetary ecosystems—the space created by suspending judgement, letting go of the past, and leaning into the future that wants to emerge in, around, and through us.

- Energy of Life — a universal organizing energetic intelligence or life force that co-creates with each individual.

- FISC™ — Your FISC™ is a unique treasury that, when acknowledged and coordinated by your inner CEO, equips you to excel. The "fisc" was the emperor's treasury. In more recent times the fisc became the name used for the knight's money holder as he set off on his quest. Properly appropriated and refined, your Facts, Influences, SoulDNA™, and Characters (your FISC™) will show you your purpose and equip you to show up with confidence and a unique essence.

  - FACTS — Data related to the details and realities of your life and circumstances from the earliest to the present.

  - INFLUENCES — Persons, events, or things that affected and/or continue to affect your actions, behaviours, and beliefs—positively or negatively. Influences can include people, relationships, genetics, religion, culture, education, or experiences.

  - SoulDNA™ — The unique essence and distinctive qualities, gifts, and abilities that were often evident in you from your time of birth.

  - CHARACTERS — Different points of view offered through your 'inner selves', voices, archetypes, and ego states.

- Purpose — The positive energetic difference you uniquely contribute to life, work, and relationships. The 'why' of your existence that guides your leadership. The difference you can make when you're in flow.

- Greater Good — The best outcomes we can achieve—individually and collectively—for the care, development, and management of Self, others, and the relational and living systems we are part of.

- Small 's' self — A poor representation of your potential—sometimes referred to as social or false self—that is primarily influenced by social expectations. It is fragmented, chaotic, dysfunctional, under managed, unaware, with unknown inner parts and an excessive need for external validation.

- Big 'S' Self — The confident, coordinating, organizing Self —the lead Character, the CEO—who provides a proactive, collaborative, conscious, and transformational style of leadership and takes responsibility for the overall operations, development, and performance of Self, Inc.™.

- Self-leadership — The act of engaging in processes and practices that synergize the elements of your FISC and increase your Difference Making Quotient™ in service to Self, others, and the greater good.

- Self, Inc.™ — The system of 'You' that is equipped to meet a need and pursue individual and collective goals through effective management and utilization of resources. Self, Inc.™ is an interactive system that affects and is affected by its internal and external environments.

· Vision — Your best hope for the emerging future.

Moving Along the Path

The Self-leadership work at the end of each Step is not just an 'add-on'. This is where you will gain your real benefits from personalizing the work. In these sections, we will offer a number of questions, queries, and discussion starters. We encourage you to get a special Self-leadership journal that will be your log book for this exploration. Journal at least once a day with whatever comes to mind. As you read, copy quotes, doodle, draw pictures, and explore possibilities. The **Moving along the Path** sections at the end of each Step will contain two sections.

Stepping Stones will involve a series of questions and exercises that will deepen and extend your understanding and embodiment of the concepts in the Step.

Travel Tips will offer additional encouragement and support on your journey.

New Perspectives

As leaders, too often we get caught up in the constant barrage of information about our failings as humans and the challenges of health and well-being that impact us personally and collectively and forget that life in all its rawness is the material from which our heroic journeys are shaped. We can become hypnotized by the incessant spinning of decisions, demands, possibilities, and opportunities. Our progress can be arrested. We can become entrenched or overwhelmed.

There is no one simple solution to the complexities of life, but there are many processes of discovery and awakening that can address the issues of a fragmented self and provide a framework for building a life that has meaning and purpose. In this book, we invite you to embark upon a courageous journey of creating and discovering, of visioning and remembering, of hoping and achieving.

Freedom doesn't necessarily come easily, for the truth is not the exclusive possession of any religious or philosophical perspective. Each of us drags a bag with us that contains the beliefs and traditions of our family, our culture, our community, and country. We encourage those joining us on this life quest to take only the most basic beliefs about Self and others as a starting point. True wholeness and authenticity is as much about letting go of the extraneous as it is about reaching out for something new.

This book is inspired and encouraged by the hopeful dialogue that we see developing between young and old, rich and poor from all parts of the globe, allowing Difference Makers of all ages to move beyond the materialism and politics that have kept people focused on the trivial while the essence of life is whispering in the breeze. We believe that there is a better way. We want to join you and other leaders in being part of the solution.

As Rumi wrote in the thirteenth century:

> Out beyond ideas of wrongdoing and right doing,
> there is a field. I will meet you there.
> When the soul lies down in that grass,
> the world is too full to talk about
> language, ideas, even the phrase each other
> doesn't make any sense.[10]

It is in this safe space that we invite you to begin this Self-leadership quest. Enter into this place where all the parts of your complex Self can "lie down in the grass" and prepare to explore a life of deeper meaning and renewed purpose. In this safe place, we encourage you to breathe deeply and open yourself in new ways to connect to the Energy of Life and to your unique inner resources. Move forward in spite of the voices of judgement, cynicism, and fear and trust the process. Our program is spiritual at its core. We believe that there is a God of Creation who lives beyond religion. We posit that a belief in a power greater than ourselves is a key element in moving beyond the existential angst that leads many today to see life as a meaningless drama that has no purpose. We believe that the Global Village calls people of all faith groups to enlarge their tents and let go of the beliefs that create 'Us and Them' divisions. Self-leadership is a call to a larger view of life and a more dynamic relationship with the Energy of Life, by whatever name—God, Allah, Infinite Wisdom, Yahweh, Bhagavān, All-Powerful, Atman, Energy of Life, Integrity, or Source—you use to describe that which initiated and continues to energize life as we know it. We are inviting you to look at life through a new broader perspective beyond a particular creed or ideology seeking only to be open to the inner call to wholeness and joy.

Guides

On any exploration of new terrain it is advisable to work with a guide at least part of the time. As you embark on this Self-leadership journey we will guide you with our thoughts and experiences and share stories of our learning. We will introduce you to heroic trailblazers who have traveled this path before us and share thoughts and experiences to inspire and encourage you.

It is our goal through this book to be one of your guides, but it will be necessary at some points for you to have someone else in real time that can hold you accountable, challenge your assumptions, and celebrate your insights. Some of you may be blessed with a wise and caring friend who can serve as a mentor and support during parts of your Self-leadership quest. However, when you get into the deeply personal aspects of the difficult things in your life it is challenging to mix friendship and accountability without temptations to rescue or fix. Often your growth will be better served by the support of a professional coach.

Ultimately though, each of you is on your own quest and although the principles and stages of the Self-leadership journey are common, the Facts, Influences, SoulDNA, and Characters are different for each of you. Choose your guides wisely. The ultimate wisdom needs to come from your evolving Self as you lean into the emerging future and are energized by the Energy of Life and a courageous willingness to follow what is trying to happen in the nexus between you and the world.

Self

Although it has been accepted for a long time that our inner consciousness is populated by a number of voices and Characters, the idea of a coordinating Self is still not widely understood. While working with families and individuals, Dr. Richard Schwartz, who developed Internal Family Systems, discovered that the "coordinating Self, which embodies qualities of confidence, openness, and compassion, acts as a centre around which the various parts constellate."[11] Whether that Sef functions well as a coordinator or is ignored and pushed aside is up to the level of inner awareness and Self-leadership you develop and practise as CEO of Self, Inc. In the past, when one Character from the inner parts—whether that was your inner critic, vulnerable child, prostitute, or warrior—was having a major meltdown in the foyer of Self, Inc. and the screaming and angst was so great that the whole of Self, Inc. was in absolute chaos, the truth of the matter was that the Character in question had either bullied or tantrumed their way into the CEO's office and demanded or assumed illegitimate leadership. It doesn't have to be that way.

The premise of our book is that you are in choice and when you choose to Self- lead you develop the inner awareness and skill to manage all aspects of your inner life, so that you can show up with new levels of consciousness and effectiveness in your outer life.

As CEO of Self, Inc. you have the responsibility as a Difference Maker to learn new skills and use your awareness and intervention skills to deal with such emotional outages. As a confident, coordinating, organizing Self—the lead Character, the CEO—who provides a proactive, collaborative, conscious, and transformational style of leadership, you can take responsibility for the overall operations, development, and performance of Self, Inc. The Steps in this book will help you develop an inner alignment that will give each of the inner Characters a sense of purpose even in the most challenging of circumstances.

As CEO of Self, Inc. you have the opportunity and responsibility to develop the practices, disciplines, awareness, and skill that allows you to lead calmly and effectively in all aspects of your life, work, and relationships. You are the person in charge. You get to decide how well you perform. The *12 Steps of Self-Leadership* will help you increase your capacity to lead Self, Inc. with a calm confidence in service to Self, others, and the systems of which you are part.

As CEO of Self, Inc. you are always in choice. You are in choice of the strategic and operating plans, the vision, determining the UVP (unique value proposition), the allocation of resources necessary to achieving defined objectives, and the development of your inner resources, i.e. the elements of your FISC. You get to decide the intentions of your daily practices, and priorities as well as the larger picture, longer term goals and objectives. All of this will become clearer as you disrupt the status quo and participate in the *12 Steps of Self-Leadership*.

Ego

For a long time the ego has been the villain in every leadership drama. Writers, speakers, leadership experts, and spiritual teachers have led us to believe that if you would only beat this part of you called ego into submission, or even get rid of it all together, you would be a better person and all your issues of pride, self-centredness, greed, and entitlement would be gone.

Here's the good news and the bad news. The ego isn't going anywhere. It is an important part of your Characters that can add value to your understanding. The more you resist parts of yourself, the more risk there is that these shunned aspects of your inner being will go into the shadows and show up in ways that will reduce your effectiveness as a leader. In the Freudian model the ego is simply the "I" that is aware and mediates between the inner desires, the spiritual urges, and reality to allow the mind to choose behaviours that are most appropriate for the moment.

Whether it is the id, ego, or super-ego, these symbolic concepts allow us to talk about the ways we show up in life, work, and relationships. Thinkers and teachers since Socrates have discussed the inner elements that are part of the complex urges and responses of the conscious human. As a Self-leader we encourage you to see yourself as a complex organism with desires, needs, aspirations, impulses, and appetites that, without awareness and leadership, will create chaos. Without thoughtful intentional Self-leadership, inner parts of your character may dominate, resulting in a limited, small 's" self, a limited behaviour repertoire, and a fragmented version of your true Self, one that lacks awareness and does not serve the best possibilities of a conscious leader.

As you work your way through the *12 Steps* you will become aware of ways in which your choices have been less than ideal. You will realize that you have let parts of you bring in elements of greed, instant gratification, fear, pride, competition, or any number of behaviours that keep you from showing up fully as your best Self.

The real issue as stated by Cindy Wigglesworth is, "Who is driving your life? Are you driven by an immature, short-sighted ego?" In *SQ21: The Twenty-One Skills of Spiritual Intelligence*, Cindy goes on to say that the ego can also mature through conscious leadership and that as we do our Self-development work the ego serves Self in very important ways. Using a car metaphor she says that the ego serves as navigator to the best Self, but should never be entrusted to drive. She writes, "It is important that ego is the navigator—it has not been thrown out of the car or shut in the trunk. My belief is that the ego is a healthy and natural aspect of the self ...We need the ego to be mature and we need the ego to be present in order for us to navigate the world."[12]

Each of you has a 'parent' ego state that contains the 'shoulds', 'musts', and 'should-nots' accumulated during your early years. Some of these powerful beliefs and attitudes are in your awareness but most exist beneath the surface. You have a 'child' ego state filled with memories of delight and hurt, pictures and bodily memories from every stage of your early life that still shape your hopes and fears. You also have an 'adult' ego state that ideally acts to allow you to calmly take in information and coordinate your responses in every situation.

Each of these aspects of your ego has both positive and negative elements and in your inner world they create some of the voices and inner Characters that you will learn to identify and lead in Steps 4, 5, and 6.

Going Inside

We will expand on the inner aspects of your Facts, Influences, SoulDNA, and Characters as you do the exploration work in Steps 4 and 5, but as you prepare for the Self-leadership quest it is important to begin to experience your inner life as more influential than you may have previously allowed yourself to admit. Many of you have been acting out a leadership script that says that results are all that matter. In many families, organizations, and businesses the outer focus and bottom line can lead you away from listening to or appreciating the inner life. You may even accept some of the get tough slogans used to prop up such an external view—ideas, like real leaders don't wear their hearts on their sleeves or cry over spilt milk, and slogans such as, "Suck it up", "Stand tall" and "Don't sweat the small stuff." If you have ignored your inner life and have pushed yourself through panic and stress, believing endurance is a necessary skill and the price of leadership success, you and your best Self are about to experience a sigh of relief.

In order to Self-lead with confidence and effectiveness you need to realize much of your life is happening beneath the surface. Our understanding of the inner life has been influenced by the work of Dr. Richard Schwartz and the previously mentioned Internal Family Systems (IFS), which were developed in response to his clients' descriptions of experiencing various parts–many extreme–within themselves.

> He noticed that when these parts felt safe and had their concerns addressed, they were less disruptive and would accede to the wise leadership of what Dr. Schwartz came to call the 'Self.' In developing IFS, he recognized that, as in systemic family

theory, parts take on characteristic roles that help define the inner world of the client. The coordinating Self, which embodies qualities of confidence, openness, and compassion, acts as a centre around which the various parts constellate.[13]

Expanding on these concepts, we invite you to begin to develop your concept of Self and to explore your inner Characters with curiosity and deep respect. We will help you realize that you as well as the people you lead and interact with have a rich multi-faceted interior which, when explored and developed, brings healing, joy, creativity, wisdom, energy, and innovation.

It is our belief that inner awareness and outer effectiveness are integrally linked in a feedback loop. When you lose connection with either the inner or outer perspectives you become disconnected from the rich interplay and synergy that each viewpoint brings, becoming entrenched, overwhelmed, and living shallowly from a reactive polarized perspective. Self-leadership is a call to serve both Self and others through more comprehensive perspectives of inner and outer life.

Stages of Development

Our openness to complexity shifts over time. When I first tried to read Neale Donald Walsch's book, *Conversations with God* in 1995, I was not ready. Neale's experiences and spiritual beliefs challenged my ideology so I pushed the book aside. Twelve years later when I watched Neale's story in the movie *Conversations with God*, I found I was no longer edged against Neale's experience. I was now able to read his book and understand what Neale Walsch had experienced—I got it. My spiritual emotional journey during a decade had transformed my openness and my inner life. I was at a new stage of spirituality. My perspective had shifted.

Each of you is on a developmental path. There are many different ways of expressing the process but one that we have found very helpful is the four stages of development from M. Scott Peck's book, *The Different Drum*.

Using M. Scott's framework, here is how we describe the four stages of development on the Self-leadership journey:

Stage One is the chaotic/antisocial. Most people experience elements of this during early childhood and the teenage years. In this stage it is all about "me." We may act loving or disciplined in order to serve our purposes but it is not coming from inner principles. We may act calmly on the outside but we are often terrified and out of control on the inside. In this stage we can be very disordered and reckless and rebel against others' expectations. Our sense of spirituality is lacking. We are seldom in touch with our authentic Self and have no real connection with the the Energy of Life. Most people naturally grow out of this stage by early adulthood. Many of those who do not, end up struggling for years unless highly organized religion, meaningful work, the military, prison, or a recovery group helps them move to Stage Two.

Some of you have learned to dress for success and have developed the outer skills to live a life that seems ordered and meaningful to most of those around you, but inside you live in chaos and the older you get the harder it is to maintain the illusion of having it together. The *12 Steps* will help you move to new levels of awareness and effectiveness.

Stage Two is the formal/institutional. For people in this stage, routines, traditions, group mission, protocols, and hierarchy are a life raft or fortress. Any change to the accepted approach will be vigorously defended and there is a strong tendency toward a 'we/they' mentality. For those of us who grew up in an organizational environment most of the beliefs and attitudes were accepted without question. For those of us who found sanity and safety in the organization as we escaped from a life of chaos, the formal/organizational stage is embraced with even fiercer loyalty.

The organization frees us from the burden of constant decision-making by giving us a set of prescribed views packaged and promoted with a focus on helping those in chaos and keeping them safe from the errors of the skeptical and the woo-woo of the mystics. Routines, policy manuals, and guidebooks like the *The Big Book* of Alcoholics Anonymous become sacred. Uniforms or dress codes give a sense of belonging. Blue jeans and a tattered shirt can be just as important as a little black dress or a tailored suit. For the religious in this stage, God is an external being—a giant benevolent all-knowing power in the sky. For the scientific in Stage Two there has developed a strident atheism popularized by people like Richard Dawkins. Adherents to this line of belief are as a loyal to their cause as any soccer fan or religious fundamentalist. The majority of good, law-abiding citizens never move out of Stage Two. People in the formal/organizational stage are helpful toward Stage Ones and threatened by Stage Threes and Fours.

If the organizational framework helps you live well, the Self-leadership journey does not require you to abandon the benefits you gain from a structured life. However, for you the challenge of the quest is to open your heart and mind to other perspectives, learn to lead your inner parts and to become more real with the people in your circles of influence and more accepting to those who see life differently.

Stage Three is the scientific skeptic/individual stage. At this stage people ask why and begin to see contradictions in the rules and practices of their organization or affinity group. Faith groups, recovery groups, and organizations see questioners as troublemakers and often encourage them to find a different group or workplace. Religious groups see skeptics as rejecting faith and often people in this stage feel conflicted and disoriented. In this stage, skeptics are unwilling or unable to accept pat answers and see the inconsistencies in themselves and others.

During the scientific skeptical/questioning stage some people are enlivened and excited as they break free from traditional faith and creatively explore science and a world of unlimited possibility. Others are simply disillusioned and struggle for a long time in denial of their own evolution, staying in the organization and trying to conform to the tribal expectations thinking that perhaps they are flawed because they ask so many uncomfortable questions and thinking if they try harder perhaps they could learn how to fit in.

Whether you are comfortably part of the skeptical/questioning group or a disconnected exile from Stage Two seeking stability, the Self-leadership quest will help you find new discoveries all along the path and you will be encouraged to experience the the Energy of Life as an ally rather than a taskmaster. It is our hope that in the process you will regain your sense of wonder and realize how spiritual you have been all along.

Stage Four is the mystical/communal stage. Having practiced emptying themselves of surface judgements, at this stage these people have come to recognize a mysterious cohesion beneath the surface of all life. Comfortable with paradox they have learned to manage polarities rather than swing between the poles. Calmly confident in knowing themselves they understand the need for discernment in sharing their truths with others. Stage Four people are now comfortable in sharing ideas with Stage Two and Stage Three seekers and feel no need to evangelize or act superior. Exquisitely aware that the whole world is a community, Stage Four people set others at ease and their sincere interest creates both safety and fertile soil for meaningful dialogue.

If you consider yourself to be part of the mystical/connected stage, the Self-leadership quest will affirm and deepen the practices and attitudes you have already developed and encourage you to realize that there is no finish line.

Regardless of your stage of spiritual-emotional development and your effectiveness in work and relationships the quest of Self-leadership is to know and manage all your parts, choices, and behaviours and to always be creating safe spaces where larger conversations can occur. It is our belief that in the words of Ken Wilber,

> In your own growth and development, you have the capacity to take self, culture, and nature to increasingly higher, wider, and deeper modes of being expanding from an isolated identity of 'me' to a fuller identity of 'us', to an even deeper identity with 'all of us' as your own capacity for Truth and Goodness and Beauty deepens and expands.[14]

It is this larger conversation that includes the "me", "us" and "all of us" that will shape and determine the effectiveness of your journey.

Triumphalism

The purpose of the Self-leadership quest is to raise awareness and respect for the dignity and sanctity of the individual as an integral part of the whole. You will know you are successful when you have an inner flow and an outer focus that allows you to honour diversity and to think, act, interact and be, with Self and others with confidence and clarity.

We welcome those who are choosing to explore Self-leadership from diverse perspectives. We ask you to travel with integrity and humility. The goal of this journey is to increase your *inner* awareness and effectiveness while also increasing your *outer* awareness and effectiveness. We will use the ascending spiral path as a central metaphor. As you travel, the experience will be similar to making your way up a path that spirals around a mountain. The circling path will give you an opportunity to view familiar vistas from different perspectives, facilitating opportunities for new insights and ongoing growth.

As we journey together it needs to be said now that moments of clarity and mountain-top experiences can only serve the larger good if they lead to a generous spirit and a mystical connectedness that embraces both your unlimited possibility and your innate pettiness, both the luminous and the shadow. Each of us is a complex mix of strength and weakness.

Celebrate your successes. Bask in your insights. Enjoy the benefits of Self-leadership. Share generously with those who ask, but please be aware that not everyone is at the same place on the path. Using the four stages of spiritual development as a guide, remember you will benefit most from those who are a little beyond you and be most helpful to those who are experiencing life from a place you have already experienced. We do serious damage when we try to force a butterfly from its cocoon or fly too close to the sun.

Finally, seek to be humble with the rest of humanity. Whenever an individual or group, organization or country becomes triumphal and sees its truth as the ultimate and its path as the only way, it leads to tyranny, fascism, discord and pain. Whether your primary influence is academic achievement, business or personal success, devotion to Buddha, Yahweh, Jesus, Muhammad, or Peck, Jung, Wilber, Beck, or any other intellectual or spiritual guide, seek to live with spaciousness and acceptance while living your truth with dignity and respect.

Advance Confidently

In Thoreau's *Walden* we read:

> I learned this, at least, by my experiment; that if one advances confidently in the direction of his dreams, and endeavors to live the life which he has imagined, he will meet with a success unexpected in common hours ... In proportion as he simplifies his life, the laws of the universe will appear less complex, and solitude will not be solitude, nor poverty poverty, nor weakness weakness.[15]

In *Deep Change*, Robert E. Quinn writes,

> The hero's journey is a story of individual transformation, a change of identity. In embarking on the journey we must leave the world of certainty ... To do this successfully, we must surrender our present self—we must step outside our old paradigms. This venture outside our current self will cause us to think differently. To continue our journey is to reinvent the self.[16]

Trust the inner stirrings and your desire to be a Difference Maker. Advance confidently. The possibilities are unlimited.

Let's begin the Self-leadership quest.

INVITATION

As you begin your journey, the first three Steps invite you to believe transformation of Self and the status quo is possible. It is an invitation to open your mind in order to dream; to open your heart in order to love; and open your will in order to act.

This is an invitation to be an intentional Difference Maker, leading from a place of greater awareness, integrity, and effectiveness.

Cheryl and I believe that as we begin the third Millennium the global realities need all of us to lead from an evolving larger perspective. One person can make an amazing difference. You are invited to explore the possibilities and potential in new and exciting ways. We invite you to increase your Difference Making Quotient (DMQ) by committing to the Self-leadership quest.

Step 1 - The Birth of Awareness

As a leader I sense the need to lead from a place of greater awareness, integrity, effectiveness, and purpose.

The Call
By Charlotte Mew

From our low seat beside the fire
Where we have dozed and dreamed and watched the glow
Or raked the ashes, stopping so
We scarcely saw the sun or rain
Above, or looked much higher
Than this same quiet red or burned-out fire.
Tonight we heard a call,
A rattle on the window pane,
A voice on the sharp air,
And felt a breath stirring our hair,
A flame within us: Something swift and tall
Swept in and out and that was all.
Was it a bright or a dark angel? Who can know?
It left no mark upon the snow,
But suddenly it snapped the chain
Unbarred, flung wide the door
Which will not shut again;
And so we cannot sit here anymore.
We must arise and go:
The world is cold without
And dark and hedged about
With mystery and enmity and doubt,
But we must go
Though yet we do not know
Who called, or what marks we shall leave upon the snow.[17]

STEP 1...

FAST TRACK

The Birth of Awareness invites you to accept the challenge, to wake up, to become fully alive, and by living with clarity of purpose to help create a saner, safer world. The leadership quest begins with recognizing that there is much more to life and to your potential than you have yet experienced. This awakening to a more Self-led life has been whispering to you in small ways from an early age. Your true Self is ready and able to be and do more. This inner awareness, prompted by your growing realization that business as usual cannot continue, can open up unlimited possibilities for increasing your effectiveness. Although as you begin the Self-leadership journey, it may be boredom, pain, failure or dysfunction that pushes you to seek a different way, it is really your powerful interior capacity that is seeking a courageous Self-leader to bring all the inner dimensions into flow. Your inner potential needs new levels of differentiation and integration. It is time to increase your Difference Making Quotient by believing that more is possible. No matter how chaotic your present life is. No matter how many addictive behaviours you struggle with, if you have moments of clarity when you dream of a better life, there is hope. For too long you have let the negative voices and the short term energy release impulses rule your life but, like a bird outside your window early in the morning, awareness is calling to you. At Step 1 you do not have to have all the answers. That is what the journey is about. Right now all you need do is realize there is more and decide that you want to live more intentionally and fully. All you have to do is listen to the call and begin the journey.

Leadership Value: Awareness

Guiding Principle: Intuitive awareness awakens potential.

FOOTHOLD

Take a few minutes to pause and make notes in a journal dedicated to the *12 Steps* about what you're feeling, thinking, intuiting, or noticing as you begin your Self-leadership quest.

Stepping onto the Path

As Ann Voskamp wrote, "Sometimes you don't know when you're taking the first step through a door until you're already inside."[18] Whether you realize it or not you are already on the path toward a new way of leading. It started when you recognized a deep inner yearning for something more. You still may not have words for it but something is shifting and you are aware of it. It is happening both within you and around you. Conscious leaders everywhere are starting to ask bigger questions and seek new ways of leading with a deeper connection to a future that honours the best in each of us.

Each of you comes to Step 1 with a different motivation and with different needs and expectations, yet each of you has a sense of being 'called.' This awakening to a more Self-led life has been whispering to you in small ways from an early age. When you blushed with healthy shame knowing that you had just missed being all that you had hoped to be, you were being called. When you lay awake at night dreaming of better ways to do or be, you were being invited. When you looked at the starry sky and connected with the oneness of creation, you were being summoned. Your experience of awareness began with a dramatic entrance into the physical world of cold and heat, hunger and plenty. At first, your only experiences were governed by a need to survive and it seemed only by crying and a bit of cooing did the outside world respond to your needs.

Much has changed since those early days of fragile dependence. Now you have become a 'you' with your own sense of you-ness and the skills to provide for yourself and meet most of your needs. You have discovered that you have a desire to lead and that others are even willing to follow. Yet something more is trying to happen. Leadership researcher Bruce J. Avolio found that leadership ability is roughly 30 per cent genetic and 70 per cent learned.[19] Kari Keating, PhD and her colleagues found that the key to becoming a more effective leader is to believe that you can be a leader in the first place.[20] You are awakening to your own magnificence and it both challenges and intrigues you. What would shift in your life if you really took full responsibility as the leader of Self, Inc.?

In each of our lives there are moments when we are called out of isolation and self-obsession into a larger awareness of life and others. It can be a call to relationship that opens our heart and brings new levels of caring and understanding. It can be a call to help someone in need that allows us to connect with the other in a new way that awakens us to life's possibilities. As a Self-leader it can be the realization that your decisions have a bigger impact and potential than you may have realized. It can be also a realization that parts of your life are out of control and that food, drugs, alcohol, relationship, greed, fear, or any number of status quo forces have you in their grip. It can be a sunrise or starry night. It can be joy and hope bubbling up from your core and inviting spirit, body, heart, and mind to dance more joyously along the path of life. It can be an opportunity to lead others in exciting work or learning. It can be the call to show up more fully as a leader at a time when the planet needs new levels of social and environmental harmony.

Self-leadership involves stepping intentionally onto the path and moving toward a brighter future where you are engaged with your inner and outer life in a more dynamic and intentional way. Instead of life happening to you, it is time to see life happening through you. As a co-creator, you are being invited to accept the challenge, to wake up, to become fully alive, and by living with clarity of purpose to help create a saner, safer world.

Waking Up

Andrew Cohen writes about this awareness of life energy in his book *Evolutionary Enlightenment*:

> Think about your experience of those moments when you are most creatively engaged. What does it feel like? Being in a creative 'flow' can be ecstatic and, simultaneously there is an often a surprising sense of urgency to bring into being that which you can sense is possible...When you feel that creative flow, often you discover a part of yourself you are not normally aware of but which feels more like your 'self' than the person you usually think you are. It's like plugging in to a deeper source of energy and passion that transcends whatever limitations you ordinarily assume. A deeper, more authentic part of your self is creatively released. That's why such moments are so fulfilling—it's not just the creative work you produce, but the experience of being more alive, more connected, more in touch with a sense of meaning and purpose.[21]

The Birth of Awareness is simply a recognition of this inner stirring, a realization that there is so much more to life and to your potential than you have yet experienced and an inner awareness that you are beginning to seek to be and do more. There is also a growing outer awareness that business as usual cannot continue. The status quo is becoming stale. This invitation to step into new perspectives, to open yourself to new possibilities, focuses on your FISC—your own 'royal treasury', a unique mix of Facts, Influences, SoulDNA, and Characters—that, when leveraged by effective Self-leadership, gives you purpose, fulfillment, and a greater DMQ.

It is this inner stirring and outer awareness—a growing realization that there are parts of you capable of much more than you have yet achieved—that brings you to the *12 Steps*. Although as you begin the journey, it may be boredom, pain, failure or dysfunction that pushes you to seek a better way, it is really your beautiful interior life that is seeking a courageous Self-leader and an opportunity to bring all the inner dimensions into flow.

Your inner potential needs new levels of differentiation and integration. The *12 Steps* work will help you show up more fully in all aspects of leadership and life.

Refusing the Call

Often the first step is tentative. You are feeling a stirring. You are experiencing a creative discomfort. A dream of what could be is forming. The desire to change is swirling but so are the forces of inertia and entropy. There is still hesitancy. Some parts of you like things 'just the way they are.' Right now you are in a space where a creative tension is beginning to invite a response. Your inner parts may not agree. The inner voices, fears, and guardians will use many different tactics to keep you from taking action. These voices of judgement, cynicism, and fear will tell you it's the wrong day, the wrong season, or the wrong year for going on a quest. They'll tell you that this book sounds too woo-woo for a respectable leader like you. The religious voice will question our theology. The inner child will be fearful of looking silly or losing friends. Your inner critic will remind you of all the times you got excited about a new program and failed.

You have been here before. You have experienced the desire to 'be' more and 'do' more. Some of you have started on the path and then turned back; others have tried and when you experienced difficulty you decided you had failed. There is no failure in life, only mislabelling. As one person said there is no such thing as bad weather, only inadequate clothing. There is no such thing as a failed quest, only delays in completion. Every hero's journey begins with uncertainty. This may only be the awakening of awareness and Step 1 may need to sit on the back burner of your life and simmer. Let that be all right. Trust your inner Self to know when it is time to move from awareness to possibility.

One of the greatest creative minds of the twentieth century, Buckminster Fuller, faced a similar decision point in the autumn of 1927. 'Bucky,' as he was called by friends, had a knack for machinery and big ideas. However, he struggled to be consistent and conform enough to stay in school. He also struggled to be stable enough to provide a safe, secure home for his family. After being expelled twice from Harvard, Bucky distinguished himself during two years in the US Navy, and then with a wife and officer training, he felt life was moving forward. He used the energy from the death of their first child to develop and patent Stockade Building Systems, but when that business failed Buckminster was devastated.

Bucky began to drink heavily and was lost in a haze of guilt and self-condemnation. It was at a low point as he walked along the shore of Lake Michigan one day that Buckminster considered suicide. At least the family would have his life insurance. Then from somewhere deep inside Bucky had another thought. There was a Self who still wanted to serve others. A part of him became curious. What if he lived his life in complete service to humanity? What difference could one committed person make?

He became curious enough about the possibilities that he committed to living more fully as an experiment for ten years. He placed his exit from life on hold. He asked his discouraged inner parts for cooperation for ten years to see what could be accomplished.

The experiment lasted fifty-six years. During his amazing life Bucky was awarded twenty-five patents and lectured around the world encouraging people to believe in themselves and challenging us all to "do more with less." Later in his writings he stated that in his moment of decision it was as if he heard a voice saying, "You do not have the right to eliminate yourself. You do not belong to you. You belong to the universe. Your significance will remain forever obscure to you, but you may assume that you are fulfilling your role if you apply yourself to converting your experiences to the highest advantage of others."[22]

The Birth of Awareness will continue to whisper until one day it will become your call. Your hesitation will fade as you explore the possibilities of what you could do as a committed Self-leader.

Growing into Selfhood

In his book, *Let Your Life Speak*, Parker J. Palmer stated, "Our deepest calling is to grow into our own authentic selfhood, whether or not it conforms to some image of who we ought to be. As we do so, we will not only find the joy that every human being seeks—we will also find our path of authentic service in the world."[23]

Many of us hear an inner voice calling us to be more. Some of us deaden the voice with work, food, and other distractions. Some of us just tell ourselves that it is foolish to seek more, and choose to settle with the life we have. The rationalization is easy since so many around us are plodding along in the same fashion. Curiosity and the willingness to leave the herd is not mandatory.

For Tama Kieves, author of *This Time I Dance*, the awareness that there was more to life whispered to her as she became an honours graduate at Harvard Law School and as she excelled at one of Denver's top law firms. Even though she was making a very good living and everyone around her thought she had it all, there was a growing inner awareness that there had to be more. At age twenty-five, the dissonance between family and social expectations and an inner calling started to become unbearable. She asked herself this question, "If you're this successful doing work you don't love, what could you do with work you do love?"

Tama took a break from work and spent time walking and journaling on the oceanfront in Northern California. Here is what she recalls from that experience years later:

> Years ago as an overworked and under-meaning-fulfilled attorney, I walked along a beach in Northern California and breathed in salt-drenched air. I made the wild and unorthodox decision to let go of that career, to let go of what other people thought, to let go of what society told me was safe and beneficial. I found my way of tasting exaltation, walking off into a life that didn't have immediate external recognition or validation. All these many years later, I am still learning how to let go. I am still learning how to run free in my own skin in this lifetime.[24]

Tama had heard the voice of true Self calling and chose to reclaim her selfhood. She was ready to explore the unknown. She had decided to no longer live a divided life.

So here you are at Step 1 realizing that an inner stirring is birthing new levels of awareness. You are realizing as Nelson Mandela stated, "There is no passion to be found in playing small—in settling for a life that is less than the one you are capable of living."[25] You know you have more inner resources available to you than you are currently utilizing.

At Step 1 you do not have to have all the answers. That is what the journey is about. Right now all you need do is realize there is more and decide that you want to live more intentionally and fully. The journey of Self-leadership begins with the simple awareness that there is more to life than same old same old. When a moment of grace allows the clouds to clear and the pure light of loving consciousness to enliven your awareness, a shift has begun and you are beginning to hear your true Self. There is no need to rush the process. Let it unfold in its own time.

Philosopher Alan Watts stated,

> For the perfect accomplishment of any art, you must get this feeling of the eternal present into your bones—for it is the secret of proper timing. No rush. No dawdle. Just the sense of flowing with the course of events in the same way that you dance to music, neither trying to outpace it nor lagging behind. Hurrying and delaying are alike ways of trying to resist the present.[26]

The music is playing softly in your awareness. As you trust your Self and the process, the need to be certain will fade and the need to be in harmony with all creation will begin to fill your heart and soul with warmth like the sun on an early spring day. When it is time to move forward you will know that you are being invited to walk through the doorway to possibility.

Moving along the Path with STEP 1...

As a leader, I sense the need to lead from a place of greater awareness,
integrity, effectiveness, and purpose.

STEPPING STONES

- Re-read "The Call." Reflect and journal about how you are
  being invited to accept the challenge to increase your Self-
  leadership, to wake up, to become fully alive, and to live with
  clarity of purpose.

  - Each time a hero embarks on a journey they are in search
    of something special. What are you in search of? Journal
    what you know or are feeling, thinking, or noticing.

  - In what circumstances, places, or environments have you
    experienced a call to leave your place of comfort?

- At least three times this week, find a few minutes where you
  can pause. Reflect on the circumstances or people—real or
  otherwise, living or not—that are helping you recognize the
  importance of leading from a place of greater awareness,
  integrity, and effectiveness. Journal your insights.

- What will it cost you if you truly heed the call?

- How have you tried to ignore or deaden the sound of
  your calling?

- If you have refused the call before, what fears, inner voices,
  things, circumstances, or people held you back from accepting
  the invitation at that time?

- Identify the inner voices, fears, and guardians that are currently trying to dissuade you from embarking on this Self-
  leadership journey.

- If you have been actively honouring and acting upon the call,
  what barriers are you still seeking to overcome?

- At this point in the birth or rebirth of your awareness, what
  aspect of your authentic Selfhood longs to be reclaimed?

- In what ways do you already recognize that you have been living, playing, or leading small?

TRAVEL TIPS

1. When you feel a bit off or fragmented—or when you're in flow—take a moment to do a quick body scan to notice what you're feeling in your body, your posture, what you're thinking, and what your inner voices are saying.

2. Keep open to serendipities and what's trying to happen in your life, work, and relationships.

3. Trust your intuition. Learn to listen to the whispers on the edge of your awareness

Step 2 - Doorway to Possibility

I open myself to my full potential by seeking to live an integrated, vibrant, Self-authored life.

Potential
By Ricky Thakrar

Step outside of yourself.
Step outside of your routines, your safe circle of friends.
Step outside of your memories, beliefs and prejudices.
Awaken to a fresh perspective on the world,
A more visceral sense of its ebb and flow,
A new view of its entangled web.
Where are you? Who are you?
Examine your life as art, judge as for a crime.
And into your verdict pierce a pivot,
Auspicating a diasporal pilgrimage
Towards the re-introduction of fortune,
Spontaneity, serendipity and surprise.
Rebel against Lady Luck's long-laid path,
Sedate her inexorable chain reactions
And embark instead upon personal ventures.
Live a life where every moment is
More than just a precursor for the next.
And in crushing your expectations,
Welcome the unexpected.[27]

STEP 2...

FAST TRACK

The **Doorway to Possibility** is an invitation into mystery and potential—not the magical thinking of childhood but the wide awake wonder of great minds throughout history. In this space we invite you to open up your heart and mind to new possibilities both of the supernatural and the physical kind. By opening yourself up to unlimited possibility you will become more aware of the many 'coincidences' that happen every day. Step 2 is an invitation to step back from the thought patterns that typically shape your daily activities, and observe yourself and your life. Instead of trying to fix your life, just observe it. All the while notice how the Universe is working in your favour. Even the discomfort or curiosity that brought you to this book is part of your unfolding. Believing in unlimited possibility is like any other training. You have to build up to it. If you haven't believed in the impossible for a long time you will need to start slowly and build up your ability to dream. Start with just being amazed at what already exists. See the miracles all around you—the Internet, the aroma of coffee, the helpful phone call, the e-mail that comes at just the right moment. And then believe in more. Self-leadership involves leading from a place of inner freedom and possibility. It also is a call to a connection with the Energy of Life. Some of the beliefs in your family and religious community may be limiting your possibilities. Letting go of some limiting beliefs will increase your potential and sense of Purpose. You do not have to be a small 's' self trapped in life—you have the possibility of being a big 'S' Self riding planet Earth on a cosmic adventure. In Step 1 you acknowledged that there is an inner stirring that is whispering within. Now in Step 2 you are invited to open your heart and mind to new options. By accepting the invitation to believe anything is possible you immediately increase your DMQ. Get curious about your potential. Take some chances. Start to move forward into unlimited possibility.

Leadership Value: Openness

Guiding Principle: Anticipatory openness expands possibilities.

FOOTHOLD

In your *12 Steps* journal, describe or illustrate what you envision as possibilities for your life.

Embracing the Mystery

Neither Buckminster Fuller nor Tama Kieves knew what lay ahead as they stepped through the door to possibility, but each of them knew they were being called from their ordinary life to something more. As you move from awareness to possibility, a level of trust and surrender is required. Although the process cannot begin without at least part of you being willing, moving forward will require Self-leadership and inner negotiations. Parts of you may be quite ready for more effectiveness in life, work, and relationships. Other parts are not so sure.

'Unlimited possibilities' has a nice ring to it. What if that means believing in a power greater than yourself, an Infinite Mind, a Creative Energy that flows through the universe, maybe even some form of God force that could be called the Energy of Life? What if the discovery of your inner world, a world filled with possibilities that have never been explored, totally disrupts life as you now know it? What if the Energy of Life is inviting you to new levels of life and leadership that will shake up your comfortable assumptions?

Step 2 is an invitation into mystery and potential—not the magical thinking of childhood but the wide awake wonder of great minds throughout history. Albert Einstein stated, "The most beautiful thing we can experience is the mysterious. It is the source of all true art and all science. He to whom this emotion is a stranger, who can no longer pause to wonder and stand rapt in awe, is as good as dead: his eyes are closed."[28]

Our learning and experience have convinced us that in order to fully appreciate, unlock, and utilize the FISC—the royal treasury of Facts, Influences, SoulDNA and Characters, that gives each individual unique perspectives and potential—a connection with Mystery is essential. As we stated in Foundations, our *12 Steps* program is spiritual at its core. We believe that there is a Energy of Life that is available to co-create with each of us. We posit that a belief in a power greater than ourselves is a key element in allowing the energy of life to flow in, through, and around us making all creation and all of life's experiences an ally on the Self-leadership quest.

As you move from Step 1 to Step 2 we invite you to follow the Self-leadership path beyond the comfortable, beyond the predictable into a place of mystery and unlimited possibility. In this space we invite you to open your heart and mind to new possibilities both of the supernatural and the physical kind. There is so much beauty and mystery in the quantum world we inhabit. Step 1 involved awareness. Step 2 involves awe.

Unlimited Possibility

We all have experienced moments when anything seemed possible and the world and universe seemed to stretch out into a spiral pathway of endless possibility—a newborn child or animal, a sunrise or sunset that took our breath away, a mountain vista, a beach view, a deep experience of intimacy, a team success against all odds. As you step through the doorway to possibility allow yourself to dream and hope. Look for miracles. Expect the unexpected. Trust that the Universe really does care and that your success is important to the evolutionary process.

That is what Buckminster Fuller and Tama Kieves did. That is what many who have set out to accomplish and experience more have done. Julia Cameron, whose books, *The Artist's Way* and *Vein of Gold,* have helped millions step into a place of unlimited possibility writes, "As long as we remain closed to the possibility of spiritual help in our unfolding, we are choosing to operate off the battery pack of our limited resources. When we open to spiritual assistance—however tentatively, however experimentally—we tap into an unlimited supply."[29]

As you work through Step 2 we are inviting you to believe in coincidence, synchronicity, quantum flirts, happenstance, and whatever name you give to the Energy of Life at this time. In Step 1, as you tapped into greater awareness, you acknowledged a yearning for more. Now, it is time to become the leader in your own life and start to dream this inner desire into reality.

As a result of his 1845 experiment with Self-leadership, recorded in his book *Walden; Or, Life in the Woods,* Henry David Thoreau, wrote, "I learned this, at least, by my experiment: that if one advances confidently in the direction of his dreams, and endeavors to live the life which he has imagined, he will meet with a success unexpected in common hours."[30]

By opening yourself to unlimited possibilities you will become more aware of the many 'coincidences' that happen every day. As we shared in the introduction, William Hutchison Murray, mountaineer and prison camp survivor, claimed with confidence from his observations and experience that,

> ...there is one elementary truth, the ignorance of which kills countless ideas and splendid plans: that the moment one definitely commits oneself, then Providence moves too. All sorts of things occur to help one that would never otherwise have occurred. A whole stream of events issues from the decision, raising in one's favour all manner of unforeseen incidents and meetings and material assistance, which no man could have dreamt would have come his way.[31]

Inner Potential

What we are proposing in Step 2 is that you learn to listen with all parts of your entity and from multiple perspectives, rather than just with your ears, that you increase your perception to include the unseen, and that you move beyond your conditioned social self to a creative awareness of your unique potential. There is a deep truth in Marilyn Ferguson's statement that, "No one can persuade another to change. Each of us guards a gate of change that can only be opened from the inside. We cannot open the gate of another, either by argument or emotional appeal."[32]

Ultimately you will have to decide. Will you continue on with your present set of insights and prejudices or will you open yourself to unlimited possibility? It doesn't have to happen all at once. Just soften your focus. Step back from the organizations, relationships, perspectives, and thought patterns that typically shape your daily activities and observe yourself and your life like a wise and caring mentor would watch and listen. Do the same with your inner Characters. Hear the voices of the playful child, the pessimist, the cynic, the saboteur, the anxious child, the protective parent, the warrior, the addict, the blamer, the poet, and any other parts of your rich interior without judging or trying to evict them.

In her amazing story of a brilliant son whose autistic tendencies nearly doomed him to a life of silence, Kristine Barnett tells how the inner genius can be nurtured in each of us. In *The Spark*, her story of nurturing inner potential in her son Jake, she writes,

> I wrote this book because I believe Jake's story is emblematic for all children. Though his gifts are unique, his story highlights the possibility we all have of realizing what's extraordinary in ourselves, and maybe even opens the door to the possibility that 'genius' might not be all that rare.[33]

For many of you, believing in unlimited possibility was abandoned along with your childhood toys and the magical thinking of your inner child who believed in tooth fairies and Santa Claus and that, if you prayed, you could keep Daddy from drinking or Mommy from abandoning the marriage. The belief in possibility that we are inviting you into in Step 2 is not magic fairy dust but it is also not harsh pessimism. Your inner child still has hopes and dreams and wisdom that will allow you to dance in the rain, see elephants in the clouds, forgive your enemies, and love without expecting anything in return.

Things may not always turn out just the way you envision, yet believing in the impossible is the essential basis for transformation and quantum leaps in awareness and innovation. Reclaiming your inner dreaming is what moves essence into reality. Reopening your heart means that you need to let go of the disappointed dreams of the past and realize that hope is more powerful than cynicism and that the mystery of unanswered prayers and failed quests doesn't deny the metaphysical, it just makes it all the more intriguing.

Now is the time to reclaim your power and explore the mystery of this unique incarnation, this Self, Inc., called you. Cherie Carter-Scott author of *If Life Is a Game, These Are the Rules* states, "Ordinary people believe only in the possible. Extraordinary people visualize not what is possible or probable, but rather what is impossible. And by visualizing the impossible, they begin to see it as possible."[34]

This 'extraordinary' is not just way out there. It is within each of you. That little boy or girl is still a part of your inner world. You also have untapped inner resources for courage, wisdom, compassion, playfulness, caring, creativity, intuition, collaboration, and curiosity.

Marianne Williamson, in *A Return to Love*, claims that our deepest fear is not our weakness but our strength. She says,

> Our deepest fear is not that we are inadequate. Our deepest fear is that we are powerful beyond measure. It is our light, not our darkness that most frightens us. We ask ourselves, 'Who am I to be brilliant, gorgeous, talented, fabulous?' Actually, who are you not to be? You are a child of God. Your playing small does not serve the world. There is nothing enlightened about shrinking so that other people won't feel insecure around you. We are all meant to shine, as children do. We were born to make manifest the glory of God that is within us. It's not just in some of us; it's in everyone. And as we let our own light shine, we unconsciously give other people permission to do the same. As we are liberated from our own fear, our presence automatically liberates others.[35]

Believing in the Impossible

A story of unblinking belief in the impossible is told of Henry Ford. In 1929, in the midst of the Depression, Henry decided to produce the world's first affordable V-8 engine cast in one block. This had never been done before. The engineers said it was impossible, but Ford never wavered and by 1932, the Ford Model 18 with a V-8 engine transformed automotive history.

Believing in unlimited possibility is like any other training. You have to build up to it. If you haven't believed in the impossible for a long time you will need to start slowly and build up your ability to dream. Start with just being amazed at what already exists. When you power up your cell phone it responds and can pick up calls from the far side of the world. Be amazed. When you turn on your car a controlled explosion takes place and you have the power of many horses pulling you wherever you choose to go. Allow yourself to be impressed. When you drive through a busy city during rush hour think of how astounding it is that there are so few accidents. Thousands of drivers of all ages and experience negotiate turns and multiple lanes with a finesse that would have had your ancestors in awe.

See the miracles all around you—the Internet, online banking, the phone call, the cheque, the e-mail that comes at just the right moment. And then believe in more. As St. Francis of Assisi wrote, "Start by doing what's necessary; then do what's possible; and suddenly you are doing the impossible."[36] You are capable of so much more than you give yourself credit for. You are more than you realize. Think back through your life. You may not be a thriver yet but you are a survivor and at times you have overcome impossible odds.

Canadian Ray Zahab, was a poor student and the last kid picked for team sports. After dropping out of college and living aimlessly he was broke, bored and unhappy. As he came up to his thirtieth birthday he said his life was like one big "so what?" In 1999, inspired by his younger brother John, Ray quit smoking and took up adventure sports and over the next four years through discipline and by believing anything was possible he became a personal trainer and entered adventure and mountain-biking races, barely scraping by financially but feeling totally alive as he got into the best physical and emotional shape of his life. In December of 2003, he read about the Yukon Arctic Ultra, a 160-kilometre multiday race through sub-zero conditions and decided to enter. Three months later, he won. Zahab won four other 200-km-plus, multiday races and in 2007 he completed a 7,500 kilometre, 111 day trip across the Sahara. Since then he has traveled to the South Pole and participated in several other extraordinary adventures. Ray says that running has taught him that we all are capable of the extraordinary in our lives. "I like to say that this type of running is 90 percent mental, and the rest is in your head," he says, repeating his well-worn mantra.[37]

No matter your age or present reality you are capable of doing more and being more. It starts with a belief deep within, a whisper from your best Self inviting you to let go of 'what has been' and 'what is' in order to experience 'what could be.' When was the last time you sat in a comfortable place and daydreamed for half an hour? Isn't it time to allow yourself to believe with futurist, John Schaar, that,

> The future is not a result of choices among alternative paths offered by the present, but a place that is created—created first in the mind and will, created next in activity. The future is not some place we are going to, but one we are creating. The paths are not to be found, but made, and the activity of making them, changes both the maker and the destination.[38]

Thinking Outside Your Tribe

Much of this chapter has been for those of you who feel disconnected and struggle with a belief in a Power Beyond Yourself or in something metaphysical, something beyond your reach, or something seemingly impossible. Now we want to challenge those of you who are part of a vibrant faith community. Although you may have had moments of doubt and maybe even some teenage rebellion, many of your beliefs have been passed on to you from parents, friends and community. It will take courage to think outside your tribe and explore possibilities beyond the traditionally accepted thinking. In the past in Jewish, Christian, and Islamic cultures such variance from the accepted dogma was often punishable by cruel practices. Unfortunately, some of those practices still exist today and even outside the traditional religions, shunning and group or parental disapproval are still real and powerful forces.

In *Sacred Choices: Thinking Outside the Tribe to Heal Your Spirit*, Christel Nani writes,

> Your ancestors taught you how to work, how to grieve, and why bad things happen. You have taken for granted that in their desire to protect you, they prepared you

adequately for life by teaching you the way of the tribe—what they valued and what they believed to be true. These tribal beliefs are the inherited ideas about the way life works, passed down to you from anyone who had power or authority over you as a child. Some of these beliefs cause you to make choices that make your life harder than it needs to be, creating conflicts and inner turmoil.[39]

All book-based religions deal with the same issues—literalism and the contradictions that exist within the writings. This has placed Rabbis, Priests, Ministers, Theologians, Imams, Gurus, Brahmans, and Ulama in a place of power and authority. This often leaves seekers caught in a tension between the letter of the law and the spirit of the law. Rule-based belief systems and unlimited possibility are not always compatible. We are not saying that Self-leadership and organized religion are incompatible, but we are saying that as you say "yes" to a life of heightened awareness and unlimited possibility you may bump into some thorny bushes along your new path. Some of the beliefs in your family and religious community will limit the possibilities for women, lesbians, gays, scientists, thinkers, and nonconformists. Some of you will not be able to achieve your full potential in your present tribe and will have to seek out new affinity groups that allow you to continue your quest for freedom and wholeness; however, not all the challengers will be on the outside. Notice even as you read these ideas how the inner voices start to become active.

Self-leadership involves leading from a place of inner freedom and possibility. It also is a call to a connection with the Energy of Life. Leaving the tribe for most of you is a call to be aware of the ways in which you are giving your power and authenticity away. However, that does not necessarily mean that you have to physically leave. What it does mean is that you have an opportunity to decide whether or not, and the extent to which, these practices help or hinder you on your Self-leadership quest. If aspects of your current religious traditions can refresh, renew, and inspire you, by all means keep them. If you have to abandon some or all of your tribal beliefs and practices in order to connect more fully to the Energy of Life, your inner awareness of love, possibility and purpose will guide your steps.

Deciding whether you are able to continue to actively participate in your traditional religious practices will be part of your hero's journey. Some of you will need to move out in order to get the freedom and perspective you need to enlarge your view of the Divine. Others of you will benefit from staying in and using the practices of your community's spiritual traditions as a springboard to a more profound connection with the Creative Energy of Life.

Free Your Genius

Once you accept that you are not just an insignificant speck in the mass of humanity and start to allow possibility to emerge you will find as Katie Byron says, "Life is simple. Everything happens for you, not to you. Everything happens at exactly the right moment, neither too soon nor too late. You don't have to like it... it's just easier if you do."[40]

This is not some new presentation of the prosperity gospel or a secret path to allow you to succeed while those around you continue to flail. Your cancer may be fatal. Your circumstances may not improve in your lifetime. Your war-torn country may be devastated. As Scott Peck said,

> Life is difficult. This is a great truth, one of the greatest truths. It is a great truth because once we truly see this truth, we transcend it. Once we truly know that life is difficult—once we truly understand and accept it—then life is no longer difficult. Because once it is accepted, the fact that life is difficult no longer matters.[41]

The ultimate goal of the hero's journey in Step 2 is to experience unlimited possibility in each and every circumstance. Viktor Frankl, a survivor of the Holocaust, witnessed incredible acts of purpose and courage even in the most difficult circumstances, which led him to state, "Everything can be taken from a man or woman but one thing: the last of human freedoms to choose one's attitude in any given set of circumstances, to choose one's own way."[42]

Martha Beck writes,

> Today, look upon your life, your bank account, your family, each person you meet, as a wild horse. If a problem looks difficult, relax. If it looks impossible, relax even more. Then begin encouraging small changes, putting just enough pressure on yourself to move one turtle step forward. Then rest, savor, celebrate. Then step again. You'll find that slow is fast, gentle is powerful, and stillness moves mountains.[43]

The Invitation

Once you accept that you are a part of the great unfolding of life and open yourself to unlimited possibility, you are no longer trudging along the path. You have accepted the invitation to experience greater awareness and possibility. As you continue on, each encounter, each challenge, each reward, each coincidence is an ongoing invitation to continue on the adventure of embodying your best Self. In *The Spontaneous Fulfillment of Desire*, Deepak Chopra states,

> As our attention creates energy, intention brings about the transformation of that energy. Attention and intention are the most powerful tools of the spiritually adept. They are the triggers for attracting both a certain kind of energy and a certain kind of information. So the more attention you put on coincidences, the more you attract other coincidences, which will help you clarify their meaning. Putting your attention on the coincidence attracts the energy, and then asking the question, 'What does it mean?' attracts the information. The answer might come in a certain insight or intuitive feeling, or an encounter, or a new relationship... Once you can see and interpret the coincidences, your path to fulfillment emerges.[44]

In her book, *If the Buddha Came to Dinner*, Halé Sofia Schatz writes,

Spirit is as vast as the ocean. Just as the seas gave birth to the first life forms on earth and shaped continents, so, too, our spirits have the potential to grow and transform our lives. Saying yes to our spirit is one of the most daring things that we can do in life, if not the most courageous. Every time your true Self is challenged, you will always be supported. The right person or the right circumstances will suddenly appear. The right job. The right book. The right words uttered by a co-worker or stranger standing next to you on the subway. That's because the natural impulse of spirit is to become manifest ...When you're aligned with your spirit, your whole life opens up.[45]

In Step 1 you acknowledged that there is an inner stirring that excites your imagination and whispers to your soul. Now in Step 2 you are starting to dream. Accept the invitation. Get curious about your potential. Move forward into unlimited possibility. Prepare to cross the threshold on your quest.

Moving along the Path with STEP 2...

I open myself to my full potential by seeking to live an integrated, vibrant, Self-authored life.

STEPPING STONES

- We refer to the Energy of Life as a source of power and inspiration. What belief do you have that allows you to believe in unlimited possibility?

- What are you curious about regarding the metaphysical and its role in leadership?

- If you already have a religion or specific set of spiritual beliefs, write a brief description of how these beliefs will strengthen and guide you as you undertake your Self-leadership journey.

- Journal how you may be challenged to step outside some of these beliefs and/or the 'religious culture' in order to lead from a larger perspective.

- Reread "Potential." In your journal, list some of the possibilities that you have dreamed about, hoped for, or imagined—as a child or more recently.

  - What serendipities or coincidences have you noticed so far on your Self-leadership quest?

  - Since starting to read the *12 Steps of Self-Leadership*, what hopes or dreams have emerged or brightened?

  - What do you already know or intuit about your potential—personally and professionally?

- How may you be sabotaging your genius by trying to manage your fears through exerting excessive control in parts of your life, work, or relationships?

TRAVEL TIPS

1. When you start to doubt yourself or the Self-leadership quest, release your doubt to a power or energy beyond yourself—by whatever name you give 'it.' Doing so will help open you to new and unknown possibilities.

2. It's no coincidence that you're reading the *12 Steps*. Get curious—really curious—about what's trying to happen in your life, work, or relationships.

Step 3 - Crossing the Threshold

I commit to trusting both Self and other wisdom as I embark on the journey of exploring, discovering, and integrating my inner and outer life.

There is a Grace Approaching
By Stephen and Ondrea Levine

There is a grace approaching
That we shun as much as death
It is the completion of our birth.
It does not come in time
But in timelessness
When the mind sinks into the heart
And we remember who we are.
It is an insistent grace that draws us
To the edge and beckons us
To surrender safe territory
And enter our enormity.
We know we must pass beyond knowing
And fear the shedding.
But we are pulled upward
Nonetheless through forgotten ghosts
And unexpected angels
Realizing it doesn't make sense
To make sense anymore.
This morning the universe danced before you
As you sang — it loves that song![46]

STEP 3...

FAST TRACK

Crossing the Threshold is a very real commitment to being intentional about opening yourself up to discovering all that is possible in and through your life. Step 3 involves both decision and action. The decision is to keep open to the invitations to learning and growth that life provides and to say 'Yes!' each day to the continuing adventure. Use the opportunities and challenges that life is presenting right now to cross the threshold and commit to connecting with the best Self you can be. In the quest, your approach to life, failure, disappointment, losing your way and having to retrace your steps is a necessary part of the process. As you move forward on your journey, heighten your awareness to be fully present. Instead of getting caught up in the inner and outer dramas and confused by the multitude of voices it is a time to relax and listen to a deeper wisdom of what is trying to happen in your life and leadership. You need a soft focus at the same time as you develop exquisite attention to the coincidences and whispers in your life. We encourage you to embody the commitment you make in Step 3 in some real way by taking a physical action to symbolize your decision to step forward into a new way of living and being. Once you have crossed the threshold and embarked upon the adventure of exploring, and discovering the dimensions of your inner and outer life you will begin to access dimensions of your Self that have been hidden or underused. Through a quest to live in integrity with clarity of intention, you commit to face everything and avoid nothing in a desire to discover the best in yourself and to become a Difference Maker in the larger community. As you choose the hero's journey, life becomes an adventure and each day is an opportunity to reach new levels of awareness and effectiveness.

Leadership Value: **Commitment**

Guiding Principle: **Intentional commitment attracts support.**

FOOTHOLD

Find or buy a something that will serve as a symbol of your decision to cross the threshold and embark on your Self-leadership quest.

Stepping Across the Threshold

Crossing the threshold is a commitment to more than just a few hours reading a book. It is an acceptance of a different way of life, a pledge to continuous learning, a commitment to the quest. It is a statement of letting go of the old in order to experience the new. In *Healing the Soul in the Age of the Brain,* author, psychiatrist and psychoanalyst, Elio Frattaroli says that there are two main ways of experiencing life—the swimming pool philosophy or the quest philosophy. According to the swimming pool philosophy, the purpose of life is to stay afloat, to function smoothly, maintaining the equilibrium of the status quo. Swimmers should seek to stay in their own lane. No one likes someone who makes too many waves. Bumping into other swimmers is to be avoided as much as possible. In this philosophy making mistakes, floundering, letting others see your weaknesses is to be avoided. Life is about keeping your head down, minding your own business and avoiding failure.

The second philosophy, which Elio calls the quest philosophy, is an adventurous seeking of a higher or better state. According to the quest philosophy,

> the purpose of life is to pursue this higher state—enlightenment, wisdom, self-actualization—by progressing through a series of difficult, dangerous trials. The successful mastery of each trial brings the seeker to the next level in his or her gradual ascent toward the ultimate goal, which though it may be unattainable, is inherently worth pursuing. In the quest, failure, disappointment, errors and retracing your steps is a necessary part of the process. The process of undergoing a trial inevitably involves some error. You can't find your way to a higher level without learning from your missteps. In the quest falling down is therefore good.[47]

Until very recently leadership has too often been about maintaining the status quo, taking care of your interests, and being seen as flawless by others. Attack politics and a corporate cronyism approach to life and leadership has become pervasive in many business and not-for-profit environments. Yet, quietly, new ways of being and doing are emerging. In the corporate world a group of successful entrepreneurs have chosen to march to a different drummer and serve a higher calling. Over the last thirty years these leaders have developed very successful organizations around a quest philosophy they have chosen to call Conscious Capitalism. Those leading the movement see it as a heroic journey. They state it this way,

Our dream for the Conscious Capitalism movement is simple: One day, virtually every business will operate with a sense of higher purpose, integrate the interests of all stakeholders, develop and elevate conscious leaders, and build a culture of trust, accountability, and caring.[48]

Crossing the threshold is a very real commitment to learning and growing and to being intentional about opening yourself up to discovering all that is possible in and through your life. Step 3 is a call to action. This call to action is not about more doing or doing more. It is a call to the inner quest to be more so that all you're doing is energized by a sense of joy and purpose. Performance coach, Dr. Brett Steenbarger, states, "Self-leadership begins when we stop prioritizing tasks and start prioritizing the elevated state in which we are most productive."[49]

As you experience Step 3, life will provide the opportunities for learning and growth. At Step 3, it is time to stop waiting for the perfect moment to embark upon the adventure of embodying your best Self. This is your time. Use the opportunities and challenges that life is presenting right now to cross the threshold and commit to connecting with the best you can be. For most of you this will be a 'both—and' experience. You will be able to participate in both a quest for increased awareness and engagement, and maintain your current work and relationship commitments. For others the quest will involve a much bolder and demanding threshold. For you to break with status quo will mean a radical shift in how you live and lead.

There will be mini journeys, detours, and delays within the larger unfolding of this Self-leadership quest. Opportunities for growth and new levels of awareness and effectiveness will arise once you start, but nothing will really change until you step across the threshold with a sense of adventure, curiosity, and intentionality. It takes courage to overcome old patterns and the voices of judgement, cynicism, and fear.

For a friend of ours, whose aging mother became quite ill, such an opportunity for evolving came with the rapid deterioration of her mother's health and a realization that her mother would probably be bedridden for the weeks or months until she died. Accepting the challenge, our friend began making regular visits to her childhood home where an angry father still guarded the door and where uncomfortable old memories returned to challenge and refine. After four months of daily visits our friend was amazed at what she learned about her mother, about herself, about life and death. She and her father came to appreciate each other in new ways. It required a commitment to cross the threshold each day. As a result of this experience, the strength in her voice and the twinkle in her eye, makes it obvious that our friend found inspiration and new levels of awareness through this dance with life and death.

When he was a boy, my son, Jason, and I read *The Hobbit* together and came to delight in the main character, Bilbo Baggins, who is invited on an adventure with the wise wizard Gandalf, and a group of thirteen dwarves. Bilbo enjoys the simple pleasures of home and prefers the safety and comfort of the familiar over the thoughts of being far away from the well-worn paths near his hobbit-hole. However, like all of us, he has a conflict between his desire for sameness and his curiosity about the larger world. With a great deal of hesitation Bilbo accepts the invitation to cross the threshold and, although during the travels Bilbo has momentary regrets as he dreams of bacon and eggs and the comforts of home, he discovers that he is more ingenious and brave than he had ever imagined. During the adventure Bilbo gets in touch with an inner wholeness and realizes he is capable of much more than he had realized. As his confidence and leadership qualities emerge, Bilbo proves himself a hero, his quest succeeds, and he returns home with a newfound wealth and deeper sense of Self.

In the later book called *The Fellowship of the Ring*, recalling the life lessons he learned from Bilbo, the adopted heir, Frodo Baggins states of Bilbo,

> He often used to say there was only one Road; that it was like a great river: its springs were at every doorstep and every path was its tributary. 'It's a dangerous business, Frodo, going out of your door,' he used to say. 'You step into the Road, and if you don't keep your feet, there is no telling where you might be swept off to.'[50]

By crossing the threshold in Step 3 you have stepped out of your door onto the Road. Now the path that looked so inviting at the start will likely become more challenging. As you responded to the whisperings and possibilities of Steps 1 and 2 you experienced a mix of exhilaration and fear. Now you're not so sure. Now as you cross the threshold and commit to the quest, there is no telling where you might be swept off to. Can you let go of the old scripts? Can you be with 'what is' in the moment and what is trying to happen?

Step 3 has its own dynamics because at this stage for the first time your inner voices and deepest desires will begin to be consciously engaged. Something is shifting. Life is less predictable. You are becoming more aware of the inner dialogue—the functional and dysfunctional—you are starting to notice when the inner voices are not supporting the best Self that is seeking to emerge. As you start to live from a deeper place and more engaged awareness, people around you will also start to notice the shift and, just as there will be coincidences and amazing support, there will be both inner and outer voices that will want you to stay the same. Your courage to move may start to make both others and parts of you very uncomfortable.

The Web of Life

Although we have chosen to use the hero's journey as a framework for your Self-leadership quest, this is not a solitary venture. John Donne's affirmation that "no man is an island" is an essential tenet of leading with awareness. It is only through awareness of the 'me, us, and all of us' that you begin to see yourself more clearly and understand your purpose as part of the larger whole. It is in your interactions with others that your ability to lead more effectively develops.

The reason the famous Camino de Santiago has been a transformative path for pilgrims for centuries is not just in the rugged path through northern Spain. The transformative power of the quest is in the interactions between the questor and other pilgrims, the innkeepers, the helpers and volunteers along the way. In order to lead Self and others you will need to be more aware than ever of the interplay of the inner and outer life and of your relationship with Self, others, and the environment. As you engage in your Self-leadership quest there will need to be times of isolation and quietness in order to experience your inner dynamics and bring order and tranquility through purposeful intent. You will also benefit from both casual and formal interaction with others so that you can gain new perspectives and refine and improve your interpersonal awareness and skills.

> **The paradox about the Self-leadership quest is that it both calls you away from the crowd and deeper into community at the same time.**

The paradox about the Self-leadership quest is that it both calls you away from the crowd and deeper into community at the same time. It is a call to gain a deeper awareness about Self and an increased awareness about others. It is a call to increase your ability to effectively lead Self and to influence and lead others. The hero travels away from the known, not to escape the web of life, but to engage more fully with a greater sense of Self and greater love and compassion for the whole.

The Long Walk to Freedom

This is perhaps not your first attempt to become free. You have been taking some aspect of this step since as a toddler you declared, "Me do it!" and tried to put on your own pyjamas or pour the milk on your cereal. You may have had some successes in those early days, but overall the message from the 'bigs' to the 'littles' is consistent across cultures that the 'bigs' are OK—stronger and smarter—and 'you' are not. In hundreds of little ways, mostly unintentional, parents and teachers, older peers, advertising campaigns, movies, culture and social media, old memories, and inner voices have been telling you that you are not OK, you are not enough.

By the time you reached your teens, your inner Self was often hidden and enmeshed beneath layers of conforming, rebelling, and escaping. Whether you became the successful student or the dropout, most of your motivation came from outside rather than from your core. Your sense of Self was being shaped by others' expectations. Therapists call this co-dependent conflicted Self a "false self" because it is really an illusion, a hologram, a reactive response generated at the expense of your best Self. In dealing with the inner and outer confusion you learned how to survive. You created personas that worked in different parts of your life. You became like Teflon. In the process, consciously or unconsciously, you lost touch with the essence, the birthright, that inner wholeness that your true and best Self brings. The shift from inner wholeness to outer survival and performance created the illusion that there was no choice. It seemed like the price of growing up. With the challenges of emerging sexuality, relationships, education and career decisions, parts of you came to believe that the quest for identity and purpose was a luxury you could not afford or didn't have the right to pursue.

Nelson Mandela, South Africa's visionary leader wrote,

> I have walked that long road to freedom. I have tried not to falter; I have made missteps along the way. But I have discovered the secret that after climbing a great hill, one only finds that there are many more hills to climb. I have taken a moment here to rest, to steal a view of the glorious vista that surrounds me, to look back on the distance I have come. But I can only rest for a moment, for with freedom come responsibilities, and I dare not linger, for my long walk is not ended.[51]

When you accept the challenge to provide leadership for the aspects of your inner Self and embody your true Self in a world where conformity and constant approval-seeking are the norm, you risk conflict and loneliness; however, it is only on a path that includes times of solitude and silence that all the inner voices, inner parts, possibilities, facts, beliefs, influences and Characters can be fully examined.

Step 3 is an opportunity for discovery, which will include lonely walks and inner turmoil. Jean Vanier in his book *Becoming Human* addresses this loneliness when he writes, "When we refuse to accept that loneliness and insecurity are part of life, when we refuse to accept that they are the price of change, we close the door on many possibilities for ourselves; our lives become lessened, we are less than fully human."[52] Step 3 requires a heroic commitment. This step opens the way to Self-confidence and inner awareness that will allow your inner light to shine and your actions to flow from a deep sense of purpose and energizing inner meaning.

Step 3 involves both decision and action. The decision, as with all the Steps is to keep open to the invitations to learning and growth that life provides and to say 'Yes!' each day to the continuing adventure. This may not be the first time you have undertaken a hero's journey. You may have learned enough through some earlier exploration to know that if you fully commit there is even more that you could be and do. As you undertake this Self-leadership quest we encourage you to fully commit and go all the way down the rabbit hole of discovery with curiosity and a belief in the process. Commit and surrender. You don't need to push the process, just begin each day opening yourself to awareness and possibility and trusting that the Universe will support you on your journey.

On the journey you may be lonely but you will never be alone. There are allies and supporters that you can call upon for inspiration and wisdom. Choose some heroes living or dead, real or fictional, who have broken free and traveled the road less traveled. Read classics like *The Alchemist, Their Eyes Were Watching God, The Hobbit, or Out of Africa*. Watch inspiring movies. Let heroes like Santiago, Janie Crawford, Bilbo, or Karen Blixen inspire and encourage you. Find examples of others in your family, community, faith group, sports, arts, or everyday life who have crossed the threshold and traveled the Self-leadership path.

Face Everything and Avoid Nothing

Joseph Campbell, who opened our minds to the universality of the leadership path and the invitation to the hero's journey wrote in *The Hero with a Thousand Faces*,

> The hero goes forward in his adventure until he comes to the 'threshold guardian' at the entrance to the zone of magnified power. Such custodians bound the world in the four directions—also up and down—standing for the limits of the hero's present sphere or life horizon. Beyond them is darkness, the unknown, and danger.[53]

In the Self-leadership quest these threshold guardians can be real, but often our imagined barriers and the drama of win-lose thinking make the journey much more fearsome than it need be. When we look the monsters in the eyes with curiosity, awareness and a sense of destiny we find they are not nearly as big as they seemed. With a sense of purpose you can find joy, even exhilaration in the challenges of life knowing that these are opportunities to experience greater awareness and effectiveness.

As you choose the hero's journey, life becomes an adventure and each day is an opportunity to reach new levels of awareness and effectiveness. Through a quest to live in integrity with clarity of intention, heroes face everything and avoid nothing with a desire to discover the best in themselves and to help improve the larger community. Self-discovery and community betterment is the ultimate goal of every hero's quest. Perfection is not required. All you need to do is make yourself available.

In 1977, a quiet Canadian youth named Terry Fox who'd had a lifelong passion for sports was told his right leg would need to be amputated immediately if he was to have any chance of surviving the osteosarcoma that had infected the bone in his right knee. The night before the surgery Terry was given an article about Dick Traum, the first amputee to complete the New York City Marathon. For Terry, that was the beginning of a dream to run what he later chose to call 'The Marathon of Hope' across Canada to raise awareness and funds for cancer research.

In requesting support from the Canadian Cancer Society for his venture, Terry described a dream he had the night before his amputation. He wrote,

> I was rudely awakened by the feelings that surrounded and coursed through the cancer clinic. There were faces with the brave smiles, and the ones who had given up smiling. There were feelings of hopeful denial, and the feelings of despair. My quest would not be a selfish one. I could not leave knowing these faces and feelings would still exist, even though I would be set free from mine. Somewhere the hurting must stop... and I was determined to take myself to the limit for this cause.[54]

Terry's quest to make a difference began on April 12, 1980, when he dipped his right leg in the Atlantic Ocean near St. John's, Newfoundland. On September 1, after 143 days and 5,373 kilometres (3,339 mi), recurring cancer forced Terry to return home for further treatment. By the time he was forced to stop running Terry had captivated the imaginations of Canadians and left an enduring legacy of courage and determination.

Terry used the last of his strength to raise funds and champion his cause but his health continued to fail and he died the next year just before his 23rd birthday.

Originally, Terry had hoped to raise one dollar for each of Canada's 24 million people. By the time of his death that number had been exceeded. The annual Terry Fox Run, first held in September 1981, has grown to involve millions of participants in over 60 countries and is now the world's largest one-day fundraiser for cancer research. Over $500 million has been raised in Terry Fox's name.

Upon his death, flags across Canada were flown at half-mast and Prime Minister Pierre Elliott Trudeau stated,

> It occurs very rarely in the life of a nation that the courageous spirit of one person unites all people in the celebration of his life and in the mourning of his death ... We do not think of him as one who was defeated by misfortune but as one who inspired us with the example of the triumph of the human spirit over adversity.[55]

In a video to share Terry's story this quote from George Bernard Shaw was used:

> This is the true joy in life—being used for a purpose recognized by yourself as a mighty one... being a force of nature instead of a feverish selfish clod of ailments and grievances complaining that the world will not devote itself to making you happy.[56]

Susan Boyle, a Scottish singer, spent a lifetime believing she had "brain damage." The youngest of nine children, Boyle had learning difficulties as a child, the result of oxygen deprivation at birth. She struggled in school and was bullied by other children. Throughout her life she had taken comfort in listening to music and had proven quite competent in singing at her local church, karaoke, and community functions. She left school with few qualifications, never married and spent years caring for her widowed mother, Bridget, who died in 2007.

Susan knew she had talent, and dreamed of earning income through her singing to assist her family. She won a few local competitions and in 2002 began taking singing lessons from voice coach Fred O'Neil hoping to improve her chances for success. She made several amateur recordings for benefits and local performances but it seemed she would have to resign herself to local notoriety. Fred encouraged her to give it another try and at age forty-eight a nervous, pudgy woman competed with many younger more dynamic performers in the 2009 auditions of Britain's Got Talent.

People were snickering as she stood nervously on stage and Simon Cowell condescendingly invited her to begin. She performed a rendition of I Dreamed a Dream from Les Miserables[57] on the first round of the show, which was watched by over ten million viewers when it aired on April 11, 2009. The response from the audience and the judges was immediate amazement and admiration. A true talent had been discovered.

When Susan's performance was released on Britain's Got Talent in April 2009 the performance was widely reported, and the clip became the most watched video on YouTube.

Susan Boyle was swept from obscurity into a frenzy of adulation and curiosity. By the time of the final competition seven weeks later, Susan's performance was an Internet phenomenon with her YouTube performance viewed over 100 million times. Within fourteen months she sold 14 million albums and performed throughout Britain, Ireland, and the United States. Enjoying her newfound fame Susan has no intention of slowing down. She wants to continue to inspire and contribute. Her message is that when we believe in our gifts and face our obstacles anything is possible.

As you move forward on your journey use the skills and attitudes from Steps 1 and 2. Heighten your awareness to be fully present. You need a soft focus at the same time as you learn to develop exquisite attention to the tiny coincidences and whispers in your life. Instead of getting caught up in the drama and confused by the multitude of voices, relax and listen to the deeper wisdom of what is trying to happen in your life and leadership. Be assured that aloneness is only an illusion because you are an important part of the web of life and the Universe will honour and support your journey.

As you cross the threshold of Step 3, and move along the path, you will develop new principles and practices, and strengthen and refine others that have served you well. You will begin to connect more powerfully with the Energy of Life, your Self, and others. You will experience greater aliveness and an increased willingness and effectiveness in contributing to the larger community. One important thing you need to know as you move forward to new levels of Selfhood and confidence is that all quests do not need to involve sandstorms, disasters, illness, or privation. Your unique present circumstances and inner awakening can be the setting for your courageous quest.

Step 3 is a decision point on your Self-leadership quest. As you cross the threshold and embark upon the adventure of exploring, discovering, and integrating the dimensions of your inner and outer life you will begin to access elements of your inner Self that to date have been hidden or underused. As you continue to move forward, we invite you to the lonely and rewarding "road less travelled" where in the silence of the pilgrims' path you will begin to hear and coordinate the Self that knows that life is meant to be an adventure of learning and growing. You will discover your inner treasures and begin to experience the true joy of living.

Commitment

We encourage you to embody this Step in some real way right now. Make a decision to live divided no more. Make a decision to embrace all your inner parts in order to build a synergistic inner life led by an informed and confident true Self. Make a decision to show up fully in life, work, and relationships. Make a decision to gain the confidence and skill to live in the right relationship with Self and others starting now.

So now, wherever you are, do something to mark this commitment. Whether you are reading this in an airplane, a waiting room, your office, on the beach, or in prison, prepare to symbolically cross a threshold. This is a point of decision and action. On the airplane it may be as simple as a trip to the lavatory. Before you sit back down make a commitment. Say, "I leave my old life here. When I sit back down I will have crossed the threshold to begin the Self-leadership quest." If you are on a beach draw a line in the sand. Then thoughtfully and meaningfully cross the line as a physical act of making this commitment different from anything before. Wherever you are, as soon as you can, stand and either cross the boundary between rooms, climb some stairs, open the curtains, take a physical action to symbolize your decision to step forward into a new way of living and being.

Moving along the Path with STEP 3...

*I commit to trusting both Self and other wisdom as I embark on
the journey of exploring, discovering, and integrating my inner and
outer life.*

STEPPING STONES

- Re-read the poem "There is a Grace Approaching."

    - What "safe territory" are you being beckoned to surrender
      or leave behind as you cross the threshold?

    - What "song" from your deepest and best Self would cause
      the Universe to dance?

- What personal or professional challenge or opportunity has
  been the motivation to cross the threshold to new levels
  of Self-leadership?

- What is your best hope for this Self-leadership journey?

- What is your greatest concern or fear?

- The Self-leadership quest is a lifelong commitment to ongoing
  learning and growth. How committed are you to the "the long
  walk to freedom"?

- What possibilities will be squandered or lost if you do not stay
  committed to the quest?

- What familiar or habitual people, places, or things may show
  up as guardians to discourage or dissuade you from staying
  committed to your Self-leadership quest?

- How will you strengthen and hold fast to your decision to
  cross the threshold and keep moving forward on the path
  when you face obstacles or lose your sense of possibility?

TRAVEL TIPS

3. If you start to lose your commitment, don't give up or give in to discouragement. Revisit your journaling notes and spend time listening deeply to the whispered invitation that brought you to this in the first place, then thoughtfully repeat the action of "crossing the threshold" again ... and again as needed to renew your commitment.

4. Staying committed requires discipline—and the help of an accountability partner. Trust that you, others, and the Universe are creative, resourceful, and whole, and that you'll have the motivation and support you need when you need it. Stay open. Stay curious. Stay the course.

EXPLORATION

Steps 4 and 5 will guide you into exploration of the core of
who you are; into exploration of how your attitudes, beliefs,
and behaviours have been formed; and, into exploration of
how unexamined aspects of your inner and outer life have
impacted your best Self, as well as people and environments in
your wake.

These two chapters will help you discover inner potential,
constrictions, and outages. This exploratory work will help
you identify your strengths and wounds, fears, biases, and
inner turmoil, as well as your gifts, strengths, and wealth of
inner resources.

Here you will be introduced to the concept of seeing yourself
as an entity called Self, Inc. with you being the CEO. You will
also be introduced to FISC—the treasury of Facts, Influences,
SoulDNA, and Characters that make you 'You'.

The exploration in these two Steps will prepare you to take
corrective action and to live with increased engagement and
transformational impact.

Step 4 - Discovering Treasures Within

I acknowledge the Facts, Influences, SoulDNA, and Characters that have shaped me and continue to affect my Difference Making Quotient.

Where I'm From
By George Ella Lyon

I am from clothespins,
from Clorox and carbon-tetrachloride.
I am from the dirt under the back porch.
(Black, glistening,
it tasted like beets.)
I am from the forsythia bush
the Dutch elm
whose long-gone limbs I remember
as if they were my own.
I'm from fudge and eyeglasses,
        from Imogene and Alafair.
I'm from the know-it-alls
        and the pass-it-ons,
from Perk up! and Pipe down!
I'm from He restoreth my soul
        with a cottonball lamb
        and ten verses I can say myself.
I'm from Artemus and Billie's Branch,
fried corn and strong coffee.
From the finger my grandfather lost
        to the auger,
the eye my father shut to keep his sight.
Under my bed was a dress box
spilling old pictures,
a sift of lost faces
to drift beneath my dreams.
I am from those moments –
snapped before I budded –
leaf-fall from the family tree.[58]

STEP 4...

FAST TRACK

Discovering the Treasures Within is an invitation to discover and embrace all the rich resources and learning contained within your unique history and inner giftings—your Facts, Influences, SoulDNA, and Characters. In Step 4 you will increase your Difference Making Quotient by accepting, embracing, and preparing to leverage the inner treasury that we call your FISC. Self-leadership is an invitation to explore and awaken from the family and cultural trance while recognizing the importance and reality of who you are and where you come from. When you own your past, you accept that you have physical and emotional characteristics that you did not choose. You realize that you have been indoctrinated, acculturated, shaped, and influenced. You become curious about the giftings that lie dormant in your SoulDNA. When you face the Facts, Influences, and perspectives of who you are, where you come from, and what has shaped you, there is a power in the deep truths that will liberate your SoulDNA and your inner parts. The Characters within that may have been abused, neglected and undernourished, can begin to feel validated and acknowledged. By examining your interpretations of your SoulDNA, Facts, and Influences you will be able to begin to write your own script. As you continue on your quest this will allow your big 'S' Self to disentangle from the enmeshed impulses and voices of the past and lead with clarity and confidence. The Self that is an integral part of your FISC, when acknowledged, empowered, and integrated becomes part of seamless living and leading allowing the whole to be much greater than the sum of the parts. With the Self coordinating the elements of your FISC, you will be able to dance in the moment with conscious nimbleness in service to Self, others, and the greater good.

Leadership Value: Curiosity

Guiding Principle: Courageous curiosity discovers hidden treasures.

FOOTHOLD

Re-read "Where I'm From." When you think about where you're from, what memories are awakened of things from the past that you liked, things you were proud of, things that were precious or painful, or things that you were perhaps embarrassed about?

Where You're From Matters

Like a tree on a hill that was brought to life by spring rains and summer sun and then shaped by winds, storms, seasons, and years, you too have been shaped by many factors and influences. In the summer of 1993, in response to a poem by Jo Carson in *Stories I Ain't Told Nobody Yet*, teacher and writer George Ella Lyon decided to see what would happen if she made her own "where-I'm-from" lists, which she edited into a poem. The process was so rich she began offering it as an exercise with other writers and teachers and it immediately took off. The list outline is simple and familiar, and the question of where you are from reaches deep. Students and teachers around the globe have resonated with this challenge and used the process to explore their formative influences. As George Ella made her list, and created her poem, she discovered a rich mix of inner and outer elements that made her unique.

Where you are from matters. Each of you is a leaf that has fallen from your family tree. In order to lead Self and others you need to acknowledge where you've come from and the ways your unique experiential mix has prepared you to contribute. It has been said that a leaf doesn't fall far from the tree. As a unique person you do choose your own path yet you are part of your geography, your experiences and the legacy and influences of your ancestry. Your history shapes you and lives beneath the surface creating its own inner sources of power, challenge, tendencies, emotions, hopes, dreams, strengths, threats, and weaknesses. Your desire to lead from an integrated strong sense of Self will be filled with denial if you do not get to the root of the matter. Just as the inner Characters that left unattended will morph and conspire, the Facts and Influences of who you are and where you come from can follow you in the shadows if you do not acknowledge the push and pull that comes from the elements that shaped you during your early years.

Each family is also a part of nested systems—extended family or tribe, culture, religion, community, region, country. Like the nested Russian Babushka dolls you are part of your family, which was part of a community that was shaped and impacted by widening circles of influence of religious, political, environmental, and economic factors.

Lay of the Land

Each of you was raised in a culture that believed itself to be unique, and in some ways superior to all others. Just as your genetic realities were not of your choosing, neither was your early environment. In those early years of dependency, parents, caregivers, neighbours, and community shaped you in their image.

Just as genes shape your reality so does culture, and over time culture makes its claim on each individual. Culture is a powerful influence. From birth you were shaped and trained by your surroundings to act without thinking of Self. You may have resisted or acquiesced, but many of you were trained by your culture to be willing to sacrifice everything, even your life, for the sake of country, party, or religion.

Self-leadership is an invitation to explore and awaken from the family and cultural trance while recognizing the importance and reality of who you are and where you come from. Step 4 is about owning the best of all your background while acknowledging the wider world and a variety of cultures and perspectives. As you reclaim all of your Facts, Influences, SoulDNA, and Characters you will find a new level of comfort in accepting your life "warts and all."

In life, work, and relationships, it is always a joy to interact with people who are comfortable in their own skin. Maya Angelou, African American writer and civil rights activist, is known for her 1969 memoir, *I Know Why the Caged Bird Sings*, and for her other biographies, essays and books of poetry. Through her writing Maya faced her life and reclaimed her SoulDNA. Her writing moved millions. She wrote,

> I am convinced that most people do not grow up...We marry and dare to have children and call that growing up. I think what we do is mostly grow old. We carry accumulation of years in our bodies, and on our faces, but generally our real selves, the children inside, are still innocent and shy as magnolias.[59]

Maya grew up. She accepted her early life experiences, revisited the pain and the joy, and through examining where she came from, and how this shaped who she was, she found peace and freedom. When you face the Facts of who you are and where you come from and the powerful Influences of your formative environments you will take ownership of your inner treasury. The power of acknowledging and embracing all of the deep truths of where you came from will liberate your SoulDNA and your inner Characters. The 'parts' that may have been abused, neglected, and undernourished will begin to feel validated and acknowledged. As you continue on your quest this will allow Self to disentangle from the enmeshed impulses and voices and lead with a clarity that is not possible as long as you live within the family or cultural trance or in personal denial seeking to escape the reality of who you are and where you came from.

Reclaiming your Treasure

Although Step 4 is a homecoming of sorts, reclaiming the gifts of your early years is far from simple. Determining where you come from involves facing truths that have been pushed aside. It involves seeing the whole from multiple perspectives. It means returning to scenes that have been blurred by time. Like the ancient Eastern story of six blind men describing an elephant, every child in a family has a unique experience with each parent and with the family system as a whole. Even on the same day at a family gathering, a trip to the beach, a family argument, or illness, every child's experience is different. Your family life and early family experiences have shaped your perspectives, attitudes, and your underlying beliefs about Self and others.

Your FISC is a unique treasury that when recognized as resources of Self, Inc. and coordinated by your Self equips you to excel. This treasury is made up of the unique strengths, insights, skills, and perspectives that you have gained through the Facts, Influences, SoulDNA, and inner Characters in your experiential and psychic life. The first step to reclaiming all the benefits of your unique FISC is to examine each of these elements in more detail.

Step 4 is not some Panglossian approach in which we are seeking to tell you that all of your experiences were meant for your good and that all of life's disasters and disappointments will suddenly be seen as gifts if you just shift your view. Quite the contrary. We are saying life is difficult. Many of your experiences have been traumatic. You are a survivor. You have left your small beginnings and become someone in the larger world. In your drive to be a Difference Maker and to succeed beyond the limits of family and tribe you may have developed laser focus while sacrificing the soft focused peripheral view that allows you to see the serendipities and coincidences that have equipped and influenced you in subtle ways.

As you come to the reclamation of your Facts, Influences, SoulDNA, and Characters we will ask you to become a personal anthropologist, exploring both the inner and outer aspects of your skills, attitudes, insights, and experiences. As you look honestly at your gifts, facts and influences a "both—and" approach will be helpful. To examine your Facts and Influences from both an insider's view and as an impartial observer will help you get to the truth of the matter.

Although it is important as a Self-leader to look at where you came from with the detached perspective of your adult ego state, it is also important to see how your inner child would have experienced your earlier years and been influenced by the realities you faced. As a very young child you took in every smell, sound, taste, touch, and view even when you were not focusing on a certain aspect of the experience. Canadian medical pioneer, Wilder Penfield, in his neurosurgical exploration demonstrated that your brain stores all of these experiences as groups of neurons that are primed to fire together in the same pattern that created the original experience. This is why looking at old photos or home movies, talking with relatives, or revisiting your childhood environment in reality or imagination, will bring to life old memories and sensations that have been lying dormant.

Differentiation of Self

Differentiation of Self has been defined as the process of freeing yourself from your family's processes in order to embrace your own uniqueness. This means being able to have different opinions and values than your family members while still being able to stay emotionally connected to them. It means being able to calmly reflect on a conflicted interaction after it is over, assessing your own role in the drama, and then choosing the most effective response for the future. In systems family thinking, it is the values and interaction patterns of a person's family of origin that create internal tendencies which, if left unexamined, lead to internal conflict, enmeshment, and polarization that unconsciously impact your decision making and relationship skills.

Your uniqueness is also influenced through a genetic lineage that began long before your birth. The genetic lottery determined your gender, hair colour, and basic physical features. The physical, emotional and cultural effects of your parents, grandparents, and siblings all influence who you are and the lenses through which you view the world. Sicknesses, accidents, life events, nationality, family and community history, even before you were born, have all contributed to shaping your inner and outer development.

SoulDNA

Parker J. Palmer wrote,

> We are born with a seed of selfhood that contains the spiritual DNA of our uniqueness—an encoded birthright knowledge of who we are, why we are here, and how we are related to others. We may abandon that knowledge as the years go by, but it never abandons us. Philosophers haggle about what to call this core of our humanity. Thomas Merton called it true self. Buddhists call it original nature or big self. Quakers call it the inner teacher or inner light. Hasidic Jews call it a spark of the divine. Humanists call it identity and integrity. In popular parlance people often call it soul. The soul wants to keep us rooted in the ground of our own being ... The soul wants to tell us the truth about ourselves, our world, and the relation between the two, whether the truth may be easy or hard to hear. The soul wants to give us life and wants us to pass that gift along, to become life-givers in a world that deals too much death.[60]

At a deeper level your uniqueness is influenced through an energetic DNA that we have chosen to call your SoulDNA. This refers to the unique essence and distinctive qualities, gifts, and abilities that were present from your time of birth. As you complete Step 4, through your own inner knowing and recall, and information you receive from others, you may discover aspects of your SoulDNA that have been shrouded or need to be embraced to more fully release your potential and increase your DMQ.

You came into this world trailing stardust. You have an inner SoulDNA that has shaped and inspired you. As a child of the Universe you have been shaped by your experiences in the physical world while also being coaxed to be more and do more by the spiritual-emotional DNA of your inner life. Now as a tourist in your own land it is important to revisit your beginnings with curiosity and anticipation. As a vocational archeologist when you allow yourself to see your entire history without allowing pride, fear, pain, or privilege to blur your view, you will discover the patterns and desires that have been developing throughout your life.

Several years ago we went to an art gallery and met a native artist, Joseph Jacobs. Joseph is an Iroquois from the Cayuga Nation and until he was forty years old he was one of the amazing native steelworkers working fearlessly assembling steel girders hundreds of feet in the air. Injured in a construction accident in 1974, Joseph was in transition when a friend brought him a piece of soapstone and a few carving tools to keep him entertained while he recuperated in the hospital. Joseph had never expressed himself in creative arts since his early childhood. Yet his unique SoulDNA immediately showed his hands and eyes what to do. Within a short time, he needed larger pieces of stone and better tools. Soon Joseph was carving wolves and eagles and intricate designs. Because it came from deep within, the work flowed. By 1981, his work was so well known that he was commissioned by the Canadian House of Commons to create a sculpture commemorating the Iroquois' Great Law of Peace. The twelve foot by four foot limestone, five panel relief, took four-and-a-half years to create and is permanently installed in the House of Commons. Joseph's authentic creativity had been expressed through an inner gifting that had laid dormant for the first four decades of his life.

In Step 4 as you look at the Facts, Influences and Characters in your life, your SoulDNA will be liberated as you reclaim that early "gifted form" that shaped and guided your development before outside forces, experiences, expectations, desires, and pressures caused you to lose sight of that inner light.

It's Complicated

Another aspect of your unique treasury is the cast of Characters that live in and through you. You are not just a body with genetic coding and a pawn in a culture that shapes your beliefs and actions. You are a complex human being with the ability to learn, adapt, explore, create, lead and discover. The voices, archetypes, and parts that live within are your unique cast of Characters that have developed over the years and impact how you show up. As you reclaim your treasures and learn how to effectively manage the Characters, you will increase your awareness and the ability of your Self to nimbly lead Self, Inc.

Of all the parts of the FISC, we have found the cast of Characters the most complicated to communicate. Fears of mental instability and "hearing voices" keeps many of you from listening to or acknowledging the rich diversity that lives in your consciousness. Yet knowing and leading your inner parts and their outward manifestations is key to expressing your Self and living with the awareness, compassion, and joyful spontaneity that is required in conscious Self-leadership.

As we worked with clients over the years we often observed bright capable leaders become a 'different person' in group dynamics as they exhibited angry outbursts, judgmental rigidity, childish pouting, and then sometimes rapid shifts back to a sensitive, thoughtful leader. These observations made us curious and challenged us to find new ways to describe and understand the inner dynamics that were obviously operating within us and the leaders we worked with. As we studied and experimented with ways to address the inner life for ourselves and our clients, we came to realize that unless we moved beyond just naming gremlins and finding techniques to silence the "monkey noise" in our minds we really weren't dealing with the Characters who continued to show up in our lives and the lives of those we coached and mentored.

In my own inner exploration I became aware of a needy child, I call 'Little Dougie' who is constantly seeking approval and is easily frightened and discouraged. 'Little Dougie' has a tendency to pout and withdraw. 'Little Dougie' is also spontaneous, curious, and playful. I also became aware of a warrior, a sage, a saboteur, a missionary, a teacher, a poet, and mystic. Cheryl did similar inner exploration reclaiming the little girl who lived within and other Characters that challenged and enriched her Self dynamics.

As we integrated our awareness of inner Characters into our coaching we first used Eric Berne's work on transactional analysis to help clients realize that they could choose to embody a Parent, Child, or Adult ego state at any moment. This helped. As our interactions with clients made us more and more curious about ego states, voices, shadows, personas, and archetypes, we explored the work of inner family therapists and came to understand that the concept of an organizing Self is essential to living with awareness and flexibility.

Some coaches or therapists talk of the inner team. We believe that the inner cast of Characters is too diverse, and in most our lives too dysfunctional, to be a coordinated team. However, as your coordinating Self gains awareness and skill there are always tasks that can be assigned to the inner hooligans that will keep them too busy to create chaos, and with effective Self-leadership these challenging parts can provide valuable perspectives.

Perhaps a brief review of developmental history will be helpful at this point. As humans, we have dominated the earth. In spite of our tendencies for warring with others, in most parts of the world we have managed to form communities. As individuals, we have evolved from simple hunter-gatherers and farmers to sophisticated communicators and learners. As our ancestors contributed to the community, they developed specialized roles as priests, healers, teachers, builders, farmers, planners, musicians, artists, and entrepreneurs, and the list goes on. Some members of the society have always been lazy, unproductive, dishonest, disruptive, greedy, but most of us amaze ourselves and those around us with our ability to learn and adapt. At our best, as contributors to society, we demonstrate versatility, creativity, courage, and dependability, plus a desire and willingness to contribute to the greater good.

Just as our global community is populated with changing roles and dynamic diversity, the same is true inside you. You are not just a body with genetic coding or a pawn in a culture that shapes every belief and action. You have an inner community. Within you there are elements of the priest, healer, teacher, builder, farmer, planner, musician, artist, and entrepreneur, and the list goes on. You are a complex human being with the ability to lead in many different ways, to learn, adapt, explore, create, and discover. Increasing your ability to lead needs to involve knowing and interacting with your inner Characters, the parts and voices that shape and inform the Self, Inc. that you are enhancing on this Self-leadership quest.

Persona-ly Speaking

Earlier in my work with leaders I helped them become aware that they showed up differently with different people and in different situations. We named some of these personas—the salesman, the cowboy, the jock, the good ol' boy. By raising awareness and helping them choose how and when they showed up in certain ways, I thought I was doing them a service. Now as we do the deeper work of exploring the archetypes and inner Characters I realize I was helping them get better at a bad game.

A façade is a mask no matter how you wear it and for those who want to connect with the authentic Self this surface connection will not suffice. I had fallen into the same trap that Hermann Hesse bemoans in this part of his poem "My Misery." He wrote:

> My misery comes from my great talent
> to wear too many masks too well.
> I learned to deceive everyone, myself included.
> I became a master manipulator of my feelings.
> No true song could reach my heart.
> Behind each step I take lurks a shrewd scheme.[61]

You may well have a promoter, adventurer, cheerleader, competitor, clown, or loyal friend as an Character living within. The difference in tone and content between a surface persona and an inner Character in service to the whole is profound. As you live from the inside rather than from the surface, life will flow from a deep sense of integrity not from a surface manipulation that blocks the music of your heart.

Who are 'You'?

Inside your brain's millions of neuron bundles life is experienced and a sense of Self is formed. Instead of experiencing separate needs, drives, sensations, and ideas constantly sending millions of signals, humans have developed a coordinating Self that is capable of taking charge of the domain of consciousness and deciding which thoughts or feelings should take priority over the rest. Whether that Self functions well as the CEO of Self, Inc., or abdicates its responsibilities, is ignored, pushed aside, or overpowered by poorly managed inner Characters, will be determined by the level of Self-leadership development.

You are part of an ongoing dynamic. In your holographic inner world a rich mix of voices, archetypes, and ego states vie for the spotlight and their opportunity to be recognized in the larger system. Beneath your usual level of awareness, old hurts and joys, voices from the past, images of inspiration, impulses, disappointments, prenatal influences, and emotions continue to influence your unconscious world. As a leader it is time to experience Self more fully and to become more aware of your inner Characters.

Peter Gerlach says,

These personality parts seem like a group of related people living in the same dwelling. They each have different skills, jobs, ages, values, and needs, and may not know about, understand, and accept each other. They can ally, fight bitterly, or ignore or hide from some others, just as members of any group do. And like any crowd working together, if the individual members are acknowledged, respected, and effectively led, stress drops and serenity and achievements soar![62]

As you progress through the *12 Steps* we invite you to get to know, coordinate, and lead your inner Characters. In our work we have come to realize that the subselves or inner Characters cannot be evicted. If left unacknowledged, underappreciated and uninte-grated these inner parts will wreak havoc in the most inappropriate ways undermining your effectiveness and well-being. Recognized, appreciated, coordinated, repurposed, repositioned, and leveraged, your cast of Characters can bring an inner power, clarity, and strength that will allow you to take all aspects of your life, work, and relationships to new levels of effectiveness.

Inner Director

As you become aware of the Self that is your inner CEO you will realize there is a rich diversity within. Richard Schwartz teaches,

> To experience the Self, there's no shortcut around our inner barbarians — those unwelcome parts of ourselves, such as hatred, rage, suicidal despair, fear, addictive need (for drugs, food, sex), racism and other prejudice, greed, as well as the some-what less heinous feelings of ennui, guilt, depression, anxiety, self-righteousness, and self-loathing. The lesson I've repeatedly learned over the years of practice is that we must learn to listen to and ultimately embrace these unwelcome parts. If we can do that, rather than trying to exile them, they transform.[63]

Peter Gerlach has concluded,

> One of your personality subselves is naturally skilled at harmonizing and leading all other parts, and making optimal *decisions if allowed to do so by your other parts*. When their Self (capital 'S') is trusted by, and leading their other subselves, people universally report feeling mixes of *grounded, clear, light, centred, purposeful, ener-gized, aware, confident, 'up,' resilient, focused, and serene.*[64]

Your Self, with acknowledgement and support, will increase in confidence as it accepts the challenge and opportunities associated with assessing, coordinating, developing, and leading the inner cast of Characters. As a servant leader the Self /coordinator/CEO is both part of the cast of Characters and the *primus inter pares*, Latin for "first among equals." Like an orchestra director who is accepted by the ensemble, your Self is able to become an effective inner director.

The Self that is an integral part of your FISC, when acknowledged, empowered, and integrated, becomes part of seamless living and leading, allowing the whole to be much greater than the sum of the parts. With the Self coordinating the elements of your FISC, you will be able to dance in the moment with conscious nimbleness in service to Self, others, and the greater good.

Loving What Is

Step 4 involves unconditional acceptance of all of 'you.' As you get to know your inner Characters, you will discover they are a ragtag mix of archetypes, voices, subselves, and ego states, with powerful attitudes, beliefs, and scripts. Shaped by your Facts, Influences, and SoulDNA, some of these inner Characters were introduced into your life so early and so subtly that you may not even know they are there. Others are the result of defining moments on your life journey. These inner elements carry successes, wounds, fears, desires, angers, hopes, and griefs that shape your inner and outer Self.

With thanks to Peter Gerlach[65] and Richard Schwartz[66] here are some of the inner subselves you might hear as you listen to the conversations your Characters are having inside your mind.

Inner Cynic — "I thought you were a confident leader. Now you're reading this Self-awareness mush? These coaches are just out to get your money."

Wounded Child — "All this talk of enormity and possibility terrifies me. I just can't do it!"

Catastrophizer — "This is just the sort of thinking your Board has been afraid of. If you start talking about your inner child they will sack you immediately!"

Health Director — "These Self-leadership ideas open up all sorts of possibilities. This is great."

Demanding Parent — "The last thing you need is another self-help book. Life is tough. It's time you face reality and suck it up, buttercup!"

Warrior — "I hate it when your parents start with that attitude. I don't know why you even continue to care what your parents think. Stand up for yourself!"

Evangelist — "This is an exciting new way to think about life and work. This would make great material for a study group. You should give copies of this book to all your friends."

Fundamentalist — "This 'Energy of Life' talk is New Age mumbo jumbo. You should burn this book."

Flower Child — "I can feel the love possibilities. I hope all this inner chaos can be left behind and all the parts can learn to love each other."

Impatient Child — "I thought this quest thing was going to be an adventure. I'm bored. Where's the action?"

Self — "I am starting to realize that I have been a reluctant leader and often given my power away. I realize it's time for me to begin to lead."

We could go on but you get the point. There are many inner Characters. These inner traits, voices, tendencies, archetypes, attitudes, and personalities are part of your brain's amazing storage system. Any of these can be triggered or called upon at any time. Self-leadership involves knowing who you are in all your complexity and realizing that in every moment you are in choice of how you show up.

Carl Jung's teaching that "what you resist persists" holds true with the inner subselves. Ignore the addict, angry parent, the needy child, the sensual self, the saboteur and when you least expect it, your leadership decisions will be undermined by a subself inner sink hole. In order to lead with a powerful sense of Self you need to recognize the angry parent, the righteous bigot, or the fearful child that lives in your mind-experience. Many of the emotion-based subselves were created through defining moments in your life and live on in your consciousness ready to be re-experienced at any moment. As you continue through the Steps there may be a need for desensitizing, healing, or forgiveness, but for now love what is without ignoring or warring.

As you become more accepting of your own inner diversity and more aware of the strengths and weaknesses contained within, you will strengthen your sense of Self and use your inner awareness to become more effective in your relationship with Self and with others.

Entering Your Enormity

The great historian Arnold Toynbee once said, "Nothing fails like success."[67]

Although you have achieved success, it is on an unstable foundation if you have not learned how to incorporate and manage your inner cast of Characters. Too often, as a leader, you have avoided listening to your subselves because you needed to ignore the negative voices, traits, and injunctions in order to get to where you are. In overcoming the negative or limiting inner parts you have succeeded as a leader, but at a cost. In learning to silence the inner noise you have lost touch with the desires, urges, fears, cautions, hopes, and inspiration that could provide support and insight on your journey. In avoiding the negative influences of the inner Characters you have developed a small 's' social self at the cost of the rich resources of a big 'S' coordinating Self. Step 4 is your opportunity to integrate your inner resources. Your goal in Step 4 is to identify and acknowledge the existence of the inside archetypes, voices, subselves, and ego states, with their powerful attitudes, beliefs, and scripts, and begin to Self-lead so that, as CEO, you can leverage, repurpose, and manage all the Characters in a way that enriches and empowers your life, work, and relationships.

> Getting to know the inner Characters is a step
> in becoming a conscious leader.

Without inner awareness it is quite possible to produce children, work hard, make money, have success and recognition and yet not be conscious of who you are or the impact you are having on the people around you. For most leaders, lack of awareness of the genetic and cultural imperatives and ignorance of the inner subselves creates a blind spot that leaves you vulnerable to integrity outages, pride, stubbornness, fear, and confusion. Getting to know the inner Characters is a step in becoming a conscious leader. It is also important to know that without awareness many of the inner Characters can operate like a virus in your internal operating system. Once you realize that you are creating and defining your Self and your own inner program you can choose to develop a Self, Inc. that represents the best of all your inner and outer attributes and a 'you' that is learning and evolving over time.

Without inner awareness and the development of a conscious Self there will be outages, flare-ups, and disconnects that damage relationships, confuse you and those you want to be connected to, and cause you to be less than you could be. Unless you explore your strengths, weaknesses, and inner wisdom you will often live and lead on the surface of life and relationships rather than experience the inner riches you already possess. Step 4 is a time for deeper exploration so that you can discover the challenges and gifts in the voices and subselves that are always active beneath your usual level of awareness.

Archetypes

The term "archetype" has its origins in ancient Greek. The meaning is an "original pattern" from which all other similar persons, objects, or concepts are derived, copied, modeled, or emulated. Joseph Campbell, Jean Houston and other social anthropologists who have studied archetypes tell us they represent fundamental human motifs of the human experience as society developed. This reservoir of past experiences has become a part of our cultures, embedded so deeply that certain behaviour patterns are common the world over. The villain, the hero, the lover, the martyr, the victim, the rescuer, are so much a part of us that they show up in children's play, in books, and theatre, and in our lives everywhere. Elements of archetypal subselves exist in each of us. Fairy tales, folk songs, ballads, and legends contain elements of these characters. Each type has its own set of values, meanings and personality traits.

Some of the most common archetypes are: The Innocent, the Orphan, the Villain, the Hero, the Child, the Saboteur, the Prostitute, the Explorer, the Rebel, the Lover, the Victim, the Creator, the Jester, the Sage, the Magician, and the Ruler. These types show up in people from all cultures in the world. Each of you is influenced by elements of several of these types. Although they may be dormant, life experiences can activate these archetypal parts at any time during our life journey. As you become acquainted with the diversity within, you will find several of these archetypal qualities have strongly influenced who you are and who you choose to be. Since you control the way you show up in life, knowing your archetypal tendencies is an important aspect of Self-leadership as you become more intentional in how you interact in life, work, and relationships.

Here are some examples of how you can examine the archetypes that show up in your life in order to increase your awareness and effectiveness.

Child: At its best, the Inner Child represents the part of you that is both enchanted and enchanting to others. It sees the potential for sacred beauty in all things. It also embodies qualities of wisdom, courage, and curiosity.

Victim: Many of you spend your lives in a "poor me" mentality constantly demanding attention and sympathy from others and using your difficulties as a way to get help from others. When properly recognized, the Victim archetype can be a tremendous aid in letting you know when you are in danger of letting yourself be victimized through passivity or through rash or inappropriate actions. It can also help you to see your own tendency to victimize others for personal gain.

Prostitute: The prostitute is about more than sex. Contained in each of you this archetype is about selling out to the highest bidder. It can apply to taking a job just for the money or working in an industry or career that lacks honesty because you can make easy money. The Prostitute archetype offers lessons in the sale or negotiation of your integrity due to fears of physical and financial survival or for financial gain. This archetype activates the aspects of the unconscious that are related to seduction and control, whereby you are as capable of buying a controlling interest in another person as you are in selling your own power.

Saboteur: The Saboteur archetype is made up of the fears and issues related to low self-esteem that cause you to make choices in life that block your own empowerment and success. As an ally, it calls your attention to situations in which you are in danger of being sabotaged, or of sabotaging yourself. Once you are comfortable with the Saboteur, you learn to hear and heed these warnings, saving yourself untold grief from making the same mistakes over and over.

There is an exercise at the end of the chapter that will introduce you to a number of inner Characters that will allow further exploration and identification of the archetypes that live within you.

Your Inner Treasury

Your FISC is a unique treasury that, when acknowledged and coordinated by your CEO, equips you to excel. The "fisc" was the emperor's treasury. In more recent times the fisc became the name used for the knight's money holder as he set off on his quest. Properly appropriated and refined your Facts, Influences, SoulDNA, and Characters will show you your purpose and equip you to show up with confidence and a unique essence.

Before you can fully benefit from your FISC it will be necessary to examine the times when negative aspects of the facts, influences and experiences of your life have conspired with the shadowy aspects of your inner parts to create chaos, confusion, and damage in your life. The work of Step 4 is to reclaim it all — pain and joy, dark and light, riches and deficits. The work of Steps 5 and 6 will be to examine, sort, polish, repair, and optimize every aspect of your FISC so that as you clarify your purpose and complete your Self-leadership quest you will never again question your royal lineage.

As you revisit your beginnings in Step 4 and reclaim your earliest experiences and tendencies you will activate creativity, curiosity, old wounds, and disappointments. Reclaim it all. Allow the memories of fresh baked bread, of spring mornings, of warm flannelette, of bullies and fights, of knots in your stomach, of sunlit fields, of dark basements, of good times and torments to rise to the surface. You will sort it out in later Steps. Some of your experiences were too heavy for a child to carry. Now as an adult you will be able to complete the work of becoming whole and, through doing that, you will reclaim your sense of wonder, creativity, wisdom, and inner genius.

Moving along the Path with STEP 4...

*I acknowledge the Facts, Influences, SoulDNA, and Characters
that have shaped me and continue to affect my Difference
Making Quotient.*

STEPPING STONES

The Stepping Stones section of Step 4 is dedicated to exploring
and identifying the elements of your FISC. Use your *12 Steps*
journal to document the results of your exploration.

As you work through the following questions, you may be
tempted to think you are being asked about things that really
don't matter; however, choose to believe that your answers are
pieces of a larger puzzle that, when combined with other aspects
of your Self-leadership quest, create an outcome where, "The
whole is greater than the sum of its parts."[68]

Facts: Outline some of the Facts of your life. Start by providing
details related to the following bullet points. Include other facts
that come to your mind during the process.

- Birth Date

- Birth Country

- Gender

- Birth Order, Siblings

- Family Structure, Care-givers

- Childhood Environment

- Childhood Health and Physical Development

- Favourite Toys, Books, Movies, Games, or Pets

- Early Interests, Hobbies, Activities, Sports

- Culture

- Education and Early Learning

- Political, Social, and Religious Environments

Influences: Use the following questions to help you identify the significant people, events, or circumstances that influenced your underlying beliefs, attitudes, and behaviours, and shaped who you are today.

Birth Date

- What opportunities or challenges did your birth present to your family?

- What advantages or disadvantages do you associate with being born when and where you were?

Birth Country

- Are you proud or ashamed of how your Birth Country is predominantly viewed by the rest of the world?

Gender

- What gender-based advantages, disadvantages, or discrimination have you experienced?

Birth Order, Siblings

- If you have siblings, what special responsibilities, opportunities, disadvantages, or expectations came with your particular birth order?

- What did you like best, and least, about being the oldest, youngest, middle, only, or one of many children in your family?

Family Structure and Care-givers

- What was the style of decision-making in your birth home or home of your upbringing, i.e. authoritarian, democratic, organic, laissez-faire?

- What was the communication style of your family?

- How were family responsibilities and roles assigned and shared? What tasks were you responsible for as a child or teen?

- How did your family members treat each other?

- How were the members of your family expected to behave day to day with each other in your home? With extended family? With neighbours? Within the community?

- How were extended family, neighbours, and strangers treated in your home?

- What was the family's relationship with money, e.g. never enough; spent freely; charitable; tight-fisted; scarcity minded; other (explain)?

- What discussion topics were forbidden or discouraged in your childhood home?

- What family secrets did you have to keep, that were never to be talked about even at home?

- What inner thoughts or voices needed to be kept silent in order to survive or avoid harm in your home, at school, at work, or in the community?

- What were the traditions, events, or celebrations that brought your family together?

Childhood Environment

- Was your childhood lived mostly in an urban or rural setting?

- Was the environment safe or dangerous?

- What did you like best about the environment? What did you like least?

- If you had been given a choice as a child or young person, where would you have preferred to live, and why?

Childhood Health and Physical Development

- Describe how your childhood health or physical development was a positive or negative factor in your development of Self-confidence?

- Were there any particular positives or negatives to being ill, being healthy, or maturing early or late?

- What people or events motivated you to try something new or move to a new level of maturity?

Favourite Toys, Books, Movies, Games, or Pets

- List the toys, books, movies, games, or pets that you cherished as a child or young person.

- Describe what you liked best about each of the things you listed.

- How did they serve you and shape who you have become?

Early Interests, Hobbies, Activities, Sports

- List your childhood interests, hobbies, activities, and sports, and describe what you liked or disliked about them, how they may have influenced your development, and the life lessons that they imparted.

Culture

- What were the unique ceremonies, beliefs, and traditions of your culture?

- Typically, how were decisions made in your cultural group?

- How were gender roles viewed or assigned?

- What were the traditions, events, or celebrations that brought your social community together?

- Are there aspects of your culture that you were proud or ashamed of? Explain.

Education and Early Learning

- What were your early educational and learning interests?

- What was your early learning preference, e.g. practical hands-on or theoretical research?

- Describe your early educational experiences, scholastic achievements, and memorable events related to your education.

- What educational choices have shaped or continue to shape your life?

- How did extracurricular activities contribute to your learning?

Political, Social, and Religious Environments

- At the time of your birth, during your childhood, or during your teens, identify significant political, social, or religious realities, and describe how they influenced your life and development.

- How did your family's political, social, or religious involvements, help, hinder, or influence you?

- What rules or expectations of your family's political, social, or religious groups resonated with you? What ones did you not understand or agree with?

- How were your family's involvements viewed by other family members, or other political, social, or religious groups?

SoulDNA: Use the following questions to explore the unique essence, ability, or gifts that make you 'you.'

- Based on what you know from photos, conversations, or memories, list at least three unique qualities or distinguishing characteristics, gifts, interests, skills, or abilities—elements of your SoulDNA—that were evident during your first seven years.

- What new qualities, or distinguishing characteristics, gifts, interests, skills, or abilities have become evident or emerged since that time?

- What do you know or sense about your SoulDNA that you have kept to yourself because of lack of safety or opportunity?

Characters: From the list of subselves or archetypes contained in the following table, choose at least twelve that you recognize as part of your Inner Cast of Characters—whether you like them or not. Don't play favourites. Choose predominate voices or Characters that you suspect are part of your inner world. NOTE: This partial list is based on characters from Greek mythology, Jung, Freud, Myss, Byrne, Schwartz, Gerlach, others, and our own imagination. Feel free to add your own characters to the list.

Abuser	Achiever	Addict	Aggressor
Alchemist	Analyzer	Artist	Auditor

Avoider	Beggar	Bully	Caregiver
Catastrophizer	Child	Clown	Competitor
Complainer	Controller	Cook	Coward
Craftsperson	Creator	Critic	Crone
Cynic	Detective	Devil's Advocate	Dictator
Diplomat	Director	Disciple	Diva
Doubter	Dreamer	Ecologist	Entertainer
Evangelist	Explorer	Facilitator	Flirt
Follower	Fool	Gambler	Gossip
Guardian	Healer	Hermit	Hero
Historian	Humanitarian	Hypochondriac	Idealist
Innovator	Inspector	Inventor	Jester
Judge	Learner	Loner	Lover
Magician	Manipulator	Martyr	Matriarch
Missionary	Monk	Musician	Mystic
Narcissist	Networker	Nun	Nurturer
Observer	Optimist	Organizer	Overseer
Parent	Patriarch	Peacemaker	People-Pleaser
Perfectionist	Persecutor	Pessimist	Philosopher
Pilgrim	Pioneer	Poet	Politician
Predator	Priest	Prince	Princess
Procrastinator	Prophet	Prostitute	Provocateur
Puppet	Puritan	Rationalizer	Rebel
Redeemer	Reporter	Rescuer	Revolutionary
Risk-taker	Romantic	Rule Keeper	Ruler
Saboteur	Sage	Saint	Samaritan
Scholar	Scout	Scribe	Seductress
Seeker	Seer	Sensualist	Servant
Settler	Shaman	Skeptic	Slave
Spender	Spiritualist	Storyteller	Survivor
Taskmaster	Teacher	Thief	Thinker
Tramp	Trickster	Tyrant	Victim
Visionary	Voyeur	Wanderer	Warrior
Whiner	Witch	Wizard	Worrier

FISC Review: Based on your FISC discoveries, this section will assist you in identifying the most significant elements that help or hinder your present performance as CEO of Self, Inc. In the following Step, Step 5, you will explore how these have impacted your Self and the people around you. In Step 6 you will take corrective actions so that you can lead with synergy. We'll pick this up again in Step 10 as you create your Self-leadership Development Plan.

Facts:

- List three positive Facts that you may, or may not, currently appreciate or optimize.

- List three negative Facts that are either hindering you now, or have the potential to impede your effectiveness if not dealt with.

Influences:

- List three positive Influences that you may, or may not, currently appreciate or leverage.

- List three negative Influences that are either hindering you now, or that you have been unwilling or unable to confront.

SoulDNA:

- List three aspects of your SoulDNA that you may, or may not, currently appreciate or allow to shine.

- List three aspects of your SoulDNA that this process has helped you start to appreciate, which will benefit from further acknowledgement and development.

Characters:

- Of the twelve Characters that you identified as part of your inner world, rank them from most to least according to the frequency with which they show up in your inner dialogues and decisions.

- For each of the twelve you selected, identify both their possible danger and their value as an ally.

TRAVEL TIPS

1. If you start to feel overwhelmed or threatened as you explore your FISC, step back, take some deep breaths, and stand or sit in the posture of a confident, successful, and effective CEO of Self, Inc. If that feels impossible, don't give up. Envision a successful CEO that you know or you've read about and pretend to be them to the extent that it helps you accept the opportunity and responsibility of being the CEO of your own Self, Inc.

2. Exploring and discovering the treasures within your FISC expands your options by increasing your awareness of the inner resources you have to work with. Review, affirm, celebrate, and meditate on your FISC elements often to become more and more comfortable and natural in using them to make a difference in service to Self, others, and the greater good.

Step 5 – Impact Assessment

I conduct an honest and transparent review of who I've been, what I've done, what I've not done, what I have ignored, and what I have hidden away.

My Misery
By Hermann Hesse

My misery comes from my great talent
to wear too many masks too well.
I learned to deceive everyone, myself included.
I became a master manipulator of my feelings.
No true song could reach my heart.
Behind each step I take lurks a shrewd scheme.
I know the source of all my suffering.
I have traced it to my innermost core:
Even my heartbeat is controlled and calculated.
I make sure no dream's deep, dark foreboding,
no imprisoned passion, no stirring sorrow
can break through this armor to my soul.[69]

STEP 5...

FAST TRACK

The **Impact Assessment** of Step 5 is a call to a fearless look at who you have been and how you have shown up. By reviewing your life, assessing your needs for healing, liberating, affirming, challenging, and integrating, you will prepare to lighten your emotional and relational baggage and live and lead from new levels of awareness and effectiveness. The objective of Step 5, through journaling, support, and discussion, is to help you let go of your denial and defences and honestly explore the ways your behaviour affects Self and others. Inner awareness calls for an honest appraisal of the inner parts that you have rejected or walled off, creating inner tension and addictive behaviours. As you write down the ways your behaviour has hurt Self and others, the goal is not to shame but to reclaim by honestly facing the harm you have done to Self and others. The work of Step 5 is accepting responsibility for everything you are and everything you could be, as you also honestly examine how you show up in life, work, and relationships. In Step 5 you stand as an observer in the nexus observing the Self-other relationship so you can become aware and responsible for your relationships with the people and organizations you interact with every day. Your Difference Making Quotient is directly correlated with your ability to take responsibility for your wake. Step 5 is about recognizing the repair work you need to do while holding the intention of doing no harm to Self or others. Since Step 5 involves pain and deep exploration it should be done with the support of a helpful guide or coach to witness, hold you accountable, and reflect back so that you can hear your own voice and the voices of the inner parts. Your guide will support you as you deal with the challenges of facing your pain and shortcomings. The process will help you explore the things that are hindering your potential and failing to honour your core essence. Through taking stock of everything you have stored in the back rooms of Self, Inc. you will begin to heal your wounds, right your wrongs, and recognize and reclaim your own uniqueness and magnificence.

Leadership Value: **Responsibility**

Guiding Principle: **Appropriate responsibility leads to integrity.**

FOOTHOLD

Picture yourself traveling through life, work, and relationships in a water craft. Journal thoughts about your wake. Have you been quietly gliding in a canoe, zooming in a powerboat, trawling, being towed or toured, or just desperately clinging to an overturned lifeboat?

Review and Assessment

The objective of Step 5, through journaling, support, and discussion, is to help you let go of your denial and defences and honestly explore your wounds and your wake. What have you done that may have hurt you, others, or the larger community? What wounds and stories limit or drive you? What forgives or amends need to be made to free you up and lighten your load? What possibilities need to be explored?

What you don't know can hurt you. And there is a lot that most of you don't know. You don't know the potential for good and difference making that is part of your creative make-up. You don't know how deeply you are loved by people close to you and by the Universe. You don't know how significant your contributions and withholdings are to the unfolding of possibility. You also don't realize the many ways that your failure to show up fully and lead with purpose has harmed you and others. You underestimate the significance of the hurt you have caused others.

Step 5 is about seeing clearly. It is about looking at the Facts, Influences, SoulDNA, and Characters from the perspective that you were born to be a Difference Maker. By conducting an honest and transparent inventory of who you've been, what you have ignored, what you've done, what you've not done, and what you have hidden away you will discover repairs and amends you need to make; you will begin to free up your psychic energy; you will prepare to embrace your reality and to leverage even the difficult aspects of your experience. You will increase your observation and mindfulness skills, and you will increase your Difference Making Quotient.

By reviewing your life, assessing your needs for healing, liberating, affirming, challenging, and integrating you will prepare to lighten your emotional and relational baggage and live and lead from new levels of awareness and effectiveness. The first four Steps have given you escape velocity. Now, like an astronaut, use your trajectory to move into a new level of orbit. See yourself, your relationships, and the world from an outer perspective.

The purpose of this process is to help each of you reclaim and leverage your FISC, your royal treasury of unique inner wealth, so that you can be a conscious Self-leader. As you sort through your Facts, Influences, SoulDNA, and inner cast of Characters you will discover many times when you have hurt Self, others, and the planet through your actions or lack of action. As you do an honest and thorough review and assessment, allow the constructive guilt and healthy shame to generate the creative tension that leads to better choices in the future.

Your inner Diva and inner Critic will misuse and misinterpret your findings. Let that be all right. Facing the facts of how others have hurt and failed you and how you in turn have hurt and failed others is uncomfortable. Your inner Characters will be activated and perhaps defensive and agitated as you do this exploration. Breathe. Relax. Choose to let the Facts just be on the paper and in your heart—neither the inner Judge or inner Executioner, inner Rescuer, or inner Protector is invited to get involved. Let your best Self examine it all—the good, the bad, and the ugly. Then with the help of your guide and best Self you will use the findings to liberate your SoulDNA and the rich tapestry of inner and outer Facts, Influences, and Characters that equip you to make your contribution to the world.

> "The curious paradox is that when I accept myself just as I am, then I can change." ~ Carl Rogers

Accepting Responsibility

In the 'both—and' world of Self-leadership, progress is always found in both letting go and taking responsibility. In order to benefit from the positive elements of your Fact, Influences, SoulDNA, and Characters that you have been exploring in Step 4, it is necessary to deal with the chosen behaviours, attitudes, habits and dysfunctions that no longer serve your evolving Self. It is also necessary to accept responsibility for the damage you have experienced or caused as a result of your life experiences up to this point. This is the work of Step 5—accepting responsibility for everything you are and everything you could be. This work is not an isolated examination of your inner assets. In reviewing your behaviour and assessing your needs it is often in the interactions and relationships with the world that the level of your Self-leadership effectiveness becomes fully known. Famous American psychologist, Carl Rogers stated, "The curious paradox is that when I accept myself just as I am, then I can change."[70] Keep trusting yourself and letting those parts you have judged, rejected, or hidden be examined and reclaimed.

As you go deep inside to explore the wounds, possibilities, hopes, dreams, failures, and tendencies, your challenge will be to not get overwhelmed by the defences of your inner parts as they come alive, so that as you do your assessment you avoid nothing and face everything, considering each discovery a gift from the Universe. It will take a shift in perspective to stand back from yourself and observe without getting caught up in the drama. In doing a thorough assessment and review you are on a sacred quest to discover times when you lost the path so that you can course correct and discover what is trying to happen in and through your life. As you take steps to heal old wounds and free up your potential you will discover gifts and insights that will increase your Difference Making Quotient.

Step 5 is essential in your journey to freedom and wholeness. Without it you will be forever divided. It is not a one-size-fits-all process. Some of you need to discover new aspects about your personality so that you can use your energy more effectively and make better decisions. Others will need to examine old patterns of thinking. Some of you have deep grief issues layered under other issues of loss and abuse and these need to be assessed, identified and dealt with. Some of you are wildly successful in society's terms but undernourished and miserably unfulfilled in your relationship with Self and the few people close to you. Others of you have issues of depression and anger that need to be explored. Some of you need to get better acquainted with your inner Characters and learn new ways to express your multi-faceted complexity. Most of you have only glimpsed the cast of Characters that live within. Some of you need to recognize the power that outdated beliefs and old agreements have in your life. Some of you need to explore the toxic shame that is part of your emotional DNA. Many of you need to examine your avoidance of the inner life and your routinized action-focused thinking patterns.

If your inner Characters have addictions to smoking, drinking, drugging, pornography, or overeating or other damaging tendencies it's time to gain control through awareness and Self-leadership and change the script. If significant relationships in your life have created patterns of abuse, abandonment, enmeshment or co-dependency it's time to recognize these and begin to find other ways to show up. As you accept your inner voices and Characters as they are, and trust your Self to lead, many of the inner conflicts will begin to fade away.

Step 5 is essential in order to free you from constant striving. In this Step we encourage each of you to go deeper. Your Impact Assessment needs to include an examination of your psychic and emotional basement, storage areas, closets, attics, and the back rooms of your life. To become a conscious leader and to Self-lead from this place of wholeness, it will be necessary over time to move beyond surface effectiveness and deal with core inner issues of shame, abuse, abandonment, limiting beliefs, trauma, and neglect while also exploring passions, bliss, preferences, and gifts so that you can integrate and manifest more and more of the potential of your best Self.

Although your review and assessment will focus on the inner thoughts, attitudes, feelings, and voices, your inventory will also examine how you show up in life, work, and relationships. It is in your outer life that you gain an awareness of your inner parts. Inner awareness and outer effectiveness dance in a constant co-creative rhythm. Self-leadership is an evolving ongoing process not a one-time event. As you balance inner awareness with outer effectiveness it takes time for old habits to be replaced. It takes time to grieve the loss of the false self you had known. It takes time to build new habits and to root out non-productive old behaviours.

The Seven Storey Dwelling

Accepting your life with all its parts is like realizing you have been bequeathed a seven storey building—perhaps in a style or location that you would not have chosen. When you purposefully accept life in its fullness with its givens, you begin to consciously empower your CEO to become more effective in integrating and coordinating all the inner and outer stakeholders. Just as with a real world dwelling, ownership has its privileges and its responsibilities.

If a real business building was dull and drab with poor air quality, black mold in a few of the areas, dirty and shuttered windows, a disorganized staff, an unkempt exterior, and poor signage, it would neither serve the stakeholders nor the neighbourhood.

This metaphor is one way of thinking of you and your inner world. Until the whole of the Self, Inc. is owned and examined and intentionally led there will be serious disconnects, secret files, closed areas, clutter, internal disagreements and feuds, outdated photographs lining the halls, and areas with "do not enter" signs. Parts of the inner dwelling will be dank and dim. Exterior décor and messaging will lack consistency or clarity.

You are Self, Inc. It is now time to reclaim this dwelling and make it your own. Although the interiors, exteriors, and residents may differ, the basic structure is the same for all of us. The ground floor serves to anchor and support the entire structure. It houses the practical aspects of maintenance and stability. The second floor is the creative department. The third floor houses engineering and manufacturing. The fourth floor is the heart of the structure with human resources, health and well-being and customer service. The fifth floor is communications. The sixth is research and development, and innovation. The seventh floor has a lounge, spiritual renewal centre, and balconies that allow access to the beauty and mystery of the beyond.

Taking ownership involves making all of the dwelling yours. If windows are shuttered and the air quality is oppressive you need to make changes. If unwanted memories, old voices, fears, and grief are cluttering the inner corridors it is time to take action. If parts of the dwelling are blocked off it is time to open up those areas. If negative attitudes, high judgement, anger or bitterness are affecting relationships and morale they need to be recognized and reorganized. If there has been a lack of leadership, it is time for clear vision and purposeful action.

When you first assume responsibility it's easiest to notice the things that are out of order; however, there are also many assets to be reclaimed, polished, revived, and used. Taking ownership requires an ability to see the possibilities that others might overlook, while also addressing the things that hinder effectiveness.

A Word about Guides

As you engage in the exploration of who you've been or not been, what you've done, what you've not done, and what you have hidden away, your journey will take you along winding paths where it is easy to get lost and discouraged.

Grieving and inner excavation involve challenging and painful work. And as we stated in Foundations, although you may have a best friend or confidante you can turn to, it is often difficult to mix friendship with the level of transparency required to go deep. For many of you, the best approach will be to seek out a coach, counsellor, wise mentor, or a combination of people that you can access personally and professionally.

A good guide does not set out to fill your emptiness or heal your wounds. Instead, with a sense of curiosity, they share the wisdom they have gained when it seems appropriate, but only as an illustration of how mystery unfolds. With an appropriate detachment, a space is opened up for you to fully explore all the possibilities of what lies within and what is trying to happen. The role of a helpful guide is to witness and reflect back, affirm, push, challenge, and help you dig deep with honesty and transparency so that you can hear your own voice and the voices of the inner parts and choose what is best as you continue to excavate your truths, change behaviours and lead with confidence. Ultimately, the answers must be yours.

Whether you choose a trusted acquaintance or a professional to assist you at this stage, it is important to emphasize that the only goal in Step 5 is to take a thorough and honest inventory. Actions that move you through the next steps of healing and more fully connecting with the power and potential of your FISC will come later.

Wake Up

Tip Kindell, Chairman and CEO of The Container Store, in his book, *Uncontainable*, states, "One of my firmest convictions is that our wake—those waves and ripples of consequence that follow our every action—is much bigger than we can ever imagine. Everything you do and don't do affects the people around you and your business far, far more than you realize."[71]

In Step 5 you need to become aware of and responsible for your wake. Some of you have been travelling through life, work, and relationships in a sleek, powerful speedboat. Focused on the excitement of the moment and the goals ahead you haven't even noticed the boats and swimmers that have been overwhelmed, inconvenienced and even capsized by your wake. Some of you think you have been more thoughtful since you have waited until you were out of harbour and on open water before you really opened the throttle and let yourself go. Because you were far from shore you thought your impact was diminished. Not so. The underwater impact was immediate and the waves you caused extend far beyond your awareness.

Like the butterfly in the Amazon you are an integral part of the fabric of life. Your angry outbursts, your loving gestures, your secret rendezvous, your use of food, drugs, relationships, people, and things, affects others. It's time to take make an honest appraisal of the quality of your relationships with the people and organizations you interact with every day. What you say, and how you say it has an impact on you and others. Your Difference Making Quotient is directly correlated with your ability to take responsibility for your wake.

Circles of Influence

Arnold J. Toynbee summed up the importance of relationship systems by saying, "Society is the total network of relations between human beings. The components of society are thus not human beings but relations between them."[72]

At one stage of my life, when I was a middle manager with over twenty-five direct reports, I had a rebellion where a few of my staff went to my supervisor and demanded my removal. I survived the mutiny, but I was not without fault, and a wise mentor took me to one of those long lunches where your future is discussed and the deep learning is penned on a paper napkin. My mentor drew a circle in the centre of the napkin and then lines extending to other circles all around me. Then he asked the question, "Who are the people that you depend on for your day to day survival and success?" The woman who led the mutiny was the first name I added to my Circle of Influence.[73] For the next half hour I populated my circle. I added my wife, key colleagues, and close family members, but I also added an auto mechanic and a technical support person. By the time our lunch was completed a wiser man lived to lead another day.

As you examine your relationships in Step 5, start in close and ask if you have been sincerely listening and caring about the relationships with the key people who are essential to your success. No person is an island, and if you are going to be a Difference Maker, using your FISC, you need vibrant relationships with others. Who are the people you need in order to maximize your DMQ? Have you created the types of collaborative relationships that create synergy and mutual benefit?

Facing Reality

This impact assessment is an essential step in moving beyond the small 's' self-absorbed, fragmented focus that fuels the addictive life. Waking up and seeing the damage your choices have caused is essential for taking control of your life. The 5th Step of Self-leadership can be an intimidating challenge. In her book, *Finding Your Own North Star*, Martha Beck writes, "I usually have clients start the process of emotional healing by writing down their secret history on a piece of paper, which they are to burn as soon as they've finished. It's amazing how many of them can't even put down the whole truth about their lives in this most private of venues."[74]

For some of you, your inner Rescuer is telling you that this stuff is really for the weak people around you—not for well-organized successful leaders like you. You don't wear any masks. You have no misery. There's nothing shrewd or calculated about your interactions with Self or others.

Others of you are all too aware of your wake. Your inner Persecutor is screaming, "I told you so!"

Some of you find this process familiar. Your inner Strategist thrives on analysis. You are very capable of analysing people and situations and you use your perspectives to gain a competitive edge. You also know that your calculating approach has distanced you from people and from your best Self, but you have considered it the cost of competition.

Regardless of the challenges you face as you examine your wake, this review and assessment is not about a comparison with those around you—it is about the call of your own potential. Are you being all that you are called to be? Have you maximized the possibilities that the Facts and Influences of your life have provided? Have you been true to your inner essence, the unique giftedness of your SoulDNA? Have you supported your Self so that it has been able to coordinate your inner Characters?

Being strong or nice when you need Self-care may appear helpful to those on the outside while your SoulDNA and inner Characters may be lacking attention and leadership. 'Smiley-face' and co-operation can be a mask when honest confrontation is needed. Excelling at a job that deadens your inner life can be killing your inner creativity and shrouding your inner light. Living in your head where every thought and move is calculated may be creating cash flow at the expense of inner flow of a deeper sense of purpose and contentment. It is time to admit that your outer success is not necessarily a reliable indication of your well-being.

The reason that facing the reality of who you are and what you have done is so intimidating is that we dread not only our weaknesses but we also fear our potential. Our action-focused performance-based organizations and lifestyles place little emphasis on looking inside. Yet until you do the inner work, you will always feel hollow. You will be divorced from your best and most powerful inner wisdom. As Julia Cameron said, you will be "choosing to operate off the battery pack of your limited resources."[75]

The pseudo-personalities that you have created to mask reality, look confident, hide your shadow, and protect you from others, disconnect you from authentic flow. Like Herman Hesse, your skill at deception creates a deep despair. When you get trapped in rigid roles and get stuck in identification with a specific persona you become shallow and unreal. Sometimes you have forgotten this or never realized it, thinking that the social self that you have been presenting to the world is really your authentic Self. As you review your impact you will begin to realize you have much more to offer to the world than you have been willing or able to give. Completing Step 5 is the beginning of not only healing your wounds and righting your wrongs, it is also the beginning of a growing recognition of your own power, uniqueness, and magnificence.

Moving along the Path with STEP 5...

I conduct an honest and transparent review of who I've been, what I've done, what I've not done, what I have ignored, and what I have hidden away.

STEPPING STONES

- Based on the poem "My Misery" by Hermann Hesse:

  - When have you not been aware that you were wearing a mask?

  - When have you purposely worn other people's faces to manipulate, hide from, and control others?

  - What acts of falsehood or deception have you knowingly used with others?

  - When have you withheld emotions in order to manipulate or control?

  - When have you pushed so hard, been so controlling and calculating, that you did not allow the inner spontaneity, creativity, joy, and playfulness to enrich and open your inner and outer life?

- By taking a further look at your FISC:

  - What Facts are you not owning that are limiting or diminishing your DMQ and/or hurting you or others?

  - What Influences will need to be acknowledged in order that forgives or amends can be made?

  - What positive Influences are you not leveraging?

  - What natural giftings or SoulDNA have you hidden or failed to develop in service to Self and others?

  - What toxic Characters are you allowing to dominate Self, Inc.? What impact does this have on Self and others?

- Describe at least three situations in your life, work, or relationships where you've had opportunities to be extraordinary but avoided the opportunity or self-sabotaged your success.

- In your journal, describe the things that you have done, or not done, that may haunt you, cause a sense of regret, incompleteness, or inhibit your leadership.

- What deep grief or emotional loss issues are you becoming aware of that need to be assessed, identified, and dealt with?

- What negative self-talk are you allowing to discourage, disparage, and disavow the child within?

- What non-helpful beliefs, attitudes, behaviours, or habits, do you need to own and change?

- Where in your life have you violated or compromised your life or leadership values?

- Given your answers to the preceding questions, what are the most important forgives and amends related to Self and others that will need to be addressed in Step 6 in order to free you up and lighten your load?

- As the CEO of Self, Inc., on a scale of 1 to 10, indicate how much responsibility you've taken for your wake (1 = No Responsibility...10 = Full Responsibility).

- In anticipation of the next part of the *12 Steps* journey, who could you engage as a guide—either a trusted mentor or a professional coach? Contact them to explain what you're needing, discuss whether or not they are the right person/ professional to provide you with support, and what the next steps are in formalizing that relationship.

TRAVEL TIPS

1. Being honest with yourself can sometimes be hard work— especially when you have spent years avoiding the truth or expending energy trying to keep things hidden in a closet or inner bunker. You don't need to, nor can you, necessarily uncover everything at one time. It's taken years to get where you are. Give yourself permission to go at this process as it unfolds.

2. Continue to be honest and transparent with your Self and others and you will experience a growing sense of confidence and wholeness.

PREPARATION

The journey to this point has opened up possibilities, helped
you appreciate the resources you already possess, and
increased your sense of ownership and responsibility. Your
increased awareness will give you the information you need to
begin to take action.

In Step 6, with a guide that provides support and accountability, you will move from exploration to action as you bring
resolution to inner and outer conflicts.

In Step 7, you will begin to discover ways to find stillness within,
and prepare to live fully in the wild peace of the nexus of Self
and others.

As you liberate and renew the resources of Self, Inc., and
consciously remove barriers to effectiveness, you will find
your awareness shifting to a more comprehensive level. The
insights and actions of these two Steps will free you from old
habits and attitudes, prepare you to redefine your purpose in
life, and get you ready to lead with a renewed sense of passion
and purpose.

Step 6 - Divided No More

I take restorative action to address attitudes, behaviours, wounds, or barriers that diminish my DMQ.

Unconditional
By Jennifer Paine Welwood

Willing to experience aloneness,
I discover connection everywhere;
Turning to face my fear,
I meet the warrior who lives within;
Opening to my loss,
I gain the embrace of the universe;
Surrendering into emptiness,
I find fullness without end.
Each condition I flee from pursues me,
Each condition I welcome transforms me
And becomes itself transformed
Into its radiant jewel-like essence.
I bow to the one who has made it so,
Who has crafted this Master Game;
To play it is purest delight –
To honor its form, true devotion.[76]

STEP 6...

FAST TRACK

Divided No More in Step 6 is the start of owning your life through facing the Facts, Influences, and your inner Characters, and taking appropriate actions to reduce your emotional baggage and bring clarity and alignment to your life and leadership. As you work with your guide it is time to unburden yourself by simply facing the truth about how you have managed Self, Inc. up to now. Healing and reconciliation requires an ongoing interplay of inner work and outer experience—of private growth and facilitated skill and awareness. In essence, you are pure energy. When your energy is disrupted by old pain and losses, and damage you have caused, your power is fragmented and you cannot be in flow. Clinging to moments of bliss and cherished experiences can also serve to keep you unavailable for what is trying to happen in your life and leadership now. In Step 6, it is time to be more mindful of the ways in which you choose to respond to life. Time does not heal old wounds, reduce guilt, or free you from clinging. It takes appropriate actions and that is the work of Step 6. By taking appropriate action—forgiving, making amends, releasing—you will regain your integrity and become "stable ground" once again for your Self and the people around you. As you do this work you begin to reshape both your brain and your ongoing experience by realizing that life is not happening to you, and by choosing to be a co-creator in the unfolding of your experience. Through letting go of old stories and old behaviours that no longer serve you, you will be able to relax into your own reality and settle comfortably into your Self. As you deal with the negative aspects of your wake and the painful aspects of your life you will see the glow of your SoulDNA and be ready to commit to your Self, Inc. purpose with clarity and inner wholeness.

Leadership Value: **Authenticity**

Guiding Principle: **Courageous authenticity leads to confidence.**

FOOTHOLD

As a starting point, choose one of the amends you identified in Step 5. Then, rather than making a direct amend either volunteer, donate, or pay-it-forward as a way to make an amend. Journal about your experience.

If you haven't already done so, it's time now to engage with a professional coach or accountability partner to serve as a witness as you act upon the forgives and amends identified in Step 5. Contact this person and set up at least a couple of sessions.

Getting It Together

All of us, like Humpty Dumpty, have fallen and been broken during our lives. It happens early and it happens often. Although the "King's horsemen" and outside forces can't put you back together again, you can. The collective wisdom of courageous questors throughout the ages assures us that the reassembled 'you' will be new and improved. That is the essence of Self-leadership—doing the inside work and the outside repairs again and again. More than one wise person has stated that the cracks are important because they let the light in. We might add to that that they also allow the light to shine out. The restoration work of Step 6 will help you take all of your life and use it to become stronger, wiser, and more useful to Self, others, and the greater good.

The Impact Assessment in Step 5 was a necessary step in fully accepting how you have chosen to show up in life and relationships until now. Psychiatrist Elio Frattaroli reminds us of the profound shift that is required to accept ourselves as we really are. In *Healing the Soul in the Age of the Brain*, he writes,

> To grow into full human consciousness requires not only the defiant awareness that we are wilfully alienated from others, but the shameful awareness, and ultimate awareness that we are naked—alienated from ourselves in a state of inner conflict. To achieve this level of self-awareness we need the repeated trials of the quest, falling down again and again until we overcome our need to hide from ourselves and learn to recognize, and so become, who we really are.[77]

As you accept full responsibility for who you are and realize that you are the leader you have been waiting for, you will experience a mix of emotions. At times you will feel a lightness and be almost giddy as a result of the unburdening that occurs when you begin to tell the truth about yourself and your relationship to others. At other times, you will be tormented by inner fears and dark secrets as their energy is released and they rise through your consciousness like dark balloons. You will also become more aware of the stirring within as your inner subselves become excited and protective, engaged and cautious. Inner voices will compete for your attention and some will try to get you to give up this ill-advised excavation. There will be inner fires, sabotage, and rocks thrown through your psychic windows warning you that you will be ruined if anyone finds out who you really are. Stay the course. Trust the process. It is in falling apart that you will come together.

Step 6 is the start of owning your life in exciting and powerful new ways. Through facing the Facts, Influences, and your inner Character parts, you are beginning to take actions that will reduce your emotional baggage, free up your SoulDNA, and bring clarity and alignment to your life and leadership. Although sharing your realization that at times you have been hurtful is an important step in overcoming denial, it does not instantly give you the emotional intelligence and relational skills to build healthy relationships in the present. Although examining the pain you have experienced is an important step in identifying emotional roadblocks and releasing pent up energy, it doesn't necessarily result in instant healing and confidence. Similarly, as important as sharing your insights about anger, fear, addiction, or anxiety are in gaining awareness, it will take time and practice to break the power they have had over you. Reducing the emotional baggage and becoming undivided requires an ongoing interplay of inner work and outer experience, of private growth and facilitated skill development.

Divided No More

Parker J. Palmer writes in *A Hidden Wholeness*,

> I pay a steep price when I live a divided life—feeling fraudulent, anxious about being found out, and depressed by the fact that I am denying my own selfhood. The people around me pay a price as well, for now they walk on ground made unstable by my dividedness. How can I affirm another's identity when I deny my own? How can I trust another's integrity when I defy my own? A fault line runs down the middle of my life, and whenever it cracks open—divorcing my words and actions from the truth I hold within—things around me get shaky and start to fall apart.[78]

In essence you are pure energy. When your energy is disrupted by old pain and losses and damage you have caused, your power is fragmented and you cannot be in flow. Clinging to moments of bliss and cherished experiences can also serve to keep you unavailable for what is trying to happen in your life and leadership now. Time does not heal old wounds, reduce guilt, or free you from clinging. It takes appropriate actions, and that is the work of Step 6. By taking appropriate action—forgiving, making amends, releasing—you will regain your integrity and become "stable ground" once again for your Self and the people around you.

Your Baggage

In her wonderfully personal and profound memoir of healing and Self-redemption, *Wild: From Lost to Found on the Pacific Crest Trail*, Cheryl Strayed recounts her 1,100 mile backpack adventure hiking solo along the trail. Although she had gone to the REI to get a guidebook and the recommended equipment she had never unpacked or assembled the items she had purchased. In a motel room near the trail, Cheryl packed her bag ready to start out the next day. When everything was packed and the water bottle filled Cheryl realized that she could not pick up the pack without wedging it against the wall and pushing hard with her legs. She considered removing some items but everything at that moment seemed essential. And so she started out. With a herculean effort Cheryl managed to balance it all on her back and she wobbled off to begin her quest for freedom and self-awareness.

Whether you realize it or not, you have done the same. Since your first coos and cries you have been storing your experiences with the outer world. You have stored memories of good times and of painful experiences. Multisensory memories, often raw and unexamined have been stuffed deep into your psyche. Old wounds and worn out aspirations, deep fears, superstitions, and primitive beliefs have been placed in your emotional backpack. You also carry anger and bitterness, stories, hope, and tenderness, and faint glimmers of what your ideal life could be.

As Cheryl Strayed faced the reality of the trail, it soon became apparent that she would need to lighten her load. A friend of ours who walked the Camino de Santiago had a similar experience. Arriving in the Pyrenees with a full pack and fresh legs he realized by the end of the first day that he could not complete his pilgrimage carrying so much stuff.

Step 6 is about taking a serious and honest look at that huge bag of psychic and emotional stuff that you are attempting to carry through life and exploring what is helpful and what needs to be left behind. The journey to authenticity is from a small 's' self to a big 'S' Self. It sounds simple, but the journey from being self-centred to Self-conscious is a demanding and enriching quest. Just as, when faced with the realities of the rugged trail, Cheryl began to keep only the essentials in her backpack she also began to realize how much inner baggage she had been carrying.

As Cheryl travelled the Pacific Crest Trail she journeyed deep into her interior exploring the experiences, losses, and stories that had filled her psyche and her heart. As she reflected on the rebellious short term relief behaviours that she had used in the past to cope with her grief, anger, disappointment, and loss, Cheryl accepted reality and began to lighten her load. Although she didn't have formal guides, people and coincidences helped shape her quest experience. Even a red fox served as a reminder of her mother. She began the process of forgiving Self and others. As she reviewed her life she found gifts of awareness, strength, courage, and deep inner satisfaction. Step by step she reclaimed her inner wholeness and let go of the pain, regret, confusion, and the inner conflict that had previously filled her life to the point where she was collapsing under the weight. After hiking for 94 days, Cheryl ended her quest at the Bridge of the Gods on the Columbia River between Oregon and Washington. There was still work to do, but dealing with her inner baggage and reclaiming her FISC had helped her develop a psychic bridge to a new and empowered life.

Face the Truth

In his book, *Let Your Life Speak*, Parker J. Palmer writes,

> We arrive in this world with birthright gifts—then we spend the first half of our
> lives abandoning them or letting others disabuse us of them. As young people, we

are surrounded by expectations that may have little to do with who we really are, expectations held by people who are not trying to discern our selfhood but to fit us into slots. In families, workplaces, and religious communities, we are trained away from true self toward images of acceptability; under social pressures like racism and sexism our original shape is deformed beyond recognition; and we ourselves, driven by fear, too often betray true self to gain the approval of others. We are disabused of original giftedness in the first half of our lives. Then—if we are awake, aware, and able to admit our loss—we spend the second half trying to recover and reclaim the gift we once possessed.[79]

Each of us arrives in life with many givens—race, culture, economy, family of origin, geography, health, even aspects of temperament. Coming home to your Self does not mean you have no choice but as long as you accept the mistaken belief that parts of you are unacceptable and that you need to meet the social challenge by embodying and carrying other people's expectations you are still living a small 's' life and you have not arrived at home. Step 6 is about relaxing into your own reality and settling comfortably into your Self.

As you work with your guide it is time to unburden yourself by simply facing the truth about how you have managed Self, Inc. up to now. Use the insights you gained from Steps 4 and 5 to look honestly at how you have treated yourself and others and how you have led the dwelling called Self, Inc. Face the failures and the outages, the hurts and disappointments. Share the hopes and dreams and the attempts in the past to be true to your uniqueness. Using your journal and information you have collected tell your story to your guide. The purpose of this session is not to seek advice but to just allow the truth to set you free.

When you tell your story and another bears witness without judgement or rescuing, something shifts. When you face your losses you become aware of the inner parts that have carried you through the difficult times. Turning to face your fear, you meet the warrior within. As you open all the inner doors the chaotic parts inside gain a new respect for the emerging leader and your Self gains confidence. You discover a hidden wholeness that has been covered with guilt, denial and a lack of awareness. You will feel your heart opening and new possibilities emerging.

Decluttering Self, Inc.

When effectively developed and managed, the FISC resources of Self, Inc. make a positive difference to who you are and how you show up in life, work, and relation-ships—physically, emotionally, and spiritually. In Steps 4 and 5 you looked at your Facts, Influences, SoulDNA, and Characters, and your responses to them. Now it is time to re-examine and declutter the emotional and behavioural patterns that have been your responses to the realities of your life so that you can be fully available by dealing with the unnecessary baggage of anger, regret, nostalgia, shame, or guilt that have been weighing you down and interfering with your ability to honour your SoulDNA. As you do the work of Step 6 you will increase your ability to use the experience and wisdom gained through exploring your FISC as support for your unique contribution to the world.

My partner, Cheryl Lester, does a presentation in which she uses a large plastic bin as a simple representation of Self, Inc. In the centre of the bin she places a light representing SoulDNA. Then she adds shiny packages and precious items to symbolize the gifts from the Facts and Influences of life. She goes on to talk about inner Characters and how these take up space and energy. Cheryl explains how we tend to put things that we are ashamed of, or won't or can't talk about into corners, closets, and bunkers that we construct to keep them under wraps and out of sight and sound, reducing available space. Then she talks about other things and experiences that add layers of material and more clutter. Soon the light is obscured, the inner space of Self, Inc. is darkened, cluttered, and constricted.

Step 6 is about examining that container of Self, Inc. and removing the garbage, address-ing the brokenness, barriers and dividedness, so, as CEO you can begin to explore and manage the treasures within in order that your inner light can shine and all the parts can begin move freely and operate more effectively. In the presentation, as Cheryl talks about the restorative process of Step 6, she talks about removing the clutter, opening the bunkers, dealing with the monsters in the closets, and restoring a sense of Self, of wholeness, and opportunity. By the time Cheryl completes the whole demonstration, the original inner light representing SoulDNA is once again shining brightly.

Limiting Agreements

Don Miguel Ruiz in *The Four Agreements* teaches that freedom really demands liberation from your own complicity in your loss of true Self. He writes,

> The way you are living right now is the result of many years of domestication. You cannot expect to break the domestication in one day. Breaking agreements is very difficult because we put the power of the word (which is the power of our will) into every agreement we have made. We need the same amount of energy to change an agreement. We cannot change an agreement with less power than we used to make the agreement, and almost all our personal power is invested in keeping the agreements we have with ourselves. That's because our agreements are like a strong addiction. We are addicted to being the way we are. We are addicted to anger, jealousy, and self-pity. We are addicted to the beliefs that tell us, 'I'm not good enough, I'm not intelligent enough. Why even try?'[80]

Dr. Joe Dispenza, a neuroscientist, affirms this inner dependency on old patterns. Dr. Dispenza states that by the time you are thirty-five years old 95 per cent of your brain is dominated by the subconscious and chemical imprint from the body. Joe goes even further than Don Miguel in stating that the amplitude of emotion devoted to new behaviour must exceed the emotion of the original imprinting in order to shift from thinking, to doing, to being.[81]

> The stories you tell yourself and the way you respond is in your control. You are not just an actor reciting someone else's lines.

As you do the work of Step 6 you won't just be lightening the emotional load you will be rewiring your brain. The good news is that you are not your brain and your choices don't just shift your awareness for the brief time you focus on a change in thoughts or actions. Every choice you make creates new neural pathways or strengthens existing brain formations. You are not the victim of genes, parenting, environment, or chance. Up until now you have been selectively focusing on certain stimuli and, through your experiences and the emotions, stories, and interpretations you have attached to these life events, you have helped shape your brain, and the brain's responses have helped create the life you are experiencing.

You can begin to reshape both your brain and your experience by realizing that life is not happening to you. As you take the actions of Step 6 you choose to be a co-creator in the unfolding of your experience and the editing of the stored information. Since the earliest days of your life you have been energized by chemical and energetic responses from your thoughts and experiences. Over time, your body has become addicted to the rush of adrenaline and the energy you get from your real and imagined interactions with others. These memorized experiences, feelings and responses now make up the inner being you call 'you.' Neuroscience now knows that all that can change. The stories you tell yourself and the way you respond is in your control. You are not just an actor reciting someone else's lines. With awareness and emotional intensity you can rewrite the script.

Restoration

The key practice in accepting responsibility on the Self-leadership journey involves taking ownership of all the painful memories, regrets, shoulda's, coulda's, shortcomings, failures, and outages that have surfaced through your Self-leadership journey and process so far. It means accepting and owning all of your life's experiences so that there are no parts of your life that cannot be used to strengthen and guide you on the journey ahead.

As you experience anger, bitterness, or fear when you interact with certain people or find yourself in certain situations, don't ignore or push it down. Face it. This is a message that you have further forgives, amends, or other completion work to do.

If you have been wounded or harmed by another, choose to forgive. This forgiveness does not involve condoning, minimizing, or dismissing hurtful, cruel, or criminal behaviour. What it does is it frees you up from being emotionally tied to a past experience and ongoing triggering by anything that resembles the original wound. By choosing to forgive you will let go of the stored energy that incomplete grief holds.

If your actions have harmed you, another person, or an organization you need to make amends. Just like forgiveness, this is often best done without direct involvement with the other person. In AA they say that you make direct amends unless it would harm you or the other person. Be wise. Often there can be unintended consequences. Trust your inner knowing. Talk with your guide and do what needs to be done.

Nietzsche said, "If it doesn't kill you it will make you strong." In every situation, once you have completed the work of releasing the disruptive energy through fearless examination, forgives, and amends there are gifts to be claimed even in the most unwelcome experiences. With detachment examine how the difficult things have made you stronger, wiser, more compassionate, and more aware. Notice what inner traits have developed through your struggles.

Even after you've done your restoration work, when you least expect it, other old memories, thoughts, or emotions may float into your consciousness. To stay open and lighten your load, welcome the awareness like a balloon. Grasp the string and look at it. If it reminds you of a forgive or an amend, commit to taking action. If it represents a cherished memory that you're clinging to, bask for a moment and remember the gift that it brought you. Then let it go.

As you practice facing everything and avoiding nothing, you will grow stronger and more confident and the waste places in your life will be restored. Life is meant to be lived in the now leaning into the future. Keep your heart, mind, and will open by forgiving often, making amends when you cause harm, and by letting life pass through you rather than clinging or resisting.

Doing the Work

There is no one way to free up your energy and stay present in your life. Use your journal and your coach or accountability partner as a witness as you continue to explore and refine. The goal is to deal with the past issues so that you can be fully present now. Make a list of the significant events in your life. You may choose to create a list of losses, painful experiences, precious moments, disappointments, failures, outdated agreements. The goal of Step 6 is not to erase these from your memory. Instead it is to complete the emotional process so that you are no longer fraudulent, anxious about being found out, weighed down by unresolved emotional pain, wishfully clinging to the past, or depressed by the fact that you are living a divided life. When you deal with the hurts and behaviours of the past you will be able to be fully present in your own life and you will exude a wholeness and confidence that will create safety and stability for those around you.

One person took a small file box and used file cards to track the people, experiences, forgives, and amends that needed to be made. This doesn't have to be done in a day. Just listing the items that need to be addressed and working your way to freedom will give you a sense of integrity and empowerment. In most cases with forgives the other person does not need to be involved. Letting go of the pain of the past is about letting go of the hope for a different or better yesterday. Life is what you have experienced. Accept the reality. Even with amends, in most cases it is not necessary to communicate directly. If an act of greed or unkindness is blocking your flow make a donation to a worthy cause or do a random act of kindness to amend for your earlier outage. Then forgive yourself and let it go.

Writing a letter to a person, yourself, or a part of you may be helpful. These letters are not meant to be sent or kept. Often it is helpful to read them aloud by yourself or to your coach and then burn or dispose of them as a symbolic act of completion.

Here are a few examples of the kind of letter you might write.

> Dear Uncle, I have been on a quest to discover my strengths and let go of the past. I realize your sexual interference early in my life has caused me great pain and kept me from living with joy and vitality. I have decided to forgive you. There is no longer any place in my life for bitterness and anger. I am letting go of the pain and the hurtful memories. Good-bye.

> Dear Inner Child, I am sorry for the times when I have ignored your need for fun. I forgive you for your tantrums and pouting. I will pay more attention to your needs. In return, I will ask you help me be more playful and curious in my work and interactions with others.

> Dear Inner Victim, I have been thinking about our relationship and realize I have given you too much power in my life. I no longer want to interpret life as happening to us. Please forgive me for my lack of leadership. Please help me realize when I am in danger of being victimized through passivity or a rash decision. Help me realize when I am about to victimize others for personal gain.

> Dear XYZ Corporation, My seventeen years with you has had a significant impact on shaping my life. Thank you for the opportunities your employment provided. I forgive you for the times when you demanded me to work long hours and miss important time with my family. I apologize for the times when I lied about my availability and used company resources for personal use. I forgive you for the sudden dismissal and the meagre severance package. I met many great people and learned important skills during my time with you. I will take the gifts and leave the rest behind.

In some cases you may choose to make direct amends even though you realize there are risks of being misunderstood. One man who had an awakening and made a list of people he had harmed had a business partner on his list. Several years earlier he had suddenly abandoned the business partnership with nearly $10,000 of money that did not belong to him. As he did his amends he became convinced he needed to make this right and not only repay the sum but add interest to the money owed. After calculating a generous repayment our hero wrote a cheque with interest and arranged to meet his ex-partner at a coffee shop. The partner was surprised to hear from him after so many years but agreed to meet. Almost giddy with anticipation the questor apologized and presented the cheque. The other person then launched into a diatribe expressing their anger, grabbed the cheque and left.

Hearing such a story you may be tempted to think the process didn't work. That is not true. The point of the story is that forgiving and making amends is not dependent on the person or institution you are dealing with. It is all about completing the experience and freeing yourself of the psychic energy so that you can leave the past behind and move forward with a renewed sense of integrity and purpose. As you deal with the negative aspects of your wake and the painful aspects of your life you will see the glow of your SoulDNA and be ready to commit to your Self, Inc. purpose with clarity and inner wholeness.

Moving along the Path with STEP 6...

I take restorative action to address attitudes, behaviours, wounds, or barriers that diminish my DMQ.

STEPPING STONES

- Using your journal and information you have collected from Steps 4 and 5 share your life and leadership experience with your coach, accountability partner, or guide. Share the details of your FISC exploration and impact assessment in order to have someone witness and mirror back the insights you're gaining, the discoveries you're making.

- As you take responsibility for your attitudes, wounds, and barriers, it's time to act on the most important forgives and amends that you identified in Step 5.

  - In conversation with your coach, go through each forgive and amend identified in Step 5 in order to prioritize and create an appropriate plan of action, noting that a direct forgive or amend should not be made if it will harm either you or the other person. In the case of an amend, often an indirect and anonymous act of charity will free up your psychic energy.

- In the case of a loss or experience that is still highly charged with emotion that involves forgiveness, write a letter to the person, entity, event, or organization that is involved in this painful experience. See the example in the Doing the Work section of Step 6. In your letter express forgives and other thoughts that will release the pent up feelings that have been weighing you down and need to be expressed. **This letter is not to be sent.** Instead, read it aloud with your coach. Once you have read the letter, burn or shred it as a symbol of letting go and releasing you from the painful energy from the past. Do this with other losses or painful experiences as needed.

TRAVEL TIPS

1. Although taking full ownership for yourself can be a bit daunting at times, it is one of the most important and freeing actions you can take on your journey. Even if you begin to lose some of your courage, stay the course, trusting that the outcomes are worth every bit of effort and energy you put into the process.

2. While dealing with the actions of Step 6, meet with or speak with your coach or accountability partner at least once a week, more often if needed. Be intentional. Stay on task. You may only need fifteen minutes to work your way through an action with your coach. At other times, you may need more time; however, given the emotional demands of this work, we recommend that your sessions never exceed two hours.

3. Your courage and confidence will grow as you take restorative actions.

Step 7 - Integral Pause

I regularly engage in times of pause, retreat, and reflection.

old and new
Maya Stein

We have such awe for the caterpillar. Reverence, even,
for its slow molting, for the poetry of its transformation. We watch, transfixed,
as it wrestles out of what was — that permeable, earthbound skin –
and catches the first whiff of flight. It's not that the metaphor is lost
on us. We recognize the magnificence and rigor of metamorphosis, the ache
and necessity of change. But the turn of our own body we thwart and battle.
Our hearts cleave from an outgrown home but we groove claw marks in our wake –
departure like a hostile beast. Perhaps it's the fulcrum in the see-saw that alarms.
That pause between the past waving its farewell and the future opening its arms.[82]

STEP 7...

FAST TRACK

The **Integral Pause** of Step 7 is a call to a different kind of awareness. We propose four types of pauses—the daily pause, the micro pause, the renewal pause, and the annual pause. The process of transformation at this stage requires a combination of awareness and new ways of acting in response to the stimuli that you encounter. As you learn to pause in conversation, in decision making, in judging, and in speaking, the pause will often be so brief that others won't even notice the space, yet in the pauses Self-leadership will give strength, insight, power, and confidence. Step 7 is an invitation to take time each day to be still. Let go of all control and let life begin to unfold. This process is an unfolding, a hatching of sorts. There is no need to hurry or force the process. This is a time when all the inner parts need to be discovered, heard, and assessed. This is a time for allowing dissent and for the marginalized inner voices to challenge attempts to quickly gain consensus. As a Self-leader you will need to pause to listen to the subtle whispering of your soul and the wisdom and gifts of your inner parts. As you pause in Step 7, keep an open mind so that you suspend judgement and old habits of thought. Keep an open heart so that you can let go of cynicism in order to empathize and see situations through the eyes of your inner parts and other stakeholders. Keep an open will so that you can move beyond fear and let go and let the new come. It is time to reflect on and edit the stories that you tell yourself about who you are and what you are called to do. It is time to take charge of the narrative in your life and realize you are free to write your own story. Trust your emerging Self. Ask big open-ended questions. Anticipate a dynamic new style of Self-leadership. Visualize the emerging future. Let go, and let come. As you use your pauses to ask why not instead of why, you will be shaping a future of unlimited possibility and becoming a conscious Self-leader.

Leadership Value: Stillness

Guiding Principle: Focused stillness facilitates clarity.

FOOTHOLD

Take time to reconnect with the symbol you chose to mark your commitment to crossing the threshold in Step 3. Use it as reminder to pause and meditate each morning, in the middle of your day, before important calls or meetings, and at the end of your day. Use it as well as a reminder to do regular body scans in order to listen deeply.

Coming to Your Senses

Step 7 is about coming home to yourself and showing up fully with all the wonder and joy you were intended to have.

The Pause is both a skill and a practice. As a skill it involves specific behaviours that shift awareness, release impediments, increase energy flow, activate deep knowing, and allow Self to lead. As a practice it is a commitment to pausing each morning and evening and several times during the day. It is also a practice of having longer purposeful pauses at least four times during the year. The integral pause will allow you to move from a mechanistic view of yourself, like a autotron moving through life with a little person sitting somewhere inside the brain taking in information and pulling levers and pushing buttons to optimize your performance, to a holistic, organic awareness and action. From this purposeful pause you Self-lead from the perspective of a spiritual being, in an energetic body, integrally connected to a web of relationships and the natural environment. Step 7 is about coming home to yourself and showing up fully with all the wonder and joy you were intended to have. The previous Steps have been an archaeological dig. You may not have discovered all the answers but you are now much more capable of living the questions. Trust yourself and trust the process.

With practice, pauses can be so integrated that they take very little time and can be accommodated into any environment or life circumstance. Whether you are headed for the boardroom or the battlefield, on the beach with family, or on a gurney headed for the operating room, a deep breath, letting go of judgement, cynicism, and fear, affirming your connection with the Energy of Life, and connecting to the emerging future with optimism and curiosity will allow life to flow for you and positively impact all those in your immediate Circle of Influence.

For generations most of us have been stuck in our heads. Suffering from the mechanistic maxim that Descartes put into the phrase, "I think, therefore I am", we have become disconnected from Self, our own bodies, nature and the Universe. By pausing with purpose you can reconnect to your sensate body, your energetic field, and your spiritual awareness. With these regular recalibrations you will experience new levels of aliveness, awareness, and effectiveness.

The Basics

We propose four types of pauses—the daily pause, the micro pause, the renewal pause, and the annual pause. Each type will have its own elements and each of you will find the process that works best for you. Here are some suggestions as you begin or refine your process.

Each morning, pause as you awake from sleep. Before you do or say anything find a quiet place to sit for few moments and in this pause breathe deeply, welcome the new day, visualize living and leading with integrity and joy. Breathe deeply again and allow any amends or forgives from yesterday to arise into consciousness and commit to dealing with those today. Set your primary intentions for the day. Stand, stretch, breathe deeply again and begin your day. Obviously if you awake with a knock at your door, a crying child, or an emergency phone call your day will begin very differently. Don't lose the concept of the pause even as you rush to a bedside or the fire truck. A deep breath and a commitment to serve Self and others with integrity will improve your response. With practice you do not need to sit cross-legged for an hour to begin your day. If you turn off the radio for a few minutes, a commute can allow you to begin your day with a non-anxious presence and a renewed sense of purpose.

As you settle into your workplace for the day, pause. Take a few moments to set your intentions for the day. It has been wisely said that energy follows attention. Wherever you place your attention that is where your energy and the larger energy field you are part of will focus. In order to make the most of the awareness that "energy follows attention" you need to shift your energy from what you are trying to avoid to what you are trying to bring into reality. Be specific.

During the day when faced with a challenge, an important decision, a confrontation, or an opportunity, take a micro pause. This can be done in a meeting, as you rush to catch a plane, in the midst of a game, or at a social event. It involves a deep breath that intentionally connects head, heart, gut, and best Self. In this integral pause you allow profound awareness to inform thought and action. With practice it can happen so quickly that others will only be aware of a brief thoughtful pause. In this quick pause, you will let go of judgement, cynicism, and fear, listen to your inner wisdom, and embrace possibility. This short pause will enable you to act knowing that when you engage all of you, Self, Inc. is creative, resourceful and whole.

At the end of each day, pause again just for a few moments of quiet reflection. Breathe deeply and express gratitudes, even for the tough stuff. Let go of regrets by committing to corrective action, send positive thoughts to loved ones and special situations.

In the *7 Habits of Highly Effective People*, Stephen R. Covey devotes Habit 7 to the principles of Self-renewal. In a section entitled Sharpening the Saw he stresses a weekly pause that focuses on the four synergistic elements of a successful life—Physical, Social/Emotional, Spiritual, and Mental. By pausing and looking at where you have been in the last seven days in each of these areas you can make the course corrections that will restore balance to your life and ensure that you are ready for purposeful choices and effective action in the days ahead. The pause does not have to be passive. You can plan menus for the week ahead, exercise, read, journal, write notes, call or spend time with one of the important people in your life.

The renewal pause involves one to three days away, preferably every three or four months, where long walks, good meals, rest and relaxation create an opportunity to review recent experiences in the context of your personal and professional goals. Too often leaders are so focused on 'doing' that Self-care is ignored. Production is pushed at the expense of production capability. Like a manufacturer that runs expensive machinery without regular pauses for maintenance and renewal it is too easy to let work take over your life. You need regular longer pauses to evaluate and renew your body, mind, and spirit. As a conscious leader it is necessary to have regular pauses to rest, reflect, realign, and reinvent. Thich Nhat Hanh teaches that,

> Self-love is the foundation for your capacity to love the other person. If you don't take good care of yourself, if you are not happy, if you are not peaceful, you cannot make the other person happy. You cannot help the other person. You cannot love. Your capacity for loving another person depends entirely on your capacity for loving yourself, for taking care of yourself.[83]

If you take this pause with a life or business partner, agree in advance to times of individual solitude and reflection combined with intentional times of deep conversation, reflection, and assessment. This is a time when your current Self and your best future Self meet and explore what is trying to happen. This is a time to journal, dream, review your ability to be fully present and live with a clear sense of purpose.

The annual pause we suggest is in the style of a personal retreat. This time away will serve you best if it is in a place where you can enjoy long walks in a woods or on a beach, and where you can experience sunrise and sunset, and starry nights. We cannot over-stress the importance of the environment. A space that has been dedicated to thoughtful retreats has its own sacred energy that will speak to you as soon as you arrive. This is not a time to be next door to a rock band or on the same lake as screaming Seadoos. This needs to be a safe place physically and emotionally where you can relax and all the parts of your FISC are welcome and honoured.

We encourage you to not only set aside five to seven days alone, but also to unplug from everything other than some instrumental music that you may choose to use during times of meditation. As part of your resources take a few poems, readings, and a book or two that will inspire and guide your own journey. Choose books like *Let Your Life Speak* by Parker J. Palmer or *Gift From the Sea* by Anne Morrow Lindbergh. If you play an instrument take it along. Other ways to open up your connection with Creativity might include some carving tools, drawing or painting materials. Cheryl has taken a week for a "Me, Myself, and I" retreat for several years now. She travels to a lakefront retreat space and rents a cottage for just herself. During the week she reads, journals, walks, writes, rests, observes nature, draws and paints. I have benefitted from silent retreats at the Loyola Centre in Guelph, Ontario. This past summer I spent a week in student residence at York University in Toronto watching Pan Am Track and Field and spending hours walking, reading, and reflecting.

The pause does not always bring a quick and simple answer. Sometimes the greatest gift is in the form of a tightness of the gut or an inner voice that says, "Not yet," or a part of you that says, "This sounds like selling out." It will take courage in a results oriented world to pause and admit to yourself and others that you don't know what's next. When you are honest about your lack of clarity, you invite others and the wisdom of the Energy of Life and your inner parts to bring new insights.

Aside from your planned pauses, once you accept the rhythm of activity and renewal, you will realize how often life provides occasion for a few deep breaths and an opportunity to move from head to body, from reactive to proactive living. Soon line-ups at the grocery store, wait times at the dentist or doctor, delays on the highway, a brief illness, a cancelled meeting, or a restless night, can go from imposition to invitation and from a time waster to a gift of awareness.

Trust Your Self

We often live on the surface of our lives, telling ourselves lies and half-truths in some distorted way believing that at the deepest level our sensitive Self could not face the truth. Nothing could be more untrue. Your challenge as you pause is to remember that even though some parts of you may be uncomfortable with the truth and the renewal process of Step 7, your spirit is being nourished and as Martha Beck writes, "No matter how difficult and painful it may be, nothing sounds as good to the soul as the truth."[84]

Leading from within is an evolution—a natural awakening. Embrace what resonates now, and brings vibrancy to your life. As Rainer Maria Rilke wrote,

> Have patience with everything that remains unsolved in your heart. Try to love the questions themselves, like locked rooms and like books written in a foreign language. Do not now look for the answers. They cannot now be given to you because you could not live them. It is a question of experiencing everything. At present you need to live the question. Perhaps you will gradually, without even noticing it, find yourself experiencing the answer, some distant day.[85]

This wisdom, written by Rainer Maria Rilke in his *Letters to a Young Poet*, still speaks to us today.

Allow the new life to emerge from Source with a childlike wonder and curiosity. The Buddhists call this place of simplicity and openness "beginners mind." Jesus said, "Unless you become like a little child you cannot enter the kingdom of God." Both of these perspectives remind us that at the soul level we knew more before we knew so much. The answers you have been searching for are within. You are creative, resourceful, and whole. You have spent most of your life judging and comparing, competing, and striving. The Self-leadership quest is not to some distant destination but to the faraway nearby. It is a process of Appreciative Inquiry where you allow yourself to emerge from the old life into a dynamic newness while realizing that at the core you are more yourself than you have ever been before. That is what Marianne Williamson meant when she wrote, "And as we let our own light shine, we unconsciously give other people permission to do the same."[86]

The process of transformation at this stage requires a combination of awareness, new ways of seeing the inner and outer world, and new ways of acting in response to the stimuli that you encounter. When you breathe deeply and trust your inner voice you will notice that there is a space between the stimulus and the response. This space is the secret to your newfound freedom. In that brief moment you can choose to live from your best Self rather than from conditioned responses and primitive instincts.

Trust yourself at the deepest level. Not the superficial social 'you' that often lives on the surface of Self and relationships and flits like a dragonfly skimming the surface, seldom landing. As you experience Step 7, expand your understanding of best Self. Let your definition of best expand to include words like truest, essential, authentic, core, foundational, most real. Explore the parts of you that you have told yourself were too much like someone you don't like, or too loud, or too much, or too little. Relax and observe. Trust.

Hatching Into New Life

So Step 7 begins with a call to a different kind of awareness. This process you have been called to is not an endurance race. It is an unfolding, a hatching of sorts. There is no need to hurry or force the process. Hatching is a complex procedure. As with many things in life, the process is as important as the destination. As a young boy I didn't know that, and I learned a harsh lesson. On a visit to my aunt and uncle's farm I was delighted to see some eggs in the process of hatching under a heat lamp. I was fascinated and as the beak and foot began to break through I thought I could help. I gently began to break away some of the shell. Soon I was horrified to see blood and then my cousin realized what I was doing and intervened. "You can't help them!" he said, "They have to do it themselves."

Since then, I have learned how wonderfully complex the hatching process is. As the embryo grows it starts to run out of space in its constrictive shell. Instinctively, a pipping muscle begins to twitch. Change is happening. This causes the hatchling's head to come up and out from under its wing, and the sharp egg tooth on the end of its beak will puncture the inner shell membrane. The piecing of this inner membrane will cause changes in the blood vessels that have covered the embryo. As the supply of oxygen in the air sac is gradually used it is replaced with carbon dioxide exhaled by the chick. This imbalance again begins to suffocate the nearly hatched chick, and as it does so it will begin to twitch in its death/birth throes once more, and it is this violent twitching which causes the chick to "pip" through the eggshell. The eggshell is now "pipped" and the chick can once more breathe fresh air.

As you pause and integrate the learning from the exploration of Steps 4 through 6, the unfolding will feel natural and flow from your inner awareness and all the work you have already done. As you continue to develop emotionally and spiritually, the restrictive shell of old habits and old thinking will become too tight and a process of pipping and hatching will continue. Through the work you have done in Steps 4 through 6 you have a great deal of information to integrate into this renovated Self you are becoming. Trust the process and your instincts. You may twitch a bit and your new ways of thinking and being will feel awkward at times. You are building new muscles. Be gentle with yourself. Find new ways to nurture the calm confidence that is emerging. You will need times of rest to allow the new ways to solidify.

The Path of Transition

The transition process begins with letting go of something. In Step 6, we helped you start to let go of the old in order to make room for the new. Next in this important process, after the letting go, comes the neutral zone. This is a desert land between the old reality and the new. It's the limbo between the old sense of identity and the emerging Self-leader. It is a time when the old way is gone and the new way doesn't feel quite comfortable yet. What we admire about the caterpillar is its non-anxious acceptance of metamorphosis. When accepted, the pauses in our life can serve as cocoons where important transitions can occur. As an essential part of the *12 Steps of Self-leadership*, Step 7 serves as an important pause on your leadership quest.

Like hatching, there is no specific timetable and no one else can force the process as your new life emerges. If you escape prematurely from the neutral zone, you'll not only compromise the change but also lose a great opportunity. As challenging as it is to simply and patiently trust the process, the neutral zone is the individual's and the organization's best chance for creativity, renewal, and development. This space between the old and the new is the time when innovation is most possible and when revitalization begins.

During this Self-transition process restrain the natural impulse to push prematurely for certainty and closure. It's tempting to avoid discomfort by seeking safety and certainty through quick decisions. This is abdication rather than acceptance of the challenges and opportunities. The integral pause is a time when all the inner parts need to be discovered, heard, and assessed. This is a time for allowing dissent and for the marginalized inner voices to challenge attempts to quickly gain consensus. As a Self-leader you need discernment and you need to pause to listen to the subtle whispering of your soul and the wisdom and gifts of your inner parts. There is no need for a pendulum swing of change. A one per cent tiller change will, over time, take your life to a whole new destination. Trust the process.

Learning to Listen

Effective listening—whether listening to Self or others—is a very important skill to develop. In order for your pauses to be most effective your listening needs to be at the highest level. Listening to Self—all the parts of Self, Inc.—does not occur in a vacuum. In many of the pauses that we suggest you will be alone. Yet part of your reflective process will involve listening and learning from what the people, situations, coincidences, and experiences in your life are saying. If you don't get past a defensive level of filtered awareness you will miss the opportunities that reflection and renewal present.

Lower level listening originates from the centre of your habits. When you listen at this level, everything is filtered through what you already know—or think you know—about past experiences and inherited beliefs. From this perspective, what you think you know gets in the way of what is really happening. Your mind, heart and will are closed. The results are predictable old behaviours and unwanted outcomes. You are listening as a defence lawyer for your old small 's' self.

As you learn to listen with more openness and curiosity you realize that the message is more than the words. You realize that your body, mind, and heart, and the people you interact with, share information through the tone, the pace, and the feelings expressed. By pausing you can say a quiet, "Thank you," and learn from the messages life is speaking to you. Pauses let you listen and choose what to respond to and how you will respond so that you can bring your best to the dialogue.

When you listen at the highest level you are fully present. You listen with openness and a soft focus, sensitive to subtle stimuli, ready to receive information from all your senses. At this level of awareness it is as if you are at the centre of the universe, receiving information from everywhere at once. As you develop this level of listening you listen with more than your ears and inner awareness. Your listening includes everything you can observe with your senses: what you see, hear, smell, and feel—the tactile—as well as the emotional sensations, and the voices of your intuitive knowing. As you learn to listen to the whole you will notice coincidences and serendipities and see them as part of the flow as well—a bird flying by, a door slamming, an interruption, an invitation to coffee, or an ad about a weekend retreat. Everything becomes part of the larger conversation as you listen well and discern what is trying to happen.

The Silent Witness

Step 7 is an invitation to become a non-judgemental observer of Self in real-time situations. As much as possible refrain from making a plan to reform yourself into some preconceived idea of what is best. Just start with observing yourself as a curious detached silent witness. Listen to how you show up and how you speak and interact with others. Notice your reactions and observe your responses without trying to do more or different, just observe. Become aware of the thoughts and stories as they fly through your mind. Notice the thoughts that roost. Observe how these thoughts shape your response, your posture, your facial expressions, and your choices. Notice how you show up in your actions, reactions, attitudes, and judgements with Self and others.

Starting with your breath, become aware of how your body moves. As you start your day, feel your fingers, toes, shoulders, and facial muscles. Notice how you move in your home, at work, in social situations. Notice your stance in different environments. Feel your smile as it shapes your face. Notice your forehead and eyebrows as you frown.

Observe yourself in store windows, in the mirror. Notice where you carry your stress and fatigue. Notice how joy and excitement show up in your body and face. Notice how you touch the things around you. Be aware of how you shake hands, hug, and caress.

As you explore your relationships with others, notice your responses as soon as you see an e-mail, hear a voice on the phone, or see another person. What do you notice in your breathing, your facial gestures, your inner resonance or resistance? Who energizes you? Who drains you? When do you become competitive? When do you go silent? Do you pout if the interaction does not go the way you hoped? Do you become loud and aggressive? Do you script your interactions and then get frustrated when the plot does not unfold as you had visualized?

As you notice the conflicts in politics, religion, workplaces and families, observe also the conflicts and polarizations within you. Eavesdrop on the inner dialogue. This is not a time to try to fix or eradicate the parts of yourself that you may have a tendency to reject. So much of the journey to wholeness and wisdom is not some strict regime of this or that, but a wise and continual management of the polarities within and without.

Accentuate the Positive

As you take a pause, one of the tools that will help you explore possibilities is Appreciative Inquiry. Appreciative Inquiry is an approach to listening and observing that starts with a strong belief in the capacity of individuals and systems to evolve. Rather than looking for what's wrong, an appreciative inquiry focuses on what is working and exploring how to bring more of this positive energy to life.

Here are a few essential concepts adapted from Appreciative Inquiry [87] that will help you ask better questions when you pause:

1. Better questions lead to better outcomes.

2. The moment you ask a question, you begin to create a change.

3. What you choose to focus on shapes the emerging reality.

4. Human systems move in the direction of their vision of the future.

5. The more positive and hopeful your image of the future, the more positive the present-day action.

As you complete your quest and continue to learn and grow, your pauses may also benefit from the 4 "D's" of Appreciative Inquiry: [88]

Discover the best of what is.

Dream of what might be.

Design systems, structures, and processes aligned with your highest potential.

Allow your *Destiny* to emerge as you lean into the emerging future.

As you use your pauses to ask 'why not' instead of 'why', you will be shaping a future of unlimited possibility and becoming a conscious Self-leader.

Moving along the Path with STEP 7...

I regularly engage in times of pause, retreat, and reflection.

STEPPING STONES

- Be intentional about scheduling your regular times of pause. Block dates in your calendar for the renewal and annual pauses. Decide on your destinations and book your reservations now.

  - Daily pauses—Pause for a few moments as you awaken each day to set intentions for the day, centre yourself, let go of old things from yesterday, and choose to be present in the now. At the end of the day pause for a few moments to review the day, express gratitude, let go of negativity, and send positive thoughts or prayers regarding loved ones.

  - Micro pauses—Do a micro pause anywhere, anytime you need to reenergize, get in touch with inner wisdom, reground, defragment, or refocus.

  - Renewal pauses—Book 1-3 days at the end of each quarter alone or with your life or business partner for long walks, good meals, rest, reflection, and review. Explore what's trying to happen in your life, work, and relationships.

  - Annual pause—Set aside 5-7 days to be alone in a safe, quiet space where you can unplug from distractions, rest, renew, journal, create, and open yourself up to the emerging future. Instead of trying to run a marathon your first time out, set some reasonable and achievable goals. Finances and work/life realities may challenge you to find other creative ways and times to pause, unplug and renew. If you're not keen on doing a multi-day pause/retreat all on your own, then a programmed group retreat may give you a more productive structure for your time away.

- Whenever you lose your balance, confidence, or poise, take a moment to remember a time when you felt very confident and in the flow, then take three deep breaths and embody the posture and energy of that experience.

- Use your journal often to make notes about what you notice before, during and after times of pause including the insights and ideas that surface.

TRAVEL TIPS

1. Effective pause takes practice. Keep practicing.

2. Use regular times of pause to gain clarity.

3. Stillness facilitates synergy. Embrace all parts of your FISC and listen to the inner wisdom during times of pause.

APPLICATION

The last five Steps will help you move from concept to application. As desire shapes reality, with engaged awareness you will notice your performance naturally improving in all aspects of life, work, and relationships.

As you re-examine your purpose and the processes you will use to serve Self, others, and the greater good, you will find a renewed joy in living with meaning. From this enlarged perspective you will be able to create short- and long-term plans to transform vision into more effective ways of learning and leading.

As you complete your leadership quest, the ongoing work will develop attitudes and practices that will keep your vision fresh and all aspects of your Facts, Influences, SoulDNA, and Characters continuously engaged in synergistic and transformational flow.

Step 8 – Call to Conscious Leadership

I accept the call to effectively manage, develop and employ the elements of FISC in conscious service to Self, others, and the greater good.

I Will Not Die an Unlived Life
By Dawna Markova

I will not die an unlived life.
I will not live in fear
of falling or catching fire.
I choose to inhabit my days,
to allow my living to open me,
to make me less afraid,
more accessible;
to loosen my heart
until it becomes a wing,
a torch, a promise.
I choose to risk my significance,
to live so that which came to me as seed
goes to the next as blossom,
and that which came to me as blossom,
goes on as fruit.[89]

STEP 8...

FAST TRACK

The **Call to Conscious Leadership** is not about perfect flawless management of Self, Inc. and others. It is about being comfortable in your own skin. Conscious leadership is about confidence and wisdom that flows from within while being exquisitely aware of every detail of the present moment. It is about being able to be so much in flow that the errors, disagreements, challenges, and surprises are just helpful information as you lead with clarity and relaxed intensity. Conscious leadership allows you to lose your balance without losing your Self. As a conscious leader you are called to be a mindful, non-anxious presence in the midst of the messiness of life. When you do that, you inspire others to do the same. Your Difference Making Quotient dramatically improves. As a conscious leader you step back and witness, even in the midst of the action, so that you can sense the whole, while focusing on a specific part. In touch with your authentic Self, you listen to intuition and act without second guessing. With Self-trust, decision making and action steps are confident and swift. You recognize the power and potential that is in you and everyone you meet. As a conscious leader you develop the inner awareness, confidence and sense of Self to make it safe to lower the emotional drawbridge. When this is done with curiosity, authenticity, and caring, deep meaningful connections and dynamic work results. As you listen to and empathize with your inner parts, you develop even more confidence and ability to empathize with others around you who are experiencing challenging realities. Conscious leadership practices create a level of awareness that allow you to bring your best to life, work, and relationships. As you lead from this new place of consciousness, you will find that inner Characters that once dominated your old unaware and fragmented small 's', will now cooperate with the growing vision and inner clarity of Self, Inc. Conscious leadership involves trusting your Self to show up fully and not only to be enough but to be *amazing*.

Leadership Value: Service

Guiding Principle: Compassionate service engages the best of Self and others.

FOOTHOLD

As you practice conscious leadership, follow the win-win way. Stand in your truth in gentleness. State preferences rather than positions. Practice deep listening and vulernability in order to stay open and fully conscious.

Conscious Leadership

To lead consciously is to lead with intent. From this awakened perspective conscious leaders realize that they are not an insignificant speck in the mass of humanity but a vital part of the emerging future. You are now ready to step fully into your role as a Difference Maker. Your unique combination of life experiences, skills, attitudes, spirituality, and inner diversity that we have referred to as your FISC, positions you to make a contribution to Self, others, and the greater good that no one else could make.

For the earlier stages of the journey we were using an invitational tone, cheering you on and seeking to inspire and engage you. Now you have completed your exploration and preparation and as a Self-leader you are ready to live and lead with increased awareness and effectiveness. Our purpose in the final five Steps is to act as your mentor-coaches, calling you to new levels of awareness and effectiveness and giving you reminders and processes that will equip you to be a transformational leader.

Conscious leadership is not some vague collection of ideas but a practical and purposeful style of leadership that is conscious of Self and others and knows that you can only truly be successful when others and the greater good also benefit. Conscious leadership is a commitment to personal mastery and genuine caring for others. Through conscious leadership you will choose to live from your passion and your giftedness with a maturity, calmness, and effectiveness that will allow you to sustainably perform at a high level while inspiring and engaging others. Step 8 is both a call and the beginning of applying the learning and clarity you have gained through the first seven Steps.

Purposeful Imperfection

The goal of Self-leadership is becoming real and embracing all that you are and all that you can be. During the Exploration phase of your leadership journey you have discovered and refined your FISC—your inner treasury of the gifts and strengths from the Facts, Influences, SoulDNA, and Characters. As you took responsibility for leadership of Self, Inc. and, through an impact assessment and appropriate actions, eliminated your outstanding debts, you learned to pause when needed and create a habit of continuous learning and improvement.

Steps 8 to 12 will apply your growing skills as you lean into the emerging future with awareness and optimism as a conscious leader with a clear purpose and thoughtful plans of how you will apply your learning for Self, others, and the greater good.

Effective decision making is not possible without the motivation and meaning provided by conscious input. Whether it is on a sports field or in a boardroom, conscious leadership is about being so in touch with Self that confidence and wisdom flow from within while you are still fully present and exquisitely aware of every detail of the present moment. In this elevated state you are so much in flow that errors, disagreements, challenges, and surprises are just helpful information as you lead with clarity and relaxed intensity. The people around you are transformed by your presence.

Conscious Self-leadership is not about perfect flawless management of Self and others. It is about being fully present and fully aware. It about being comfortable in your own skin. It is about using the skills of mindfulness and Appreciative Inquiry to ask what is trying to happen when your heart beats quickly, your breathing becomes shallow, your palms sweat, your memory fails, your least favourite parts start screaming in the back rooms of your consciousness. It is about managing your enthusiasm when your adrenaline flows, you have an insight, or you experience success.

In *Conscious Capitalism*, John Mackey and Raj Sisodia write,

> To be conscious means to be fully awake and mindful, to see reality more clearly, and to more fully understand all the consequences—short term, and long term—of our actions. It means we have greater awareness of our inner self, our external reality and the impacts we have on the world. It also means having a greater commitment to the truth and to acting more responsibly according to what we know to be true.[90]

What keeps many leaders from being more conscious of the inner life is the constant demands of the outer life. Because most leaders focus on the game, the construction site, the battlefield, the operating room, or the runway, they discount the amount of inner preparation, constant awareness, and Self-management it takes to work at the highest levels of skill and action. Of the river of sensory data we take in, about 80 per cent of it is dominated by two billion messages of visual information per second. Although we believe we see the world in detail, details can only be acquired via a tiny focus point in the centre of our view.[91] This means we have to rapidly dart our focus point around to build up a detailed view of a scene. Similar demands take place in your inner life as the voices, thoughts, emotions, and inner parts are constantly being scanned as well. As a conscious leader you are quite capable of developing the awareness and skill to take in information, attend to your inner parts, and manage your real life relationships, while performing at the highest level in the midst of the action.

> Conscious leadership allows you to lose your balance without losing your Self.

Life is messy. As a conscious leader you are called to be the non-anxious presence in the midst of the messiness. Conscious leadership allows you to lose your balance without losing your Self. It helps you stay the course in the midst of a confusing, exciting, or frustrating part of your life without any "fear of falling or catching fire." When you do that, you inspire others to do the same. Your focus and performance improve. Parts of you that have lain dormant start to come alive. You are more accessible and feel more engaged. People in your life begin to show up more fully. Serendipities happen.

Emotionally Available

The paradox of becoming a conscious leader is that when you do your own inner work it isn't just your mind that is liberated. As you face your own grief, inner turmoil, stored emotions, conflicted values, and underlying beliefs, your whole energy system begins to open up. Your heart has increased capacity. Your inner and outer hearing improves. You are more grounded and more creative. You may not always be fully present but you know when you are absenting and as you show up fully, others around you will too. You may still be surprised by the intensity of judgement, cynicism, and fear in yourself and others but as you learn to face the issues with yourself and others you will find that relationships begin to take on a whole new level of authenticity.

Mitch Albom, in *Tuesdays with Morrie*, describes the powerful effect of being emotion-ally available—"I believe in being fully present," Morrie said. "That means you should be with the person you're with. . . . I am talking to you. I am thinking about you." In sharing his learning during fourteen Tuesdays with his dying sociology professor, Morrie Schwartz, Mitch goes on to say,

> He did this better than anyone I'd ever known. Those who sat with him saw his eyes go moist when they spoke about something horrible, or crinkle in delight when they told him a really bad joke. He was always ready to openly display the emotion so often missing from my baby boomer generation. We are great at small talk: 'What do you do?' 'Where do you live?' But really listening to someone—without trying to sell them something, pick them up, recruit them, or get some kind of status in return—how often do we get this anymore? I believe many visitors in the last few months of Morrie's life were drawn not because of the attention they wanted to pay to him but because of the attention he paid to them. Despite his personal pain and decay, this little old man listened the way they always wanted someone to listen.[92]

Being emotionally available involves inner awareness and outward honesty. M. Scott Peck said that during a client session he would mentally leave and plan his evening commute or connect with an old memory while feigning interest in what being said. When he realized this, he started saying to his client, "I'm sorry I missed that last part. Please say that again." Rather than being offended, the other person felt validated and truly listened to. Conscious leaders are emotionally available to themselves and others and honest in their interactions.

Relationships

As a conscious leader your awareness and skill in relating to others and dealing with disconnects is essential. In his book, *Leading Consciously*, author Debashis Chatterjee writes,

> An organization is a web of intimate relations. This indefinable energy of intimacy is a factor that determines the effectiveness of leadership. The ability to listen, the virtue of patience, the art of accommodating and understanding a person in context are the attributes of intimacy.[93]

Relationships are in constant interplay. Expert John Gottman's studies have shown that we are always either 'turning toward' or 'turning away' from relationships. As a conscious leader, relationship awareness is necessary in all realms of life. Your ability to notice when a relationship needs attention and your ability to make and respond to repair bids is important. View Gottman's YouTube tutorials. Read his book, *The Relationship Cure*.

Dr. Gottman calls the best predictors of relationship failure or continued misery the "Four Horsemen of the Apocalypse."[94] If these four damaging behaviours—criticism, defensiveness, stonewalling, and contempt—go unchecked, a relationship is doomed. When these behaviours show up at home or at work, conscious leaders recognize the tension and explore what needs to be done to restore safety and respect. Rather than fearing such fierce conversation, as a conscious leader, you can become skilled at starting softly and talking about the important issues with openness and honesty. As you continue to listen to your inner voices and create calm within, you will be able to be a non-anxious presence when stakes are high and emotions are aroused.

Another destroyer of safety in relationships is inappropriate sexual innuendo, language, and behaviours. Leaders have an added measure of responsibility to ensure that they do not violate these sexually-related boundaries. Conscious leaders are aware of their own and others' sexual energy and set respectful boundaries for themselves and others in social and workplace environments. When inappropriate actions, touch, or comments occur these are addressed with dignity and respect. As a conscious leader you will know when further dialogue or action is required.

A "Fierce Conversation" has been defined as one in which you "come out from behind yourself, into the conversation and make it real." We live in a culture where it seems many of us are sleepwalking through life and because of our lack of awareness many of our conversations remain at the surface level. Conscious leaders seek deeper connections with Self and others. A blog by Jaime at Fierce Inc. states,

> A Fierce Conversation encourages you to switch from this surface mentality and instead get more engaged. What we mean by this is to bring more of yourself to the conversation by peeling off the masks you may wear around certain topics—this doesn't mean it's always about having long conversations or inappropriate disclosure. Rather focus the time you have on making your conversations count.

Remember that one of the four objectives of a fierce conversation is to enrich the relationship.[95]

In *Choice Theory*, Dr. William Glasser states, "If there is one truth that no one can dispute, it is that the success of any endeavour is directly proportional to how well the people involved in it get along with each other."[96] Conscious leaders develop the inner awareness, confidence and sense of Self to make it safe for others to show up fully. By sharing your inner dreams, hopes, fears, disappointments and emotions with others you lower the relational drawbridge and invite others to become more conscious and more available. By connecting well you build meaningful relationships. When this is done with curiosity, authenticity, and caring, deep meaningful connections and dynamic work will result.

Conversations Matter

Consistent, effective, compassionate communication is an essential part of leadership and business. Conscious leadership is about showing up fully and being aware. In her book, *Fierce Conversations*, Susan Scott makes this David Whyte inspired statement, "The conversation is the relationship. If the conversation stops, all of the possibilities for the relationship become smaller, and all of the possibilities for individuals in the relationship become smaller."[97]

In her writing and her work with leaders Susan challenges us to be fully conscious. She writes,

> Begin listening to yourself as you have never listened before. Begin to overhear yourself avoiding the topic, changing the subject, holding back, telling little lies, and being imprecise in your language, being uninteresting even to yourself. At least once today, when something inside you says, 'This is an opportunity to be fierce,' stop for a moment, take a deep breath, then come out from behind yourself into the conversation and make it real. Say something that is true for you.[98]

As you move forward and bring your gifts to a world that needs you and your leadership, it is important to learn how to open safe space so that real conversations can occur about what really matters. "There can be no vulnerability without risk; there can be no community without vulnerability; there can be no peace and ultimately no life without community."[99] As you show up in life, work, and relationships, this M. Scott Peck quote is a reminder that the quality of your conversations will determine the quality of your leadership effectiveness.

Compassion

When you not only see a person's pain but also feel moved within, you place yourself in the shoes of the individual. For the conscious leader compassion calls for action. As you answer the call to conscious leadership be aware of the ways in which life will call you to respond.

The 2014 Nobel Peace Prize laureate Kailash Satyarthi shifted from a career in electrical engineering at the age of twenty-six to working full time to eradicate child labour. In 1980, Satyarthi founded the Save the Childhood Movement and began raiding factories, brick kilns and carpet-making workshops where children and their indebted parents often pledged themselves to work for decades in return for a short-term loan. Satyarthi told Epoch Times that compassion is needed "to ensure sustainability and peace" in the world, and that it comes from a connection with one's Self. He states, "A connection of everyone with her or his inside is what makes you a global citizen and helps you find solutions to persisting problems especially in countries where corruption and mismanagement are common."[100] He practices compassion by connecting transparently, and honestly with others, he said, and maintaining his "child inside." He also says that compassion for him is about action, and translates into his work for justice, equality, and peace. Over the last thirty-four years Kailash has raided sweatshops, organized marches, spoken, advocated, and in the process directly liberated over 80,000 child laborers.

Sometimes the call to compassion comes suddenly. When an assisted living home in California abruptly shut down in the fall of 2014 many of its frail and elderly residents were left behind, with nowhere to go. The staff at the Valley Springs Manor left when they stopped getting paid—except for cook, Maurice Rowland, and janitor, Miguel Alvarez. With sixteen residents the cook and janitor's roles quickly changed in order to care for the residents, who needed round-the-clock care. Miguel would only go home for one hour, take a shower, get dressed, then be there for 23-hour days. Abandoned by his parents as a child, Miguel knew what it felt like and his compassion called for action. Maurice Rowland, the cook, also chose to be a compassionate leader and handed out medications during those long days. He says he didn't want to leave the residents—some coping with dementia—to fend for themselves. Alvarez and Rowland spent several days caring for the elderly residents of Valley Springs Manor until the fire department and sheriff took over. The incident led to legislation in California known as the Residential Care for the Elderly Reform Act of 2014.[101]

In his book, *Uncontainable: How Passion, Commitment and Conscious Capitalism Built a Business Where Everyone Thrives,* The Container Store CEO, Kip Tindell, tells of his compassion test during the tough financial times in 2008. As sales dipped, The Container Store faced a crisis. Other businesses were laying off staff to reduce losses. Kip knew in his heart there had to be another way. After much thought, CEO Kip, and his team decided that the compassionate way to provide conscious leadership was to honour their commitment to their staff and keep all their employees. In order to avoid layoffs The Container Store froze wages and stalled 401(k) matching. After a significant turnaround in the following year, the company lifted the freeze and reinstated its matching retirement support. As they regained stability, the conscious leaders of the Container Store strengthened the already generous benefits package enjoyed by full-time workers and part-timers alike. "While conventional wisdom may tell us downsizing automatically drives a company's stock price higher and increases productivity, it actually doesn't," said Tindell. "Layoffs take a huge, lasting toll on morale and productivity in the work place. Laying off people is not the best way—it's the easy way. Putting our employees first is not only the right thing to do, it also happens to be more successful than any other business methodology," he said. "If you take great care of the employees, they take great care of the customers."[102] By 2010, The Container Store emerged from the recession and began posting record numbers.

Conscious leadership will awaken compassion as you use the strengths from your FISC to respond to your call to be a Difference Maker.

Consciousness Conditioning

Being fully present, passion-filled, energetic, focused, and aware of Self and others is a set of foundational skills based on consistent practices. Here are some reminders of daily habits that will increase your capacity for consciousness.

1. Be Grateful.

Start every day with a moment of gratitude. Be thankful for the opportunities, the people, and the learnings that are in your life. End every day with a time of reflection focusing on the positive experiences and serendipities that have enriched your consciousness.

2. Use Deep Intentional Breathing.

Breathe through your nose drawing the breath to the deepest part of your abdomen. Do this several times each day—especially if you tend to sit at a desk over a keyboard for hours at a time. Exhale through your mouth releasing the negative energy in your shoulders, back or wherever you hold it. Just three deep breaths held and then released will refresh and regulate the oxygen flow in your blood, making you more alert.

3. Read the Emotional Field.

When you enter a room be aware of the emotional energy. In a meeting observe the mood. See the indicators but also pay attention to what your intuition is telling you. When you realize your inner emotions are out of control, take a micro pause and a deep breath to recalibrate. When you are leading a meeting and the room is filled with negative energy ask everyone to pause and take a deep breath. A wise leader once stopped a rancorous meeting and changed the whole tone by simply asking, "Did you notice how the energy just left the room?" She paused and restated her intention and the emotional field shifted.

4. Exercise.

Get at least 150 minutes of moderate aerobic activity or 75 minutes of vigorous aerobic activity every week. Do strength training exercises at least twice a week. Moderate aerobic exercise includes such activities as brisk walking, swimming and mowing the lawn. Vigorous aerobic exercise includes such activities as running, water exercises, and dancing. Strength training can include use of weight machines or activities such as rock climbing or heavy gardening. You can add opportunities for re-energizing by parking a distance from the entrance and using stairs instead of elevators. Seek to spend time out of doors every day and thoughtfully connect with natural sources of energy—the sun, the trees, the wind, and bodies of water.

5. Pray or Meditate.

Meditation and prayer offer many health benefits, including reduced stress and anxiety. This is a way to satisfy the basic human need to make a connection with something larger than yourself. Depending on your preferences, you may offer prayers to a specific divinity or more general thanks and requests to a more expansive sense of the Beyond. Whether you use a more traditional model of prayer or a meditative approach, scientific studies continue to show an enhancing of the brain cortex associated with regular meditation or other spiritual or religious practices and that these activities also guard against depression. These daily practices will help you feel more alive, increase feelings of calm, and heighten your awareness.

6. Honour your Preferences.

Introverts need time out of the hustle and bustle to ground themselves, recharge, and contribute through their most natural abilities. People with a preference for introversion draw energy from an internal world of thought and reflection. If this is your preference, you will serve your Self and others best if you regularly have time doing things alone or with one or two people you feel comfortable with. Take time to reflect so that you have a clear idea of what you'll be doing when you decide to act.

Extroverts need interaction with others. People with a preference for extraversion draw energy from an external world of interaction and doing. You get energy from active involvement in events and a variety of activities. You often understand a problem better when you are able to talk about it and hear what you and others have to say. You can enhance your performance and energy flow by meeting regularly with creative thought partners.

7. Rest.

It has been estimated that as many as 70 per cent of North Americans are sleep deprived. In order to bring your best energy to life most of you need seven or eight hours of sleep each day. As a conscious leader you need to listen to your body. Although a 20-minute nap can refresh and renew you, when that's not possible, even two minutes of calm, deep breathing can help you show up more fully in an important meeting. However, there is no substitute for a good night's sleep.

8. Eat Well.

There has never been a time where more information is available on foods. Listen to your body. Avoid the latest fad. Eat foods that are closer to nature: whole grains rather than processed chips or crackers from a box, whole fruit rather than juice or fruit bars. If you eat meats, choose wisely and reduce the amount of red meat. With the understanding that there is value in all things in moderation don't depend on caffeine or sugar to give energy boosts. Let your body answer the vegetarian-carnivore debate, not your peer group or your thoughts. You can find thoughtful healthy leaders on both sides of the forks over knives debates, as well as many experts who have found health through a blended approach. Food writer, Michael Pollan, says everything he's learned about food and health can be summed up in seven words: "Eat food, not too much, mostly plants."[103]

9. Eat Mindfully.

Stop multitasking at meal times. Unplug. Set aside time for eating without other entertainment. Mixing food and business should be the exception. As often as possible sit to eat. Make time to prepare at least some of your own meals, preferably from fresh ingredients. Preparation, even the night before, can add to the enjoyment and awareness of renewing and strengthening your body. Create variety and pay attention to presentation. Appreciate the appearance and the beauty of the food you are about to eat. Focus on each mouthful. Think about the flavour, texture and even the sound of the food in your mouth. One of the joys of eating is sharing a relaxed meal with others.

10. Activate Your Energetic Self.

You can decide at any moment how you will show up in any situation. How you stand, breathe, relax your face, and the tone you choose are all in your control. Choose to be the most alive person you know. Laugh as much as possible and have a sense of humour. As you consciously increase your ability to choose the ways you want to believe, act, speak, and respond to life, you stop living at the mercy of everything outside of you. When you focus on peace, love and calmness at all times, these high vibrational frequencies impact everything around you. By showing compassion for every situation you encounter, the frequencies of that situation will be raised. When you tap into your soul energy you are no longer an isolated individual but a transformative force of life in the flow of the cosmos.

11. Tune into Positive Vibes.

Energy is like a radio signal. You are a receiver. You can choose what you focus on. You have the ability to receive multiple frequencies at any time. By setting positive intentions moment by moment and recalibrating when the negative comes in, you can create your own playlist and a powerful alliance with all the positive people and forces in the Universe. Focus on the positive energy of your Circle of Influence not on the negative energy of other people's Circles of Concern.

12. Be a Giver.

Practice random acts of kindness and expect nothing in return. Give some money to someone less fortunate than you. Donate to a cause you believe in. Pay for the coffee of the person behind you in the drive-thru. Send a thoughtful gift to someone you haven't spoken to in years. Donate clothing to a shelter. Pick up a piece of garbage and throw it away. Always have compassion and gratitude for everything in your life. By being a giver you join with the creative energy of life and you will experience an unlimited supply of energy.

13. Smile

Mindfulness teacher, Thich Nhat Hanh says, "Sometimes your joy is the source of your smile, but sometimes your smile can be the source of your joy."[104] Smiling is recognized around the world as a sign of friendliness. Through your smile you also communicate feelings about your immediate environment, your mental well-being, your personality and mood, even your physical health. A genuine smile will increase your credibility with others. Researchers now know that a smile brings many other benefits to you—lower heart rate, reduced stress levels, and a boost in your immune system. As you practice smiling regularly at yourself and others it will become more natural and flow from deep within. When your inner peace flows into your smile you will be living the teaching of Hanh who states, "If we are peaceful, if we are happy, we can smile, and everyone in our family, our entire society, will benefit from our peace."[105]

14. Have Fun

The late Christopher Reeve, in his 1998 autobiography, *Still Me* tells of the important role that fun played in his recovery after he shattered his first and second vertebrae in a fall from a horse. The cervical spinal injury had left him paralyzed from the neck down and Christopher was in a great deal of pain at the hospital as he awaited a life-threatening surgery to reconnect his skull and his spine. "As the day of the operation drew closer, it became more and more painful and frightening to contemplate," Reeve wrote, adding:

> In spite of efforts to protect me from the truth, I already knew that I had only a fifty-fifty chance of surviving the surgery. I lay on my back, frozen, unable to avoid thinking the darkest thoughts. Then, at an especially bleak moment, the door flew open and in hurried a squat fellow with a blue scrub hat and a yellow surgical gown and glasses, speaking in a Russian accent. He announced that he was my proctologist, and that he had to examine me immediately. My first reaction was that either I was on way too many drugs or I was in fact brain damaged. But it was Robin Williams. He and his wife, Marsha, had materialized from who knows where. And for the first time since the accident, I laughed. My old friend had helped me know that somehow I was going to be okay.[106]

For some of you playfulness and fun will come naturally. For others, these will be new skills you will need to develop. One of the definitions of fun is "lighthearted pleasure." What a great way to describe the leadership pilgrim. As you deal with the heavy issues of life and open your heart each day you will develop the ability to have fun and to experience some elements of lightheartedness even when the going is tough.

Be Real

The purpose of the Self-leadership quest is not to reach some Teflon state where you are above and beyond the pain and grief that life brings. There will be illness, disappointment, perhaps even violence and death. Be real. When it hurts allow yourself to cry. When your Inner Child is frightened, listen with compassion. When you are angry, agitated or disappointed allow yourself to be fully present with what is. When you are weary, rest. Self-leadership is not intended to be another religion or dogma that becomes your castle safe on a hill above the strife. It is meant to be a road map with signposts and a guidebook with words of inspiration and wisdom from others who have traveled a similar path.

When you show up fully you give your inner parts—intuition, deep wisdom, and compassion—opportunity to grow and mature. The learning loop of inner awareness and outer effectiveness will provide the feedback you need to make meaningful course corrections as you continue to learn and grow. As you manifest the new life in real time in real situations, accept the messiness of life. As David Noer reminds us, "Breaking free and learning how to learn is a subjective, inside-out messy process that is at odds with the avowed, external, objective reality of the old paradigm."[107]

As you move along the path of Self-leadership into the daily realities of community life, managing your inner and outer worlds will determine your effectiveness in helping to create a saner, safer world. Step 8 is about managing the polarities of life and managing yourself so that you live in harmony with your soul while extending grace and understanding to those who do not see the world the same way as you do. You will not always be on a high. There will be nights of despair and seasons of desolation. The goal of Self-leadership is not to eliminate the ebb and flow of life but to increase awareness of your inner and outer life so that you can show up fully with honesty and integrity and through being real, bring a freshness and vitality to each day of your life.

Being You

The world needs you now—in your imperfection—in your formative processes. Whenever you show up fully as yourself, you make a difference. Trust your inner knowing. Your FISC equips you with wisdom and power. Caroline Myss states that,

> We often hesitate to follow our intuition out of fear. Most usually, we are afraid of the changes in our own life that our actions will bring. Intuitive guidance, however, is all about change. It is energetic data ripe with the potential to influence the rest of the world. To fear change but to crave intuitive clarity is like fearing the cold, dark night while pouring water on the fire that lights your cave. An insight the size of a mustard seed is powerful enough to bring down a mountain-sized illusion

that may be holding our lives together. Truth strikes without mercy. We fear our intuitions because we fear the transformational power within our revelations.[108]

Stay conscious. When you are in touch with your authentic Self, listening to your intuition and acting without second guessing, decision making and action steps are calm and confident. Whenever you lose your way, remember that no matter how much your present reality may seem like a barren desert, deep within there is an oasis. When you feel stuck remember these words from Martha Beck, "The best way to break through any barrier is to access a point of perfect stillness at the center of your being, a Self deeper than your senses or your mind."[109]

Conscious leadership practices create a level of awareness that allow you to bring your best to life, work, and relationships. At the start of this journey we encouraged you to see yourself as a complex being with desires, needs, aspirations, impulses, and appetites that without Self-leadership would create chaos. As you lead from this new place of consciousness, you will find that inner Characters that once dominated your old unaware small 's' self, will now cooperate with the growing vision and inner clarity of Self, Inc. Conscious leadership involves trusting your Self to show up fully and not only to be enough but to be *amazing*.

Moving along the Path with STEP 8...

I accept the call to effectively manage, develop and employ the elements of FISC in conscious service to Self, others, and the greater good.

STEPPING STONES

Use your journal to explore your responses to the following questions.

- In what situations, events, circumstances, or relationships do you find it particularly challenging to remain in the moment and fully present?

- In what situations, events, circumstances, or relationships do you find it easy to be fully present?

- How conscious and present are you with the key people in your Circle of Influence—personally and professionally?

  - What can you do to strengthen your relationships with these key people?

- What does being real mean to you?

  - How do you know when you're not being real?

- Co-opt a part of yourself, a trusted colleague, or your coach to let you know when you exhibit criticism, defensiveness, stonewalling, or contempt.

  - What work do you need to do to address these behaviours?

- Where and how does stress show up in your body?

  - What message(s) is your body sending you?

- How does lack of confidence show up for you? What clues come from your body, energy, posture, or inner Characters? What patterns do you observe?

- How is compassion calling you to take action in your Circle of Influence?

TRAVEL TIPS

1. Just as we often under recognize, under appreciate, and under use our material resources, the same can be true regarding our FISC. Use regular pause techniques or *12 Steps* journal reviews to stay consciously connected with your inner treasury of Self, Inc. resources.

2. Consciousness is risky. Give your Self permission to open up, loosen your heart, take some risks, and step fully into your life, work, and relationships.

3. To be effective as a conscious leader you need to develop caring awareness regarding Self, others, and the systems of which you are a part.

Step 9 - Purposeful Leading

I clarify my purpose in order to effectively contribute to the well-being of Self and the systems that I am part of.

Don't Settle
By D.H. Lester

Don't settle
For edicts from popes
And political schemes
Tired half-hopes—worn-out dreams
Don't settle
For the latest hit song
And bright shiny things
Just going along—birds without wings
Don't settle
There's greatness within
You're destined to lead
It's time to begin—plan to succeed.[110]

STEP 9...

FAST TRACK

Purposeful Leading involves a realistic optimism that states that even in the midst of suffering, pain, confusion, or failure as long as you have a willingness to learn and grow you can find purpose. The call of Step 9 is for you to move beyond the self-serving attitudes and behaviours of surface living and, by accessing the unique assets of your FISC, become a Difference Maker wherever you find yourself today. We believe that each of you arrives in this world trailing stardust and containing a unique essence or soul. In your deepest core there is a resonant sense of purpose that, once claimed, will provide an inner compass that will always point you to your true North. It is in the interplay of inner subselves, your unique SoulDNA, your givens, experiences, hopes, and dreams, and the people and realities you face now, that your awakened purpose finds meaningful and synergistic ways to make a difference. The benefit of having a clearly stated purpose is that once you have a long view you can be fully present in the current process. Your processes are the things you do to follow through on your purpose—the things you do to bring it to life. Often purpose seems distant and far off. By asking how can I find meaning in my present moment you may find a process that makes sense in the here and now. Step 9 is an affirmation of who you are and the beginnings of a plan to take the next steps on your vocational journey with a clearly stated purpose and a process that honours and resonates with your SoulDNA. Lean into the future. Follow your heart. Keep moving. Trust the journey. Follow the urgings of your FISC and let your life shine. As you live your truth the path ahead will become clear.

Leadership Value: Purpose

Guiding Principle: Recognized purpose gives meaning to life and leadership.

FOOTHOLD

Think of someone you respect and know well who you've seen in numerous settings. Think about the unique 'something' that they bring to any situation, interaction, or conversation. Now, imagine you're that person being observed. What do people see in you? Journal about this unique 'something' or essence that you bring to life, work, and relationships.

Let Your Life Shine

When our youngest son was fourteen, he decided he wanted to go to the Philippines for the summer as part of an international youth program centred in Florida. After discussions and research into the organization my wife and I agreed to his adventure. The main focus of the project was to use available materials to construct a building which would be used by Philippine youth in the future. As soon as school ended, James was off to Florida, with his ten-inch boots, sleeping on a platform over the water. For two weeks our son and the group of young people, ages fourteen to eighteen that had signed up for the summer program, spent long days improving physical fitness, building team work, discipline, and awareness skills. At the boot camp there were over 1,000 young people from all over North America. Some would climb a mountain in Africa, some would ride motorcycles across the desert, and others would ride horseback in Brazil or work in inner city missions in the USA.

> By letting your light shine you really do make a difference.
> Follow the urgings of your FISC and let your life shine.

As the training time came to an end, Cheryl and I travelled to Florida to check on the progress and participate in the send-off celebration. After packing their belongings, the teams gathered under a large circus tent with parents, friends and family looking on. There were over 2,000 of us under this tent. As the evening sky became dark the leaders on the stage thanked each of the young people who had been involved in the program to this point. With a positive attitude and a generous spirit they acknowledged the illnesses and homesickness that had already eliminated some of the would-be adventurers and then outlined what would happen next. Each team member was handed a candle. Soon all the lights would be extinguished and the program director would light one candle to represent the difference the participants would make during the summer ahead. Each team member would then be called upon to declare if they would continue on with their summer opportunity. The leader made it very clear there would be no shame in listening to their inner wisdom and choosing not to go. For those who lit their candles the exit would take them to waiting buses and off to the far reaches of the globe.

The lights were extinguished and the darkness was total. Then the director lit one candle in the middle of the tent. There was a collective gasp as we all realized how much difference one small light can make. Then one by one the leaders and their teams came forward and each team member made a commitment to action by lighting their candle. Soon the tent was aglow with the hopes and excitement of over a 1,000 young people with candles in hand. Having already said our goodbyes, we watched as our son walked to the exit on his way to a bus and his flight.

That summer was a life-defining experience. For us it was a lesson in the power of one. One candle can light up a large circus tent. One life can change a city or a country. One Self-leader can transform a business, an organization, a faith community, or a social agency. By letting your light shine you really do make a difference. Follow the urgings of your FISC and let your life shine.

Your Unique Call

Each of you leaves a unique fingerprint on the people, places, and processes you touch. Each of you brings an essential something to the unfolding of the evolving whole. With over seven billion people on the planet and the fast pace of life it is too easy to discount the importance of one. The message of this book is that each of you matter. As you follow your passion and live with a sense of purpose you increase the vibrational level of the whole. When you allow disappointment, fear, anger, and aggression to dominate your view, all of us are diminished.

Step 9 is not some saccharin solution to the pain and suffering that is a part of many people's lives on a daily basis in a world where everyone faces the realities of living as part of a society where violence, illness, severe weather, natural disasters, addictions, crime, suffering, and death are part of the ebb and flow of life. It is, however, a realistic optimism that states that even in the midst of suffering, pain, confusion, or failure as long as you have a willingness to learn and grow you can find purpose in your next breath.

The call of this book is for you to move beyond the attitudes and behaviours of surface living and, by accessing the unique assets of your FISC, become a Difference Maker wherever you find yourself today. As Viktor Frankl states in *Man's Search for Meaning*, "The meaning of life differs from person to person, from day to day, and from hour to hour."[111] He goes on to state, "Everyone has his own specific vocation or mission in life to carry out a concrete assignment which demands fulfillment. Therein he cannot be replaced, nor can his life be repeated. Thus everyone's task is as unique as his specific opportunity to implement it."[112]

Respond to your call to make a difference in the well-being of the systems that you are a part of through finding meaning in the unique opportunities you face today.

A Dream of Life

We believe that each of you arrives in this world trailing stardust and containing a unique essence or soul. Your SoulDNA is unique, as are your Facts, Influences, and inner Characters, so at the core of you there is a distinctive call to bring life and a distinguishing style and verve to the larger system. This is what the famous dancer, Martha Graham, meant when she said, "There is a vitality, a life force, an energy, a quickening, that is translated through you into action, and because there is only one of you in all time, this expression is unique."[113]

In your deepest core there is a resonant sense of purpose that, once claimed, will provide an inner compass that will always point you to your true North no matter what storms assail your inner or outer life. In moments of insight or powerful emotion you have touched this essence of life. When you have experienced this inner aliveness it's like you have been plugged into a power source. You feel a powerful call to experience more of this aliveness, but the answer may take time to coalesce. The bridge from this inner call to reality is in dreaming.

> **Dream. Open your heart. Trust the process. Ask for what you want. Dare to act. You are enough.**

It is this dream that empowers and inspires Rachel Naomi Remen, MD, the Clinical Professor of Family and Community Medicine at UCSF School of Medicine. As a medical educator, therapist and teacher, she has enabled many thousands of physicians to practice medicine from the heart and thousands of patients to remember their power to heal. Her ground-breaking curriculum for medical students, *The Healer's Art*, is taught in ninety of America's medical schools and in medical schools in seven countries abroad. Rachel's dream comes from the depths of her being and shapes her life. She says it this way,

> My dream of medicine was not to become competent. My dream was to become a friend to life. It was that dream that enabled me to endure the relentless pursuit of competency required of me. But competence did not fulfill me then and could not have fulfilled me for my medical lifetime. Only a dream can do that.[114]

As you take the learnings from the *12 Steps* and use the inner awareness that you are developing to live with a greater sense of purpose and aliveness, remember, that beneath all the parts, voices, influences, and experiences that have shaped you since you were conceived, there is a river of life flowing, carrying purpose and meaning. It is this pure Essence that gave birth to you and it is from this Source that your most profound sense of Self, Inc. and the dreams that bring purpose to your life originate. However, you cannot decide what to do solely from within. It is in the intersection where the two worlds meet that you will more deeply understand your purpose and ways that you can manifest it. It is in the interplay of inner subselves, your unique SoulDNA, your givens, experiences, hopes, and dreams, and the people and realities you face now, that your awakened purpose finds meaningful and synergistic ways to make a difference. You have been exploring possibilities throughout your life and even though you may presently be seeking a larger more fulfilling path to your purpose, the seeds of greatness are within, stirred and cultivated by the emerging future. Dream. Open your heart. Trust the process. Ask for what you want. Dare to act. You are enough.

Living on Purpose

Life Coach, Elizabeth McKenzie, recently stated, "Your purpose is the BIG HAIRY thing that you want to accomplish in your lifetime. It's the change you want to effect in the world. When you're old and grey and reminiscing on the years gone by, it's the thing you want to be able to say 'WOW, I did that.' "

She goes on to state, "Your purpose is broad enough to take you in different directions. It's got enough scope that you can achieve it in a number of different ways. And it's expansive enough that it can be reinterpreted and reimagined at different stages of your life. But it's so, so connected and engrained in your being that once you've tuned in to its siren song, it will always be your guiding light."[115]

The benefit of having a clearly stated purpose is that once you have a long view you can be fully present in the current process. One of the most important ironies of clear purpose and engaging processes is that as a conscious Self-leader you will lose all track of Self and time as you experience flow in your life. When you have a clear purpose and a process that engages, you will experience the complexity and joy that George Bernard Shaw championed when he wrote,

> I am of the opinion that my life belongs to the whole community and as long as I live it is my privilege to do for it whatever I can. I want to be thoroughly used up when I die, for the harder I work, the more I live. I rejoice in life for its own sake. Life is no 'brief candle' to me. It is sort of a splendid torch which I have a hold of for the moment, and I want to make it burn as brightly as possible before handing it over to future generations.[116]

People want to know their purpose, the why of their existence, the reason that they're here. However, a sense and understanding of purpose seems to still elude many. Over-use of a word can diminish its original meaning or 'purpose.' As you clarify your purpose it may be useful to shift your perspective by changing the language. Many people link purpose to some ginormous accomplishment or achievement, for instance to paint the Sistine Chapel, fly to the moon, make a billion dollars, raise a large healthy family. What if, instead of limiting it to achievements, we redefine purpose to mean—"the positive energetic difference you uniquely contribute?"

Although Elizabeth McKenzie uses the word purpose, she indicates that the big "WOW, I did that" difference that she makes, wherever she is, whatever she is doing, is that she raises the vibrational level of the world. Your WOW doesn't have to be loud or showy. Sometimes the difference a person makes is subtle, quiet, and unnoticed by the masses.

For my partner Cheryl, the difference that she naturally makes is that she "raises aware-ness and increases effectiveness by creating safe spaces for meaningful dialogue." One of the ways or processes that she uses to carry this into the world is through her leadership coaching. For me, my difference making contribution is "creating a safer, saner world through transformational teaching." One of the ways I do that is through deep and meaningful conversations, and by connecting people to books and teachings that I believe can be helpful in making their lives, and by extension the world, safer and saner.

Viktor Frankl taught us that you can always find meaning in the moment. William Glasser similarly taught that you can always live in choice. Even in the midst of crisis or experiencing the last moments of your physical life, you have the opportunity and choice to make a difference by embodying your Difference Making gifts, attitudes, and natural skills by allowing your positive energetic essence to flow in and through you. One of our beloved mentors, Lillian Broad, made a difference in the lives of everyone she interacted with. Even in the nursing home during the last years of her life as she experienced pain and failing sight, she continued to nourish and draw from her FISC, bringing a positive energetic energy to every interaction. Like Morrie Schwartz, who we reference in Step 8, Lillian was always emotionally available. Her family, friends, and caregivers knew that they mattered, they were precious, and the unique 'something' that made them 'them' was important, special, and needed. Even though we visited her to bring comfort, we often received more than we gave and left feeling inspired and enlivened.

Vocation

In *Let Your Life Speak*, Parker J. Palmer writes,

> Before you tell your life what you intend to do with it, listen for what it intends to do with you. Before you tell your life what truths and values you have decided to live up to, let your life tell you what truths you embody, what values you represent.[117]

> Vocation does not mean a goal that I pursue. It means a calling that I hear. Before I can tell my life what I want to do with it, I must listen to my life telling me who I am. I must listen for the truths and values at the heart of my own identity, not the standards by which I must live—but the standards by which I cannot help but live if I am living my own life.[118]

For some of you, the exploration and learning of the Self-leadership quest has confirmed that you have been in the right vocation all along. Now with new skills and a renewed focus you can make life even more rewarding for yourself and others by embracing and deepening your sense of purpose, and increasing your DMQ by being intentional about utilizing, repurposing, and managing your unique FISC.

For others, the Self-leadership quest has changed everything. As you have become fully present, listened to your heart, and dreamed of the future, you now realize there has been a disconnect between your best Self and the person you have been trying to be. You now understand that you are uniquely gifted to do much more and to be much more effective as a conscious leader. In order to fulfil your calling to be a Difference Maker a major shift will be required.

In *The Reconnected Leader*, Norman Pickavance addresses the question of vocation. He writes, "Vocation is about connecting with a sense of self, about being clear on what we stand for beyond the specifics of the immediate task and job and being true to this." He goes on to write,

> There are typically three ways that leaders can answer this question. The first is seeing work as a job and all about the money, the next bonus or paying for the next holiday or new car. This view of work comes wrapped up with the notion of acquiring things. The second answer for many leaders is that it's all about the career, about achieving things, about doing more. The issue with these answers is that they fail to address a wider question: What am I living for? ... when people work just for the money, work satisfaction goes down while giving everything over to a career is too small to hold the human spirit. Significantly both of these outlooks are oriented towards what we can get out of work. If, on the other hand, we can find a wider sense of what work is about and connect it with what we are living for, our emphasis shifts to what we can give through our work. This third answer lies at the heart of what developing a sense of leadership vocation is about. Vocation in the broadest sense requires a shift of perspective from the narrowest sense of a job (a series of tasks) and a career (a progression and development of responsibility and earnings) to a more holistic sense: a cause worth pursuing for the benefit of many, bringing a stronger connection to all.[119]

David J. Powell, PhD, stated,

> Soon after graduating high school or college, we're expected to get a job, choose a career, as if work is a single conversation with some unknown forces. Work is a constant conversation, a back-and-forth of what I think is and is not me. It is the edge between what the world wants of me and I want of the world in terms of labor. Yet, we are constantly changing. And deciding. I am often asked 'how did you choose to go to China, to write about clinical supervision?' My typical answer is 'it chose me, I didn't choose it.' The only decision we have to make is how or whether we will respond or turn away from that calling. When you turn towards that calling, you have already begun your journey home.[120]

Step 9 is an affirmation of who you are and a commitment to respond to your calling as you take the next steps on your vocational journey, directed by a clearly stated purpose and processes that honour and resonate with your SoulDNA. Because each of you bring different life experiences, inner urgings, capabilities, and combinations of temperament, strengths, weaknesses, and opportunities, each process will differ. Again, as Elizabeth McKenzie reminds us, "There are many, many different processes you can use to bring your purpose into form. Both a doctor and a life coach could have the same purpose: to heal others and help them on their journey."[121]

Frances Moore Lappé in her book *Getting a Grip* says that for many of us the calling in our life may come from a rude shock. She writes,

'Seizing the Moment' typically refers to a positive moment of opportunity, one not to be wasted. Gradually it dawned on me, though, that such a moment can come as a disconcerting shock, dissonance that might not feel too good at the time. It is these precious moments—when something shakes us up, rattling us from our resignation or depression, or galvanizing that vague sense that there must be more to life—that we can break free.[122]

This learning from discomfort was true for two teachers that shifted their focus in helping others. Both Muhammed Yunus and Timothy Gallwey were teachers when they realized that their theories and teaching were actually interfering with what needed to happen. Nobel Peace Prize laureate, Dr. Yunus, went on to start microcredit and revolutionized economic development. World renowned coach and consultant, Timothy Gallwey shifted his sports coaching and created the *Inner Game* concepts that have had a significant impact on Sports Coaching, Corporate Coaching, and Health and Fitness. Your purpose may not start with your groove but your rut. When you ask the right questions amazing results can occur.

Lean into the future. Listen to your calling. Follow your heart. Keep moving. Trust the journey. As you live your truth the path ahead will become clear. Set your intentions and continue your practices. Don't wait any longer. Act when the opportunity comes. Learn from each experience and know that when you act from a place of positive intentions each setback is just more information as you continue to find your way.

Shift Happens

Just like vocation, purpose has discovered you as much as you have discovered it. The awakening that has brought you to a place of inner and outer exploration is happening across the globe. The exciting innovations and massive population growth of the twentieth century brought us into the third millennium with a growing awareness that the future was going to ask more of us than we had given during the raucous growth of the last quarter century. Mihaly Csikszentmihalyi speaks to this realization when, in *The Evolving Self*, he writes,

> Now we suddenly realize, that unless we take things in hand, the process of change will continue under the sway of relentless chance, a chance blind to the human dreams and desires. Like horrified passengers on an airplane who are told that the pilots have mysteriously vanished from the cockpit as the plane is cruising miles above the ground, we know we must find a way to master the controls or the trip will end in disaster.[123]

You are not the first generation of leaders to realize you live at a pivotal time in history, but you are probably the first to live at a time when the web of relationships and the impact of your next steps have such a profound interconnectedness with the whole planet. We truly have become a global village and no matter where you are you can be one of the ones who helps shape the emerging future in a positive way. As you awaken to the possibilities of choosing your path, the purpose you embrace and the process you choose to move toward your purpose will either advance the global society or deplete it.

It is important as we explore this topic that we honour the contributions you have already made. Your life up until now has been for a reason even though you may not have been living on purpose. It is just that you, and all of us on planet earth, are being called to new levels of consciousness and higher purpose. In their book, *Conscious Capitalism,* Mackey and Sisodia share the story of how one company shifted its processes in a way that increased meaning and engagement for everyone connected with the organization. Founded in 1968, Waste Management spent its formative years "Helping the world dispose of its problems." The company's greatest asset was enough landfill space to bury over forty years' worth of waste. Employees simply collected and disposed of waste. Then attitudes and awareness started to shift and individuals and organizations began to reduce and commit to eliminating waste. Facing a major downturn in waste revenues, CEO David Steiner turned these challenges into opportunities. Now Waste Management is focusing on facilities that use sophisticated technologies for waste-to-energy projects and is treating waste as a valuable asset rather than a problem. Waste Management's tagline is now "Think Green" and its refined purpose is to be "North America's leading provider of integrated environmental solutions."[124]

Perhaps your realities are changing. Your skills, experience and circumstances, combined with your unique FISC, give you a distinct Difference Making opportunity. Perhaps it is time for you to rethink and shift your processes.

Processes

Your processes are the things you do to follow through on your purpose—the things you do to bring it to life. Often purpose seems distant and far off. Be intentional. By asking how you can find meaning in your present reality you will clarify processes for expressing your DMQ right where you are.

Viktor Frankl said that you can discover meaning in three ways:

1. By way of achievement or accomplishment

2. By experiencing something such as goodness, truth and beauty—by experiencing culture or nature or loving another human being

3. By accepting the challenge to suffer bravely up to the last moment. There are many different processes you can use to live with meaning and these can shift over time.[125]

Terry Fox found meaning through sports, friends, and family until an experience with cancer changed his life. Then he found meaning in what he called "The Marathon of Hope" to run with a prosthetic leg across Canada to raise funds for cancer research. When the cancer moved into his lungs and forced him to abandon the run, Terry found meaning in dying with courage and dignity.

The purpose statement that Nobel laureate, Albert Schweitzer, embraced was—"The purpose of human life is to serve, and to show compassion and the will to help others."[126] During his ninety years he was a theologian, musicologist, organ technician, physician and surgeon, missionary, philosopher of ethics, lecturer, writer, and the builder and chief force of the famous hospital at Lambaréné, in Gabon, in Equatorial Africa. Each of these processes helped Albert show up fully and make his unique contribution to the greater good.

Shining Moments

All of these quotes and ideas of dreams, purpose, and processes may sound good, but for some of you finding meaning in life still seems elusive. You want a practical way to explore what is trying to happen, and discover your unique Difference Making potential.

One of the ways to do this is through telling stories of your shining moments by looking back over your life at times when you were so engaged that you were in flow. Times when you were at your best. Times when it felt like you were plugged into some amazing power source.

Contained in these shining moments is your FISC illuminated by your SoulDNA. Follow the light and it will lead you to your present opportunity to find meaning and purpose.

You'll explore this in more detail as part of the work you do in the Stepping Stones that follow.

Moving along the Path with STEP 9...

I clarify my purpose in order to effectively contribute to the well-being of Self and the systems that I am part of.

STEPPING STONES

- In your *12 Steps* journal under these three headings—the **early years** (up until you left home or graduated), your **formative years** (when you stepped into adulthood), and the **last two to five years**—describe three 'shining moments' in each timeframe when you were at your best; when you felt like you were plugged into some amazing power source, and were experiencing flow.

  - Share your stories with your mentor or coach. Then together simplify each story to one sentence. Simplify each sentence to one phrase to describe how you showed up in the 'shining moment' experience or action. Then reduce each phrase to a word that describes your essence in each 'shining moment'. Play with these words. Write them on sticky notes or index cards. Doodle. Explore. Look for defining patterns that point to your larger purpose in life.

- Sometimes our failures and frustrations cause us to go deep inside. What failures and frustrations in your life, work, or relationships are causing you to rethink your purpose or the processes that you use to bring it into the world?

- Spend time reflecting and dialoguing with your future Self about how your difference making will be acknowledged in your eulogy. What do you want to be remembered for? Are your present processes aligned with your Difference Making potential? If not, what needs to shift?

- Based on your insights so far, draft your Self, Inc. purpose statement—a statement that incorporates what you know about the unique and positive energetic difference that you make. Elizabeth McKenzie said, "Your purpose is broad enough to take you in different directions. It's got enough scope that you can achieve it in a number of different ways. And it's expansive enough that it can be reinterpreted and reimagined at different stages of your life." Your purpose statement will serve as a guiding light as you move forward in Step 10 to create your Self-leadership Development Plan.

TRAVEL TIPS

1. Defining your purpose is a 'both—and' process. It comes through both inner awareness and outer engagement. It doesn't need to be perfect the first time. As you continue to evolve, your understanding and articulation of your purpose will continue to develop and clarify. Write it down. Test it out. Edit it.

2. Having your own Purpose Statement helps you assess whether your current activities or emerging opportunities are on message—or not. If not, then as CEO of Self, Inc. take steps to get yourself realigned with your purpose. Alignment creates meaning, fulfillment, and renewed energy.

Step 10 - Putting it all Together

I actively engage in regular planning and review to manage and monitor my ability to make a difference.

Don't Go Back to Sleep
By Rumi

For years, copying other people, I tried to know myself.
From within, I couldn't decide what to do.
Unable to see, I heard my name being called.
Then I walked outside.
The breeze at dawn has secrets to tell you.
Don't go back to sleep.
You must ask for what you really want.
Don't go back to sleep.
People are going back and forth across the doorsill
where the two worlds touch.
The door is round and open.
Don't go back to sleep.[127]

STEP 10...

FAST TRACK

In **Putting it all Together**, Step 10 is an affirmation of who you are and the beginnings of a plan to take the next steps on your vocational journey with a clearly stated purpose and processes that honour and resonate with your SoulDNA. It is important in Step 10 to move from reflection and analysis to planning and implementation. It is time to act on your best intentions and, in the laboratory of relationship and manifestation, discover the behaviours that generate responses that nurture and enhance the new life you are seeking. Step 10 is about putting foundations under the castles you have built in the air as you develop practices that get you in touch with the wisdom within while acting quickly to implement actions on the insights you receive. As you plan and move your insights into action, structures give form to your plans. These include daily practices, workspaces, environment, journaling, accountability, and review. Effective strategic and operational planning articulates not only where you are going and the actions needed to make progress, but also how you will know if you are successful. As you complete Step 10, it is time to create a meaningful leadership development plan. A personal Self-leadership development plan is your road map to success. Nothing speaks to commitment like a written plan with specific, measurable goals with witnesses, collaborators, checkpoints, and specific outcomes. Your Self-leadership plan utilizes the best, most meaningful components of a business plan model and mixes them together with elements of the Self-leadership quest. It is important to note that the best plan is one that is not rigid and restrictive but rather flexible, dynamic, and evolving. As you complete Step 10 and honestly examine your present strengths, weaknesses, opportunities and threats, you can intentionally and purposefully leverage from your FISC the best of your own experiences, knowledge, wisdom, skill, and inner parts to effectively lead both Self and others in service to the greater good.

Leadership Value: **Processes**

Guiding Principle: **Planned processes generate meaningful outcomes.**

FOOTHOLD

Having drafted a Self, Inc. purpose statement in Step 9, identify one action you will take in the next week that will align with your purpose and create a significant, positive shift in your leadership effectiveness and DMQ.

Rewriting the Script

Since the time when our ancestors wrote on cave walls, we have shaped our lives with collective and individual narratives. Stories of courage and endurance inspire and encourage us. They can also imprison us. For many years the story that the world was flat was reinforced by stories of sailors who had ventured too far and fallen into the abyss.

Of all the concepts in *12 Steps of Self-Leadership* no single element will have more transformative power than a realization that every aspect of your life is shaped by the stories and scripts you participate in, and an awareness of how stories shape each day of your life. Your parents had a script before you were even born. Even your naming was part of a story. As you grew you have either been a willing actor in the scripts of parents, teachers, family, community, and the larger society or you have rebelled against the script and either lived as an anti-hero or the author of your own story. As Rebecca Solnit states, "We are narrative creatures—we swim in stories as fish swim in water."[128]

As a Self-leader, choosing how you will play your role is essential to living on purpose. As David Brooks reminds us,

Among all the things we don't control, we do have some control over our stories. We do have a conscious say in selecting the narrative we will use to make sense of the world. Individual responsibility is contained in the act of selecting and constantly revising the master narrative we tell about ourselves.[129]

As you lead with purpose and define your processes you take control of your narrative. You choose to write your own script. Deepak Chopra expresses this powerfully when he writes,

In nearly everyone, this participation in the stories of our lives is happening automatically, without awareness. We live like actors in a play who are given only one line at a time, going through the motions without understanding the full story. But when you get in touch with your soul, you see the whole script for the drama. You understand. You still participate in the story, but now you participate joyously, consciously, and fully. You can make choices based on knowledge and born out of freedom. Each moment takes on a deeper quality that comes from appreciation of what it means in the context of your life. What is even more thrilling is that we, ourselves, are capable of rewriting the play or changing our roles by applying attention, grasping the opportunities that arise from coincidence, and being true to the calling of our souls.[130]

It is time to take charge of the narrative in your life and realize you are free to write your own story. In Stephen R. Covey's book, *The Third Alternative*, he said it this way,

> Our paradigms and cultural conditioning make up the story of our lives. Each has a beginning, a plot, and characters. There may even be heroes and villains. Countless subplots make up the big plot. There are crucial twists and turns in the narrative. And most crucially, there is conflict. No conflict no story. Every story turns on a struggle of some kind: a hero against a villain, a race against time, a character against her conscience, a man against his own limits... But there is a third voice in the story that is neither the hero nor the villain. This is the voice that tells the story. If we are truly self-aware, we realize that we are not just characters in our own story but also the narrator. We are not just written, we are the writer too. My story is only part of much bigger stories—stories of family, a community, and a whole culture. I might have limited influence on how those stories evolve, but I am very much in control of how my story goes. I am free to tell my own story.[131]

As you create your plan in Step 10, listen to your inner dreams. Reflect on your learning and insights. Trust your coordinating Self and all the inner parts. Re-examine your FISC. Ask big open-ended questions. Start now and let the process evolve.

Plan the Work — Work the Plan

One of our mentors on this quest, Tama Kieves stated, "It's great to have intentions. But it's better to take steps. Steps will change your life. The smallest step can open you up to the biggest possibility."[132] Step 10 is about planning, but it is also about action. If you have been doing the exercises at the ends of the chapters you have already started to make changes in the way you lead Self and others. Now as CEO of Self, Inc. it is time to move from vision to action.

In two years I went from an overweight flat-footed jogger who struggled to complete a mile run to a marathoner who finished in 3:29 placing me 1446th out of 3222 finishers in the ninth running of the Canadian National Marathon in 1983. I did this through consistent training, but mostly by following Amby Burfoot's 12-week Marathon plan. I registered for the race. I built the basic fitness level. I marked the mileage I would need to run each day for the twelve weeks leading up to the Marathon in Ottawa on my calendar. I ran the prescribed training miles keeping a log of distances and times. On race day, I knew my goal and ran my pace checking my progress at each mile along the 26-mile route. It worked and I repeated the process again four years later. Now, thirty-two years later, as an arthritic sixty-nine-year-old who fractured his left heel in a fall some years ago, I am running a couple half Marathons each year still using consistency and a 12-week plan as my guide.

You have dealt with the inner chaos and reclaimed your Facts, Influences, SoulDNA, and Characters. You have clarified your purpose and by planning processes in Step 10 you will enhance your ability to contribute to Self, others, and the greater good. By incorporating your learning into your daily activities and being a conscious leader you have increased your Difference Making Quotient. Now it is time to put structures in place so that you can consistently plan the work and work the plan.

As you bring your hopes and dreams to the world and take action there will be failures and setbacks, but each will just be helpful information as you continue to refine the processes that will allow you to make your contribution to the larger good. Action planning will help you to focus your ideas and decide what steps you need to take to achieve particular goals. Just as you prototype your purpose statement to learn through doing, we encourage you to also use a prototype approach to refining your Self-leadership plan. Don't miss the point that failing with dignity and a learner's attitude may be one of the most important gifts you give to those around you. Fear of failure paralyzes most of the people around you. If you wait for the perfect plan and the calm sea you will never set sail. When you act with curiosity and enthusiasm you become a beacon of hope to others who have yet to move from planning to action.

Perspectives

Often as we travel through life we get stuck in a particular point of view. Like a race-horse with blinkers we focus only on the track ahead. That may be useful at times when the terrain is flat, but when it comes to integrating your learning and exploring possibilities on uneven paths and unexplored territory, such a restricted view will limit your potential and slow your progress. By looking at life through multiple lenses you will gain new perspectives, and as you see life from new points of view, instead of plodding along, you will be able to make quantum leaps in awareness and effectiveness.

As you prepare for action and plan for the future, think of yourself coming back into society after a long journey far from civilization. Your perspectives have shifted. Your values are different. It will take time to find your new normal. You will need to be loving with yourself and compassionate with those who sense you have changed and don't know quite how to relate to your new attitudes and behaviours. Steps 6 to 9 are about allowing a new level of consciousness to emerge naturally to strengthen and nourish your best Self through the life-giving practices that have developed on the journey. Step 10 is about planning and initiating your re-entry process and forwarding the action.

In his work on presencing, Otto Scharmer describes this process you have been going through as going down the 'U'.[133] In this progression you have opened your mind, your heart, and your will. You have surrendered old patterns of seeing, thinking, and being but you have not yet fully established and embodied your new practices. An 'open mind' and 'open heart' allow you to begin to see a situation from the periphery of the whole, the 'open will' enables you to begin to act from the leading edge of the emerging future.

Danish sculptor and management consultant, Erik Lemcke, described his experience of
this awakening to Otto Scharmer this way,

> After having worked with a particular sculpture for some time, there comes a
> certain moment when things are changing. When this moment of change comes,
> it is no longer me, alone, who is creating. I feel connected to something far deeper
> and my hands are co-creating with this power. At the same time, I feel that I am
> being filled with love and care as my perception is widening. I sense things in
> another way. It is a love for the world and for what is coming. I then intuitively
> know what I must do. My hands know if I must add or remove something. My
> hands know how the form should manifest. In one way, it is easy to create with this
> guidance. In those moments I have a strong feeling of gratitude and humility.[134]

As you take the experiences and learnings from the *12 Steps* journey and incorporate
them into your life through Step 10, your authentic Self will begin to manifest and
you will feel yourself rising into a new life with unlimited possibilities. When you
lose your balance or feel fear or anger arising you can use compassionate listening and
mindful practices to regain your confidence. Breathe. Smile. Like the sculptor, trust your
instincts. Trust that you are not alone. You are creative, resourceful, and whole. You are
a co-creator and what emerges is exactly what the world needs from you right now. It is
important in Step 10 to move from reflection and analysis to planning and implementation. It is time to act on your best intentions and in the laboratory of relationship and
manifestation discover the behaviours that generate responses that nurture and enhance
the new life you are discovering.

It will take courage and ongoing awareness to allow your best Self to emerge. You have
had some habits and responses that have been in place for many years. It will take time
to allow your best Self to show up with consistency. Maya Angelou said it this way,

> One isn't born with courage. One develops it. And you develop it by doing small,
> courageous things, in the same way that one wouldn't set out to pick up a 100
> pound bag of rice. If that was one's aim, the person would be advised to pick up a
> five pound bag, and then a ten pound, and then a 20 pound, and so forth, until one
> builds up enough muscle to actually pick up 100 pounds. And that's the same way
> with courage. You develop courage by doing courageous things, small things, but
> things that cost you some exertion — mental and, I suppose, spiritual exertion.[135]

As you begin to manifest the new life and strength that is emerging there will be temptations to slip back into old habits or at least to take it easy on yourself. Step 10 is about
putting plans, structures, and habits in place to strengthen your vision, increase your
resolve, and provide reminders that you will no longer settle for wearing other people's
faces or settling for less than full engagement in the Self-leadership journey.

As you plan and implement, be gentle with yourself, but not too gentle. You have
come too far to disavow your SoulDNA by allowing the inner light to fade. In your
new awareness everything in life is a message to guide your journey. Look and listen.
As Canadian writer Charles de Lint, writes, "It's all a matter of paying attention, being

awake in the present moment, and not expecting a huge payoff. The magic in this world seems to work in whispers and small kindnesses."[136]

A House of Your Own

Implementation is an ongoing process of awareness and gentle course corrections. Self-leadership and championing your best Self does not suddenly make your physical and economic life easier. There will be difficulties. That is a given. When you accept the challenge to be a Self-leader you begin to live from the inside out and do what needs to be done one day at a time, sometimes one step at a time. David Reynolds in *Constructive Living* writes,

> Life isn't always fair. I can't offer any excuses for that fact and won't try to minimize it. I do know that life seems to go better for me when I pay attention to doing what needs doing rather than ruminating about how I deserve better than what life sends my way. If you want milk, it is inefficient to sit on a stool in a field hoping that a cow will back up to you. If you want riches, it's inefficient to lie in bed hoping that Congress will include you in the national budget next year. Effort is good fortune— effort is not a state of mind, but a quality of doing.[137]

When MIT professor, Otto Scharmer, asked the violinist Miha Pogacnik to describe key moments from his music experience, he told him about his first concert in Chartres.

> I felt that the cathedral almost kicked me out. 'Get out with you!' she said. For I was young and I tried to perform as I always did: by just playing my violin. But then I realized that in Chartres you actually cannot play your small violin, but you have to play the 'macro violin.' The small violin is the instrument that is in your hands. The macro violin is the whole cathedral that surrounds you. The cathedral of Chartres is built entirely according to musical principles. Playing the macro violin requires you to listen and to play from another place, from the periphery. You have to move your listening and playing from within to beyond yourself.[138]

As you forward the action in Step 10, a new level of living and loving is required if you are truly committed to letting your best Self bring joy and wholeness to your Self and others. This Step "requires you to listen and to play from another place, from the periphery. You have to move your listening and playing from within to beyond yourself."[139] Ever since Step 3, when you crossed the threshold to embark upon the adventure of embodying your best Self, your journey has been mostly introspective. Now it is time for a new level of attention and awareness in order to show up fully, and mindfully engage in life, work, and relationships. Living authentically is the ultimate 'both—and' experience. In every moment it requires all your skill and attention while at the same time requiring a complete surrender to the larger mystery of which you are a part.

> **"Live as if you were to die tomorrow. Learn as if you were to live forever."** ~ Ghandi

As you open yourself to new levels of awareness, it is a descent into a new place of being present with what is seeking to happen in and through you. In this process you suspend downloading old patterns of being, and open your mind, your heart, and your will to new levels of awareness and presence. Just as Miha Pogacnik needed to play from a different place, as you integrate your realities with your potential, you will be able to let the new come into your vision and attention, and by linking head, heart, and hand, begin operating from the whole. The amazing part of this new form of awakened integration is that even though you have gone deeper into your Self than ever before, the resulting purpose and actions will flow from a perspective that is far beyond you as you operate from the nexus of the emerging future and the possibilities that the best of you is being asked to contribute.

Regardless of your age or stage, your actions in Step 10 will send positive ripples well beyond your awareness. Like the butterfly in the Amazon your actions are shifting the energy of the larger whole. Each day as you show up fully, and mindfully engage in life, work and relationships you are living as Ghandi suggested when he said, "Live as if you were to die tomorrow. Learn as if you were to live forever."[140]

Throw off the old weights and fears and start living with confidence and openness. Serendipities will occur. The time for analysis and deepening is past. Step 10 is the season for planning and harvest. Live as Henry David Thoreau did at Walden causing him to write,

> I learned this, at least, by my experiment; that if one advances confidently in the direction of his dreams, and endeavors to live the life which he has imagined, he will meet with a success unexpected in common hours. He will put some things behind, will pass an invisible boundary; new, universal, and more liberal laws will begin to establish themselves around and within him; or the old laws will be expanded, and interpreted in his favor in a more liberal sense, and he will live with the license of a higher order of beings."

He concludes the paragraph with, "If you have built castles in the air, your work need not be lost; that is where they should be. Now put the foundations under them.[141]

Step 10 is about putting foundations under the castles you have built in the air. Continue to use wise guides, but most importantly, as we will stress more in Step 11 and 12, trust the wisdom and guidance of your SoulDNA and develop practices that get you in touch with the wisdom within while acting quickly to implement actions based on the insights you receive, and the plans you've created.

Structures

As you plan and move your insights into action, structures give form to your plans. For individuals these structures include daily practices, workspaces, environment, journaling, accountability, planning, pauses, and review. A plan is a map to help you identify and assemble required resources, take meaningful action, assess results, and choose the next steps. As you consciously seek to be a transformational leader your planning allows you to communicate your vision in realistic terms with your inner and outer team so that collaboration and synergy can develop. Effective strategic and operational planning articulates not only where you are going and the actions needed to make progress, but also how you will know if you are successful.

These structures are essential in moving the action forward, yet within the structures there need to be new levels of awareness, creativity, and nimbleness. Too often, rather than freeing you up and serving the emerging future, these structures can serve the past and keep you stuck in old ways of thinking and responding. By integrating your inner voices, intuitive knowing, imagination, and sensate wisdom you can create new structures that act as bridges and scaffolds that will allow you to move into the places of most potential—places where you are exposed to, and connected with, something new.

Structures to open your mind, to suspend old habits of judgement, old habits of perception, and old habits of thought may be questions you begin to incorporate into your daily planning. Questions like "What do I need to let go of?" will help open up possibility for innovation. Scheduling 5 to10 minutes before a meeting or an activity for a time of quiet presencing will allow you to get grounded, and tune in to what is trying to happen. Changing the meeting agendas to include times of deep listening and silence, movement, and different perspectives, will shift the whole planning and implementation process. Taking time at the end of a meeting to check in with other participants, setting up measures of success, and checking these out regularly allows you to hear from the system and begin to live and act from an inner-outer perspective at all times in all situations. With structures in place setting intentions, suspending judgement, hearing all the voices, acting in a moment, prototyping, deep listening, intuiting, naming and managing polarities, can become a part of regular practices.

In order to increase your Difference Making Quotient, how you pay attention in any given context, what you pay attention to, and how you respond, is critical. Structures that honour the inner parts and the complex social field that is created as you form community are essential in allowing you to fulfill your purpose. Agendas, meeting structures, time and space considerations can create new ways for you and your collaborators to come together to interrogate reality, explore possibilities, and move from small 's' self-thinking to a big 'S' Self-creativity. As you move from a reactive mechanical approach to a more organic, engaged 'interbeing', the structures will need to evolve to help you sustain your insights and share them with others so that ideas can be translated into innovations and prototypes.

Self, Inc. Guiding Principles

You are the CEO of Self, Inc. Your leadership values and guiding principles shape your inner and outer life. As you take responsibility for your life and all the possibilities and potential that your FISC contains, your vision and guiding principles will determine your Difference Making Quotient.

Bob Chapman was only 30 years old when he became chief executive officer of family-owned Barry-Wehmiller in 1975 after the untimely death of his father. When you visit the company website forty years later the first thing you will encounter is a powerful statement of the guiding principles that have shaped Bob's life and organization. During his first 10 years as CEO, Bob and his team stabilized the struggling bottle washer and pasteurizer business. Then they began to diversify its product line by acquiring beaten-down packaging companies and bringing them back to life through supporting and inspiring their existing leadership teams. Bob's strategy for success became his mantra of being "truly human' in all aspects of work and relationships. Today, $1.8 billion Barry-Wehmiller is a combination of almost 70 acquired companies spread among ten subsidiaries across the globe. Bob Chapman champions a culture focused on "bringing out the best in its people through communication, trust, celebration, respect, continuous improvement and responsible freedom."[142] He and his co-workers boldly declare that they are building a better world. They state:

> We're more than just a successful capital equipment and engineering solutions firm. We're an organization fiercely committed to improving the lives of our team members across the globe. By providing meaningful work in an environment of care and compassion, we send them home fulfilled by their time with us, rather than drained by it. We understand what every human being on the planet desires: to know that who they are and what they do matter. As a business, we have a unique opportunity to let them know that they do.[143]

Conscious Capitalism, a business leadership movement that Bob and like-minded visionaries have developed, states, "Culture is the embodied principles and practices underlying the social fabric of a business, which permeate its actions and connects the stakeholders to each other and to the company's purpose, people and processes."[144]

Just as Barry-Wehmiller's success stems from a clear set of values and guiding principles, so too your success and Difference Making Quotient and influence will depend on the clarity and consistency of your guiding principles as CEO of your own Self, Inc.

For Eagle Tree Leadership our core values are: deep democracy, connectedness, learning, and synergistic collaboration. These serve as guidelines for our inner and outer interactions. They shape the way we set up our home, our offices, our writing, our coaching, and our workshops. Along with the twelve Values and Guiding Principles of Self-leadership, which are summarized at the end of Step 12, they create a framework for our personal and professional lives. We dialogue regularly about our culture and find meaning and purpose through living into our calling.

The purpose I have been committed to since my mid-teens is "to create a safer, saner world." This and my natural gifting led me into elementary education as a teacher. My first school was dynamic and I felt like I had come home. As I worked with other dedicated teachers in public education I was inspired, engaged, and transformed and after seven years I chose to become a school principal so that I could have even more influence in shaping a culture of engagement and transformation. My commitment, honesty, courage, and effectiveness led to positive school cultures and exciting learning opportunities for everyone involved.

When government policies made sweeping changes to our educational system the guiding principles no longer resonated with my own, which led to my decision to leave public education and seek another process where I could live out my life purpose. I went through some desert times and a couple of false starts before I found an opportunity with a social agency as a program manager and life coach working with marginalized youth. As soon as I started at Eclypse Youth Centre it felt like I had come back home. My desire "to create a safer, saner world" has inspired and engaged me as Cheryl and I developed Eagle Tree Leadership and wrote this book.

Similarly as you honour your Self, Inc. purpose and use intuition, awareness, and courage to follow your purpose, your guiding principles will always let you know when you are in the right process to live out the giftings of your FISC. You will feel like you have arrived at your heart's true home.

SWOT Analysis

The SWOT exercise will help you look at your present strengths, weaknesses, opportunities and threats. This analysis tool has been used by businesses and organizations since the 1970s. As you examine your strengths, weaknesses, opportunities, and threats we encourage you to look at the process from a global perspective. With an abundance mentality there is no need for always being competitive and constantly comparing yourself to others. Your responsibility and opportunity as a conscious leader is to use all your innate talents, interests, desires, and goals in conjunction with consistent personal practices designed to develop and enhance skills and attitudes that will serve the larger good. Like so many aspects of the Self-leadership quest this is a 'both—and' process. You need to develop both your inner awareness and your inner competencies at the same time as you develop both your outer awareness and outer competencies.

As you become a conscious transformational leader, the SWOT is an analysis of where you are compared to where you can be as you continue to evolve. Otto Scharmer calls the space between self and Self the spiritual divide. He says it this way, "The spiritual-cultural divide reflects a disconnect between little self and Self—that is, between one's current 'self' and the emerging future 'Self' that represents one's greatest potential"[145]

Strengths: By listing natural or developed strengths or areas of passion that you are already aware of, as well as those that you are just beginning to discover and develop, you will gain confidence, increase your energy, effectiveness and flow in life, work, and relationships.

Weaknesses: One of the greatest challenges that leaders face is the misconception that they need to be all things to all people. By knowing what you do not do as well, you can effectively delegate and recruit the skills and attitudes that will fill the gaps and enhance your collective effectiveness. By asking for help, as a Self-leader you will transmute your weaknesses into strengths through acknowledging what you don't know or don't do as well, and allowing others to contribute through their areas of strength.

Opportunities: As you open your mind, heart, and will, exciting future possibilities will begin to surface. There will be opportunities in Self-development, in your family, with friends, in your larger Circle of Influence, and potentially beyond. The powerful question that will keep you open to possibilities is, "What is trying to happen?" Being open, gives your purpose-related passion an opportunity to manifest in new and exciting ways.

Threats: By acknowledging real or potential threats to your well-being and DMQ, you will continue to become a more capable and conscious leader as you responsibly make better choices and mindful course corrections. As a Self-leader you are at risk of sabotage by inner parts that have not been fully identified, owned, integrated, and aligned with your higher purpose. Owning and monitoring the threats to your inner and outer leadership, will increase your ability to lead with confidence and integrity.

Your Self, Inc. Plan

The difference between wishful thinking and effective implementation is in your ability to create and follow a meaningful Self, Inc. plan. Lester R. Bittel stated, "Good plans shape good decisions. That's why good planning helps make elusive dreams come true."[146] As the CEO of Self, Inc., a personal leadership development plan is your road map to success and fulfillment. As we have said throughout this book, the secret to success is commitment, and nothing speaks to commitment like a written plan with specific, measurable goals with witnesses, collaborators, checkpoints, and specific outcomes.

Many professional business people map out a plan of where they desire to be in the future. Studies have shown that those who create and use a written personal leadership development plan are far more successful than those who don't. There is no set formula for creating your plan, but it should include enough information to answer two main questions: "Where do I want to be in X years?" and "What do I need to do to get there?"

Your Self-leadership plan utilizes the best, most meaningful components of a business plan model and mixes them together with elements of the Self-leadership quest. It is important to note that the best plan is one that is not rigid and restrictive but flexible, dynamic, and evolving. To be useful a plan needs to work for you. Ideally, it needs to contain a definition of your higher purpose. It needs to incorporate the learnings and insights gained through your FISC exploration and impact assessment. It needs to identify processes—the ways through which you will be able to best manifest your purpose, leverage your potential, and make a difference in service to both Self, and others.

A plan is meant to be a living document. Although your higher purpose, once discovered, remains the same, the processes (ways that you choose to live out your purpose) may be many and varied, changing and evolving with time, experience, and opportunities. A plan can include meaningful 'measures' that you can use to assess whether or not you're on track, or what may need to be redefined, or recalibrated. In the business world, these are sometimes called KPIs (key performance indicators), relevant guideposts that help you keep focused and aligned with the things that you have identified as being the most important in allowing you to be successful and live on purpose as a Difference Maker.

In Stepping Stones we offer some suggested frameworks for your planning. This is not a one size fits all process. Some very successful organizations have been mapped out on a napkin during a late night conversation. Author Tama Kieves writes,

> It's easy in our culture, to think you need a plan, a map and a guarantee. But that's what keeps you stuck. Free your genius. Stay committed, true, and dogged to the one thing you can do. Your only job is to listen to the next step. Your only job is to sniff the ground, let the wind inform your cells, stay alert to your desires and the undercurrent of a Universal Intelligence. Every step is an answer to prayer. Every step is a devotion.[147]

This is another 'both—and' polarity. Some of you will need and want to have a structured, detailed plan. Others, not so much. Create a plan that works for you. The plan is always meant to be in service to your best Self and your higher Purpose. Whenever you find yourself serving the plan instead of it serving you, it's time to rethink and evaluate what's working and what isn't. Stay loose but keep your dream in focus.

Your plan is a living dream of a better future for you, others, and the planet.

Your plan is a living dream of a better future for you, others, and the planet. Once you have written it down, committed to action, and started living it share your ideas, your goals, and your needs with everyone you meet. You never know who will connect you with the next resource or idea. Your passion and commitment will inspire and engage others and as you are transformed by your leadership quest you will transform the people and spaces in your environment.

Moving along the Path with STEP 10...

I actively engage in regular planning and review to manage and monitor my ability to make a difference.

STEPPING STONES

The primary objective in this section is to help you develop a Self-leadership Plan that will be a useful and dynamic tool that provides inspiration, guidance, and accountability as you continue to increase your DMQ™ as the CEO of Self, Inc.™.

Some of you will be content to use loose leaf pages, index cards, napkins, or your journal to set your intentions and create the materials that will serve as reminders, accountability checkpoints, and breadcrumbs on the path in case you lose your way.

Others will benefit from a more formal structure and process. There are many different planning document formats. The sample Plan that is included with these Stepping Stones is merely a suggestion. Again, make it your own. Make it work for you.

In addition to the *12 Steps* work you've done so far, the following items will provide additional insights that will help you develop your Plan.

- Core values and guiding principles will always let you know when you are involved with the right processes to live out your FISC. List your core values and guiding principles.

- SWOT — As CEO of Self, Inc.™ the ability to identify and acknowledge the Strengths, Weaknesses, Opportunities, and Threats is an important part of the planning process.

  - Strengths: What areas of skills, abilities, or passion are you already aware of and/or are just discovering and developing?

  - Weaknesses: What skills or abilities do you lack, or are weaker in, that could create opportunities for others to contribute through their strengths?

  - Opportunities: As you review your *12 Steps* learning so far, and continue to listen to both inner and outer wisdom and direction, what purpose-aligned opportunities are emerging in your life, work, and relationships?

- Threats: What people, circumstances, habits, or inner Characters have the potential to hinder or sabotage your well-being, success, and DMQ?

NOTE: Use the following SAMPLE PLAN to develop your own Self-Leadership Plan

---

Chris, Inc.
Self-Leadership Plan
January 1 to December 31, 2016

Difference Making Proposition (Purpose):
Facilitate respectful, efficient, and collaborative relationships that support learning.

Core Values / Guiding Principles
- Honesty / Honesty leads to wholeness.
- Respect / Respect for Self and others improves teamwork.
- Collaboration / Collaboration optimizes diversity.
- Efficiency / Efficient processes lead to desired outcomes.
- Learning / Learning facilitates continuous improvement.

SWOT:
- Key Strength(s): Big picture thinking and ability to develop efficient systems and processes.
- Key Weakness(es): Believing I am / can be good at everything.
- Key Opportunity(ies): Leadership mentoring and success planning.
- Key Threat(s): Low / wavering Self-confidence.

Key Activities / Roles (Processes)
- Continue as VP of Finance — Jan 1 to Dec 31, 2016.
- Serve as assistant coach for child's soccer team — Apr to June 2016.
- Participate in Habitat for Humanity project — July / Aug 2016.
- Provide group-based tutoring to five first-year university Accounting program students –Sept to Dec 2016.

DEVELOPMENT PRIORITY — Self-Confidence
Objectives:
- Identify and address the inner scripts, beliefs, or people and circumstances that negatively impact confidence;
- Learn how to effectively use Self-leadership techniques strengthen my self-confidence and improve Self and other leadership effectiveness.
Motivation:
- Desire to show up more fully and effectively as a leader.
Benefit:
- Increased ability to facilitate learning and collaborative relationships.
Risk if not successful:
- Reduced trust in my ability to effectively lead my department.

- Reduced interest of others in involving me in senior-level discussions, decision-making, and strategic planning initiatives.

Action Required:
- Sign up with a leadership coach who can help identify the issues, facilitate skill development and an actionable and accountable plan.

Timeframe:
- January to June 2016.

Measures of Inner Success:
- Increased inner awareness and effectiveness in recognizing and managing inner voices and scripts that hinder healthy Self-confidence.
- Fewer and shorter occurrences of low Self-confidence.
- More frequent and longer periods of feeling strong, confident, and in flow.
- Increased Self-respect and appreciation for my unique FISC-related skills, abilities, and gifts that I can use to increase my DMQ and live out my Purpose.

Measures of Outer Success:
- Positive informal and formal performance feedback from my peers, staff, friends, and family.
- Greater degree of engagement in conversations with peers, staff, and stakeholders.
- Increased ability to own my areas of strength AND weakness and take corrective steps to recalibrate when I start to waver.

DEVELOPMENT PRIORITY -
Team Development and Relationship Dynamics Training
Objectives:
- Develop new facilitation and team development skills;
- Improve understanding related to personality differences and interpersonal dynamics.

Motivation:
- Identified department performance gaps related to collaboration and efficiency of team-based interactions.

Benefit:
- More efficient use of meeting time. Higher engagement and collaboration.

Risk if not successful:
- Individual and collective fear and resistance to transparent and engaged dialogue and open collaboration.

Action Required:
- Research and register as participant in appropriate skills training workshop.

Timeframe:
- October or November 2016.

Measures of Inner Success:
- Increased willingness to engage in relationships.
- Increased inner Self-confidence in dealing with confrontation / resistance.
- Greater appreciation for diversity and its importance in teamwork.

Measures of Outer Success:
- Increased ability to set expectations for and influence team performance.

- Improved team performance receives recognition from within the organization.
- Informal and formal feedback from staff / team members indicates greater satisfaction, higher productivity, and increased efficiency related to team-based work and interactions.

SELF-LEADERSHIP PAUSES — Keeping It Fresh

Objectives:

- Daily Pauses:
  - At the start of each day, take at least five minutes to check and choose my attitude, and set my intentions for the day.
  - At the end of each day, take time to reflect on my failures, my learnings, my successes, and record at least three gratitudes.
- Weekly Pause:
  - Take fifteen minutes every weekend to review my calendar for the upcoming week.
- Renewal Pause:
  - Friday, April 30, 2016 — Using Self, Inc. plan document, review progress. Revise details of plan and/or recalibrate actions to align with plan.
- Annual Pause:
  - August 21-26, 2016 at ABC Retreat Centre:
  - Unplug from distractions, including TV, phone, and Internet.
  - Review outcomes and performance related to Self, Inc. Plan.
  - Read at least one book related to the inner life. Reflect and journal insights.
  - Healthy snacks and meals.
  - Solitary walks.
  - Creative activities that open up my thinking and ability to dream about my envisioned future.
  - Regular journal entries related to my sleeping dreams, waking hour serendipities, emerging awareness and insights.
  - Journal reflections on past year learnings.
  - Rough draft of ideas and details of my Self-leadership plan for the coming year.

TRAVEL TIPS

1. Planning can seem like an onerous task—particularly if you've had bad experiences before around wasted or rigid planning processes. There is no perfect plan. Choose to experiment with what will work best for you by starting with the sample outline, then adapting and changing your plan as you regularly refer to and engage with it during the year.

2. As CEO of Self, Inc. envision your future, then develop a plan that will ensure your success in getting there.

Step 11 – Transformational Leadership

As a leader, I inspire, engage, empower, and facilitate transformational change in the world—individually and collectively.

Inter-Relationship
By Thich Nhat Hanh

You are me and I am you. Isn't it obvious that we inter-are?
You cultivate the flower in yourself
so that I will be beautiful.
I transform the garbage in myself
so that you do not have to suffer.
I support you; you support me.
I am here to bring you peace
you are here to bring me joy.[148]

STEP 11...

FAST TRACK

As you take responsibility for **Transformational Leadership** you realize you have an inner audience as well as an outer Circle of Influence. Through your sense of purpose, clear intentions, and a willingness to take action you are becoming a catalyst for positive change—a Difference Maker. Step 11 is your moment of declaration. You have a vision and a plan of action. It is time to invite all of your inner parts and your outer allies to support you as you choose to live with clarity and openness. It will not be just in what you say, but in the way you lead from a new place of inner wisdom, empathy, confidence, and vision. Without a meaningful connection with the Energy of Life, and regular encounters with a coach or accountability partner, integrity outages may occur. Your commitment to goals that transcend small 's' self-interest, your daily practices, and mindful pauses are essential elements of maintaining integrity, managing risk, and creating a transformative legacy. Step 11 is your opportunity to prototype and bring to life the shifts that the Self-leadership work has prompted. Don't underestimate the impact that you can have from this enlightened perspective. Step 11 is about managing the polarities of life and managing yourself so that you live in harmony with your soul while extending grace and understanding to those who do not see the world the same way as you do. Your Self-leadership journey is a balance of self-confidence and humility. Transformational Self-leadership will no longer be about doing the right thing it will be about being the right thing—the energetic, loving, forgiving authentic you. Ultimately, transformation is a commitment to always bring your best Self into the world and into every aspect of your life, work, and relationships. As you continue to live from an inner place of vision and passion you will have a calm knowing of what comes next and you will be able to forward the agenda with confidence and positive energy.

Leadership Value: Leadership

Guiding Principle: Transformational leadership inspires and engages others.

FOOTHOLD

What new or enhanced practice(s) can you introduce into your life, work, or relationships this week that will demonstrate respect, integrity, authenticity and accountability as a transformational leader?

Declaration

A very successful business acquisition specialist shared his approach with us. He finds a business that has potential but is struggling with focus and production. Once he and his team acquire ownership he takes time to listen and talk with all the stakeholders both inside and outside the organization. The reason he is so successful is that he is open, curious, and non-judgemental. People are quickly aware that this is not a fault-finding mission. He asks the leadership team to continue to use their best judgement and carry on with business as usual. He and his transformation team use Appreciative Inquiry to probe what is working and what is possible. He observes, observes, observes and then he listens some more. He asks what is possible and what is trying to happen. He assesses the stated goals and considers what needs to shift as the organization moves effectively into the future. He refines the purpose statement and goals and shares and enhances this with his mastermind group. Finally he is ready for declaration day.

He calls everyone together. No one is excluded. Using a basketball court, football stadium, or auditorium with people sitting in the round he stands in the centre. When all the employees are assembled he calmly and confidently shares the vision for the emerging future and the short and long term plans. Like his hero, Teddy Roosevelt, he uses the arena analogy and says up until now there have been players and observers. He reminds them of Theodore Roosevelt's famous quote:

> It is not the critic who counts; not the man who points out how the strong man stumbles, or where the doer of deeds could have done them better. The credit belongs to the man who is actually in the arena, whose face is marred by dust and sweat and blood; who strives valiantly; who errs, who comes short again and again, because there is no effort without error and shortcoming; but who does actually strive to do the deeds; who knows great enthusiasms, the great devotions; who spends himself in a worthy cause; who at the best knows in the end the triumph of high achievement, and who at the worst, if he fails, at least fails while daring greatly.[149]

Then he declares that as of this moment everyone needs to decide whether this is the right time and place for them to live out their skills in this organization. Everyone is challenged to leave the bleachers and either join the team on the field of action or to leave the organization with dignity and respect.

Step 11 is your moment of declaration. You have a vision and a plan of action. It is time to invite all of your inner parts and your outer allies to support you as you choose to live with clarity and openness. Your Difference Making Quotient will be determined not only by what you say, but also the way you lead Self and others from a place of inner wisdom, empathy, confidence, and vision. Let your inner light shine. You have arrived.

Daring Greatly

Using Teddy Roosevelt's 'Daring Greatly' speech as her inspiration, in her book *Daring Greatly*, Brené Brown writes,

> When we spend our lives waiting until we're perfect or bulletproof before we walk into the arena, we ultimately sacrifice relationships and opportunities that may not be recoverable, we squander our precious time, and we turn our backs on our gifts, those unique contributions that only we can make. Perfect and bulletproof are seductive, but they don't exist in the human experience.[150]

As you take your learnings and newfound sense of wholeness and purpose into life, work, and relationships it will take courage. You are ready. The time is now and it is important to have a sense of urgency. Your inner parts, your friends and family, your workplace colleagues, and the larger world have been waiting for your unique contribution. Step 11 is your opportunity to start living from a Self-directed sense of calm confidence and inner awareness. As you allow the new life that has been transforming you from the inside out to shape and inform your daily choices you will discover that the Self-leadership quest has indeed been transformative. You will realize you do have an increased capacity to make a positive difference in the world.

As you step into the arena, your declaration will be powerful since it now comes from a strong sense of inner awareness and purpose. Instead of presenting a fearless exterior you will now be able to show up without having all the answers and instead of being bulletproof you have become a transformational leader as you allow yourself to be vulnerable. As you own your wake and engage with openness and vulnerability, you give those around you the courage to do the same. Brené Brown says it this way,

> Vulnerability is not weakness, and the uncertainty, risk, and emotional exposure we face every day are not optional. Our only choice is a question of engagement. Our willingness to own and engage with our vulnerability determines the depth of our courage and the clarity of our purpose; the level to which we protect ourselves from being vulnerable is a measure of our fear and disconnection.[151]

Step 11 is your opportunity to prototype and bring to life the shifts that the Self-leadership work has prompted. Like the heroes Joseph Campbell studied, you return from your quest bringing wisdom and insight to your community. Don't underestimate the impact that you can have from this enlightened perspective. You are not the same person as you were when you accepted the challenge back in Step 3 and stepped across the threshold onto the Road.

Transformational Leadership

As you lead Self and others from a place of purpose and inner awareness you will notice that the energy shifts in and around you. You will notice that you are hearing beyond the words and listening to the whole social field. You can now lead into the future with confidence and optimism and you will begin to notice the way that Self-leadership transforms relationships.

Pulitzer Prize-winning presidential biographer and a pioneer in the study of leadership, James McGregor Burns, introduced the concept of transformational leadership in his 1978 book, *Leadership*. He defined transformational leadership as a process where "leaders and their followers raise one another to higher levels of morality and motivation."[152]

Historically, through the strength of their vision and personality, transformational leaders have been able to inspire followers to change expectations, perceptions, and motivations in order to work towards common goals. Researcher Bernard M. Bass expanded upon Burns' original ideas. According to Bass, transformational leadership can be defined based on the impact that it has on followers. Transformational leaders, Bass suggested, garner trust, respect, and admiration from their followers.

It is now accepted that there are four different components of transformational leadership:

> **Intellectual Stimulation:** Transformational leaders not only challenge the status quo; they also encourage creativity among followers. The leader encourages followers to explore new ways of doing things and new opportunities to learn.
>
> **Individualized Consideration:** Transformational leaders offer support and encouragement to individual followers. Transformation depends on open lines of communication so that followers feel free to share ideas, allowing the leader to offer direct recognition of the unique contributions of each follower.
>
> **Inspirational Motivation:** Transformational leaders have a clear vision that they are able to articulate to followers and help followers experience passion and motivation to fulfill these goals.
>
> **Idealized Influence:** The transformational leader serves as a role model for followers. Because followers trust and respect the leader, they emulate this individual and are motivated to develop their own leadership potential.[153]

To be a true Difference Maker requires the highest level of Self-leadership and moral example. History is replete with failures of leaders who allowed a lack of discipline, awareness, and moral values to erode their private and public DMQ. As a transformational leader you will need to continue to do your private work so that you can have public validity.

Historically, the seven deadly 'sins' have been:

- Lust — the uncontrolled desire for money, food, fame, or power.

- Gluttony — the overindulgence and overconsumption of anything to the point of waste.

- Greed — the inordinate desire to acquire or possess more than one needs.

- Laziness — the failure to utilize one's talents and gifts.

- Wrath — anger and bitterness that leads to inner and outer destruction.

- Envy — jealousy of another's traits, status, abilities, and lack of embracing of your own FISC.

- Pride — love of the small 's' self, believing that this 'you' is essentially better than others.

These moral failures do not originate "out there." They begin within when you as a leader do not honour your inner treasures and continuously lead Self, Inc. so that no archetypal part or inner Character will push your best Self aside and sabotage your transformational potential. As a leader you have a high calling to ensure that external power and influence doesn't lead to internal rationalization and confusion. It is a sacred trust to lead Self and others.

When others are younger, have less power or position, or are enamored by your charisma and success, succumbing to one of the historical 'sins' is far too enticing. Without a meaningful connection with the Energy of Life, and regular encounters with a coach or accountability partner, integrity outages may occur. Your commitment to goals that transcend small 's' self-interest, your daily practices, and mindful pauses are essential elements of maintaining integrity, managing risk, and creating a transformational legacy.

Transformation through Empowerment

Here is a summary of a success story from an April 1, 2013 Harvard Business Review article entitled *How SAP Labs India Became An Innovation Dynamo.*[154] It is the story of one transformational leader in action.

In April 2010, V. R. Ferose, at age thirty-five, became the youngest-ever managing director of a global multinational firm in India. As managing director of SAP Labs India, one of fifteen global R&D centres of the German software giant SAP, Ferose's mandate was to reduce employee turnover which had reached a painful 19 per cent in 2009 to below 10 per cent by 2012.

Rather than rushing into action, Ferose took time to identify the root causes of employee dissatisfaction by listening to and observing employees. He noticed that discontented employees were posting negative comments on the lab's internal blog about the local management team, which they viewed as unresponsive to their needs.

Frustrated employees were complaining about the lack of on campus amenities such as child care and the stifling bureaucracy.

Ferose realized that SAP Labs India had to engage its young employees (average age twenty-nine) differently. He believed that it is not the CEO's job to find ways to make his or her employees happier. As a transformational leader, he believed the CEO's job is to give employees the freedom to test and deploy their own solutions that will in turn make them happier at work. This belief led Ferose to overhaul SAP Labs India's hierarchical, 'top-heavy' corporate culture, allowing bottom-up creativity and innovation to blossom. He empowered his 4,000 plus employees to experiment with bold new ideas by freeing up time for staff members to work on solving the very problems they were complaining about. He believed such a move would not only directly and positively impact SAP's core business, but also improve employees' level of engagement, working conditions and morale.

Within two years of taking over, V. R. Ferose's transformational leadership had empowered and engaged employees so that production and creativity flourished and commitment to the company increased. Attrition dropped from 19 per cent in 2009 to 10 per cent in 2011, to seven per cent in 2012. The India lab now ranks #1 in employee satisfaction within SAP's global network of fifteen R&D labs.

As you lead from this place of transformation, remember you have an inner audience as well as an outer Circle of Influence. Through your sense of purpose, clear intentions, and a willingness to take action, you will be a catalyst for positive change both in yourself and in your Circle of Influence. In their book, *Transformational Leadership*, Bernard M. Boss and Ronald E. Riggio wrote,

> Transformational leaders ... are those who stimulate and inspire followers to both achieve extraordinary outcomes and, in the process, develop their own leadership capacity. Transformational leaders help followers grow and develop into leaders by responding to individual followers' needs by empowering them and by aligning the objectives and goals of the individual followers, the leader, the group, and the larger organization.[155]

The Hard Truth about Soft Skills

Whether it is your inner life, family, workplace or organization, caring, compassion, awareness, and openness are the glue that will hold it all together. Too often these so-called soft skills have been ridiculed and pushed aside in the guise of productivity. Efficiency experts and hard-nosed CEOs focused on results while ignoring what they called "touchy-feely stuff." The truth is that vulnerability and transparency is not for wimps and this transformational engagement is too difficult for many leaders to face. As you manifest your newfound inner awareness there is no need to play small. Your willingness to show up fully and be a role model for Self-leadership is essential. Since the mid-1990s, individuals and organizations have realized that the security-for-life employment agreements of the past were disappearing and without the old glue new ways of developing loyalty and engagement would be required.

Gallup's 2012 State of the American Workplace poll showed that in America 70 per cent of employees are not "engaged" at work. More than half, 52 per cent, say they are not enthusiastic or committed and are essentially sleepwalking through their day. Another 18 per cent are truly unhappy, or "actively disengaged," as Gallup states it, and they could be undermining not only their own performance but the work of colleagues. Only 30 per cent of American workers really love their jobs, according to the survey. In a note from Gallup CEO, Jim Clifton, that precedes the report, he says that getting employees excited about their jobs is the responsibility of managers. The cost of poor management is high, he writes. Measured by engagement, the top 25 per cent of teams have 50 per cent fewer accidents and produce 41 per cent fewer product defects. The top 25 per cent also rack up much less in health care costs. According to Gallup's research, workers who don't care about their jobs cost the U.S. between $450 billion and $550 billion each year in accidents, poorly produced products and health care bills.[156]

It has taken time for individuals and organizations to accept that soft skills do deliver a return on investment, but increasingly individuals and organizations realize that external results are enhanced by internal transformation. The acceptance of Self-awareness and the need for coaching has grown steadily over the last ten years as Sherpa Coaching surveys have demonstrated. "Those who say the credibility of coaching is 'somewhat high' or 'very high' jumped to 90 per cent in the 2012 report. The numbers stayed right there in 2013 and improved once again in 2014, to 93 per cent. Compared to just five years ago, the number of people who see the credibility of coaching as mediocre or worse has declined sharply, dropping from 27 per cent to seven per cent."[157]

In his 1997 book, *Breaking Free*, leadership expert David M. Noer wrote,

> Leadership in the new reality is neither a gentle nor a spectator sport. It is an against-the-grain activity requiring tenacity, courage, and faith. Seeking the difficult and elusive systematic solution, while resisting the shallow and often reinforced short-term fix, requires tenacity. Learning and behaving according to the relevant but new soft competencies, while resisting the temptation to retreat into the easier and irrelevant hard behaviors of the past requires courage.[158]

Playful Engagement

Transformation is both intriguing and intimidating. As a leader, your success will depend on your ability to create safe open spaces within yourself and within the dynamics with others where debate moves to dialogue and compliance and fear moves to exploration and transformation. As a transformational leader your influence internally and externally needs to be inspirational rather than coercive. This is an exercise in 'both—and' leadership. You need to both set clear intentions and keep open to seren-dipities and surprises; to be both resolute and flexible; to focus both on the task at hand and the bigger picture; to be tuned in to both the moment and the emerging future.

For stakeholders who have been trained to be compliant, and may find safety and security in the status quo, engaging and transforming is another 'both—and' process. By being both aware and effective, both action-oriented and reflective, both creative and reliable, you will use both example and inspiration to increase the openness and capacity of those in your Circle of Influence. Most adults think of play as childhood games. The play we refer to here could involve a wide variety of modalities including free association, art, music, dance, adventure learning, redesigning a work space, improvisational theatre, or a drumming circle.

Transformation is not for wimps. It involves letting go of the processes, procedures, and sureties that served you well in the past to move into a new uncertain reality. Transformation requires surrendering old ways of being and doing. It involves letting go of the procedures manual and exploring what's trying to happen with curiosity and openness. It involves moving from the letter of the law to the spirit of the guidelines. Your Difference Making Quotient depends on your ability to stay grounded and in the right relationship with Self and others. Creating a playful creative environment is essential for the best to emerge. To be meaningful this playfulness is not flippant but respectful while creating open space for exploring the new.

Taking a playful attitude focusing on possibility rather than certainty, embracing prototypes rather than absolutes, allows room for failure and exploration. By changing up the environment, putting aside phones and electronics, and creating a relaxed, playful atmosphere, people free up their minds and let go of cynicism and fear. In this place of discovery magic exists. There is a creative energy in the free flow of ideas and deep learning when you get out of the script and into playful engagement. Innovators like Eagle's Flight have been creating such environments for over twenty-five years with amazing success. Founded by Phil Geldart in 1988, Eagle's Flight has earned its reputation as a global leader in the development and delivery of business-relevant, experiential learning programs that achieve specific training objectives and lasting behaviour change.[159]

As you seek to be transformative, create opportunities for your inner Characters and your Circle of Influence to interact with Self, Inc. in new and creative ways. In his bestselling book, *A Whole New Mind*, Daniel Pink explores how playfulness is a key ingredient in nurturing our brain's ability to work as an integrated whole. One of your skills in being a transformational leader will be your ability to engage in meaningful play both with your inner Characters and with others.

Empathy

Empathy is one of the foundational elements for the transformational leader—empathy toward Self and others. Empathy connects us with others and allows us to create bonds of trust. It gives us insights into what others may be feeling or thinking; it helps us understand how or why others are reacting to situations; it helps us listen at a deeper level and it informs our decisions. A formal definition of empathy is the ability to identify and understand another's situation, feelings and motives. It's our capacity to recognize the concerns other people have. Empathy means: 'putting yourself in the other person's shoes' or 'seeing things through someone else's eyes.'

When you listen with empathy you really hear the other person without an agenda, inner chatter, opinions, or competing stories. Your entire focus is on the other person and you will know you are connecting at the empathic level when you start leaning forward, with a great deal of attention on the other conversation and the other person and not much awareness of the outside world. Energy and information flow. You not only hear the other person's voice but notice all that is coming to you in the form of information—the tone, the pace, the feelings expressed and unexpressed.

Simon Sinek titled his 2014 book *Leaders Eat Last: Why Some Teams Pull Together and Others Don't.* Sinek says researching his latest book has even changed the way he conducts his own life and business. "The lesson I'm learning is that I'm useless by myself. My success hinges entirely on the people I work with—the people who enlist themselves to join me in my vision. And it's my responsibility to see that they're working at their best capacity." Empathy—the ability to recognize and share other people's feelings—is the most important instrument in a leader's toolbox, Sinek believes. It can be expressed in the simple words, "Is everything OK?" It's what effective leaders ask an employee, instead of commanding "Clean out your desk" when he or she starts slacking off. It's what you ask a client when a once-harmonious relationship gets rocky. "I really believe in quiet confrontation," Sinek says. "If you had a good working relationship with someone and it's suddenly gone sour, I believe in saying something like, 'When we started we were both so excited, and it's become really difficult now. Are you OK? What's changed?' "[160]

Empathy is both an inner and outer skill of the conscious leader. It is important to understand and empathize with your inner Child, your inner Warrior, your inner Victim, or any other of your inner Characters as the challenges of life trigger emotion and a desire to act. As you listen to and empathize with your inner parts you will develop even more confidence and ability to empathize with others around you who are experiencing challenging realities.

Dynamic Leadership

As a transformational leader it is important to develop a level of awareness that helps you know when and how to change your leadership style—when is it necessary to be more directive versus coach-like? When is it appropriate to delegate? What do you or those you lead need in order to succeed? What is the appropriate level of supervision for the corresponding level of skill and responsibility? How do you help Self and others stretch and grow? How do you keep your finger on the pulse without being excessively hyper-vigilant and micro-managing?

Both in working with your inner parts and the people around you it is important to stay nimble and use a variety of ways to provide input and support. As a transformational leader you need to continuously assess the awareness and effectiveness of both your inner

Characters and your outer followers. Your skill to coach, direct, delegate, mentor and support while honouring the unique gifts of your inner and outer players is a dynamic process. At times, one of your inner or outer line-up may be very well suited to a role so you can assign a responsibility and confidently delegate. However, if circumstances shift and that part or person is triggered you may have to quickly intervene and move away from delegating and back to directing. Your inner Warrior may serve to alert you to boundary issues, threats, and challenges that require action. This delegation may serve you well until a man who reminds you of your abusive father walks into your board-room or work space. Inner awareness and a quick check with your inner Sage will tell you that this is a time for you to Self-lead and direct the inner Warrior to stand down.

Too often we either become rigid or lax in our responsibilities. Delegation without accountability is abdication. Directing without consultation is fundamentalism. Leading into the emerging future requires involvement and awareness. Challenging as it may be, a leader needs to stay firm in contributing the best from their FISC while providing leadership that is flexible and adaptable enough to help those they lead bring their best into the workplace. It is complex. What worked well yesterday or this morning may need to shift now. Transformational Self-leadership is a dynamic dance. Letting go of judgement, cynicism, fear, and baggage and stepping into the future is an exercise in improvisation based on the solid footing of established values, inner awareness, and meaningful practices.

As a transformational leader your awareness and your non-anxious presence provides a calm fluid movement through a variety of leadership styles to address the constant ebb and flow of changing needs. The shifts are so subtle and interventions so swift that it takes exquisite awareness and effective intervention. Dancing in the moment becomes your leadership edge.

Your Difference Making Quotient

As you come to this part of your leadership journey we want to ensure that you maximize your transformational power by emphasizing our formula for Making a Difference. Your **DMQ = (Facts + Influences + SoulDNA + Characters) x Self-leadership**. Your Difference Making Quotient is a dynamic interplay of the inner and outer life. The coordinating Self, CEO of Self, Inc., has the capacity to exponentially leverage your potential, when it is empowered and integrated through ongoing awareness and con-templative practices. Your level of awareness and effectiveness in applying Self-leadership concepts begins within and is the key factor in bringing the best you have to offer into life, work, and relationships in service to Self, others, and the greater good.

As Timothy Gallwey explored peak performance in athletes and corporate clients and developed his "Inner Game" concepts, he expressed his summary of the process by stating,

> In this century, if we do not learn some of the basic skills of the Inner Game, our technical progress in the outer game will be of little benefit to mankind. We have a

profound need to better understand, and learn to make changes in, the domain we call *our-selves*. And that can happen only if we change in ways that are in harmony with our true nature and not at war with it.[161]

In our work together we have helped you examine your inner life in Steps 4, 5 and 6 so that you can better understand and make changes in Self, Inc., our way of talking about you with your true nature enhanced by effective Self-leadership. Your FISC is your inner treasury. It makes up the domain of inner Self. Your ability to make a difference for you, your Circle of Influence, and all of us depends on your continued inner work so that you embrace your inner diversity and potential through Self-leadership. As you increase your Difference Making Quotient and lead with skill and confidence, you will continue to disrupt the status quo and help transform the world into a better place for us all.

Moving along the Path with STEP 11...

As a leader, I inspire, engage, empower, and facilitate transformational change in the world—individually and collectively.

STEPPING STONES

- What can you do to communicate your commitment to being a transformational leader to those in your Circles of Influence?

- As a transformational leader what will you stand for? What will you say 'yes' to, and what will you say 'no' to? What do you want for Self, Inc. and others? Write your own "I have a Dream" declaration speech that aligns with the gifts, passion, and vision of your Purpose and Difference Making aspirations.

- Imagine yourself as CEO of Self, Inc. standing in the midst of the people, opportunities and challenges surrounding you, fully aware of the resources in your FISC. Invite both the inner and outer members of your team to be your supports and allies as you move forward in fulfilling your purpose and helping them fulfil theirs. Journal your thoughts, feelings, and insights.

- What aspects of the status quo that was part of your reality at the beginning of your Self-leadership quest are you now willing to challenge and change?

- In what ways will you open up lines of communication with family, friends, colleagues, or staff in order to be more transformational in your relationships?

- Following through on the Self, Inc. plan you developed in Step 10, set up and calendar meetings with your accountability partner/coach and/or mastermind group.

TRAVEL TIPS

1. Transformational leadership is not always about doing the right thing. It is about being the right thing. Be vulnerable. Be open.

2. Remember...**DMQ = (Facts + Influences + SoulDNA + Characters) x Self-leadership.** This is a reminder that your Difference Making Quotient is directly correlated to the level of Self-Leadership awareness, ownership, and management you use with your Facts, Influences, SoulDNA™, and Characters.

3. Inner transformation results in outer effectiveness. Continue to do your inner work.

Step 12 - Keeping It Fresh

I intentionally Self-lead in ways that inspire, engage, and transform my evolving effectiveness as a Difference Maker.

I Have Arrived
By Thich Nhat Hanh

I have arrived,
I am home,
In the here,
In the now.
I am solid,
I am free,
In the ultimate I dwell.[162]

STEP 12...

FAST TRACK

Keeping it Fresh does not mean that you will always be on a transformational high. Keeping it fresh involves developing regular spiritual practices and disciplines that will ground you, renew you, and help you stay connected to the Energy of Life. Love your Self in all its complexity. Live your struggles and your triumphs. Love your successes and your defeats. Love the people and opportunities that provide dance partners for your dance of life. Live in the moment with openness and anticipation leaning into the emerging future with hope and optimism. Stay nimble. Stay curious. Developing a habit of noticing the small mercies and serendipities of life, over time, will increase your awareness and help you become more aware and more mindful, even more grateful. By choosing to focus on the positive, you can greatly increase your energy and your effectiveness. By frequently checking with your best Self, your heart's desire, your purpose, and your progress, you will flow through your days with a deep sense of integrity. Lean in to your conversations, your work, and the emerging future, using every experience as information as you stay open to what is trying to happen in and through your life. This Self-leadership quest is a lifelong commitment to regular ongoing practices that will keep you spiritually, emotionally, intellectually, and physically alive and well. As you develop your daily, weekly, and seasonal routines, trust the process. Let the rhythm become a part of your natural flow through life. May you continue to learn and grow as you explore the incredible potential and Difference Making Quotient in Self, Inc. that is contained in and through your FISC.

Leadership Value: Renewal

Guiding Principle: Regular renewal creates synergistic flow.

FOOTHOLD

In order to keep your Self-leadership insights fresh, plan to take at least one hour per week away from your usual workspace where you can nourish your creativity and inner life through a mini-retreat. This could be as simple as a walk through the park, a matinee movie, a solitary meal at an interesting restaurant, a visit to a zoo, art gallery or library. Basically, choose any space or activity that expands your energy and perspective.

Keeping It Fresh

Keeping it fresh does not mean that you will always be on a transformational high. It also doesn't mean that when things are tough and you struggle that you have lost your way. Participating in the Self-leadership quest has changed your inner programming. You are a different person as a result of getting in touch with your best Self and getting a glimpse of your soul's desire to use this earthly journey as a learning opportunity so that you can make a positive difference for Self and others in all aspects of life, work, and relationships.

Keeping it fresh involves developing regular spiritual practices and disciplines that will ground you, renew you, and help you stay connected to the Energy of Life so that you maintain and refresh your inner awareness and outer effectiveness. Keeping it fresh involves a dynamic tension between the shining moments of the past and the intriguing possibilities of the emerging future. In the nexus between past and future, inner and outer, there is the freshness of the current moment filled with newness and vitality. It is in this edge of now that life becomes fully alive. In this intensely alive state life flows in and through you and you are leading from a place of total engagement.

Using the practices that have been introduced in previous Steps, in this final Step you are encouraged to create each day from the moment you awaken until you close your eyes in sleep with awareness and purposeful attention. Keep your life purpose in mind at all times. Fall in love with your purpose and the processes you choose to bring it into the world. Treat your life as your ultimate lover and think of your daily processes as the dance of life.

Stay nimble and fresh, dancing in the moment the way that Anne Morrow Lindbergh described in *Gift from the Sea* –

> When you love someone, you do not love them all the time, in exactly the same way, from moment to moment. It is an impossibility. It is even a lie to pretend to. And yet this is exactly what most of us demand. We have so little faith in the ebb and flow of life, of love, of relationships. We leap at the flow of the tide and resist in terror its ebb. We are afraid it will never return. We insist on permanency, on duration, on continuity; when the only continuity possible, in life as in love, is in growth, in fluidity — in freedom, in the sense that the dancers are free, barely touching as they pass, but partners in the same pattern.[163]

Love your Self and your FISC in all its complexity with its Difference Making potential. Live your struggles and your triumphs. Love your successes and your defeats. Love the people and opportunities that provide dance partners for your dance of life. Live in the moment with openness and anticipation leaning into the emerging future with hope and optimism. Stay nimble. Stay curious. Keep it fresh.

Ephemeral Thoughts

Although you have been journaling since Step 1, as you live and lead with love, life passes quickly. Thoughts, like fireflies on a summer night, flicker through your consciousness and then fade. Many of you are so active that preserving an insight, a business idea, or an intuitive feeling can seem like trying to catch lightning in a bottle. These precious gifts from within and beyond will enrich your life, but only if you find a way to preserve them. Become a doodler. Journal in margins. Use bullet points, illustrations, drawings, thought clouds, whatever.

Small notebooks offer a flexible and portable format for recording ideas. Place pencils and pads in your vehicle and in the rooms of home and office. Phone apps come in a wide variety of types and capabilities. Explore possibilities and find one that works for you. Index cards are durable, and easy to carry so you can record your ideas just about anywhere. Longer sessions of free flowing journaling could be a weekly practice. Your journal should definitely be with you on your longer pauses as you reflect on where you have been and where you are going. I have a notebook that I use as soon as I return from a run. I find that my inspirational thoughts often disappear by the time I have showered. Cheryl often captures the thoughts from a vivid dream as soon as she gets up.

So write. Let the thoughts flow. Explore regrets, misdeeds, lost opportunities, outages, failures, jealousy, fear, cowardice, avoidance, confusion, and vengeance. At the same time remember and write about shining moments, successes, courage, heart, hope, joy, awareness, strength. Dream. Explore what is trying to happen. Investigate possibilities, dreams and desires. As you make it a practice to appreciate the inspiration, advice, and insight that comes from your inner Characters and the Energy of Life you will notice that the frequency and quality of meaningful insights will increase.

Homecoming

As you arrive at Step 12, you once again cross a threshold. This time you are returning to your heart's true home. You are returning to a Self, Inc. that has been enlarged and enriched as you have explored and taken responsibility for your inner life. Through the Self-leadership quest you have freed up and embraced your authentic Self. Now it is time to celebrate. Allow yourself to see your true Self with all the wonder and appreciation that T.S. Eliot referred to when he wrote, "The end of all our exploring, will be to arrive where we started, and know the place for the first time."[164]

Whether your current quest has been a profound journey from a place of deep despair, frustration, and addiction to a whole new way of thinking and being, or a gentle opening to more expansive ways of experiencing and expressing your most authentic Self, it is time to rest and affirm. You are a child of light, a unique expression of the Energy of Life. It is time to embrace the deep truths that your best Self has known all along. Now with an enriched FISC and increasing Self-knowledge you are ready to step into living your truth even more intentionally and more fully.

Take time to appreciate the transformation that has been occurring in you as you arrive at your own door as if "for the first time." Realize you are constantly evolving. Each moment, each day is filled with possibility. Look in the mirror and see this beautiful life force looking back and realize that each of the *12 Steps* has shifted your awareness and prepared you to serve Self and others with new levels of love and effectiveness.

It is time to stop learning for a while and allow yourself to bask in the warmth of your own fire knowing that you have answered the call to a more authentic life. Even as you arrive at a place of resting and a deep sense of being at home in your own body, in your own life, in the evolving reality, you will find an inner stirring inviting you to assist others who are at various stages of the Self-leadership quest. Just as you have found solace and support from others, you are now more consciously available to the call from the Universe to make a positive difference for others in all aspects of life, work, and relationships. There is no need to start a campaign. Just rest in your knowing and live your truth in your relationships, in your work, in the marketplace.

Other Calls to Learning

As you settle into the new normal, since life is a series of quests, there will be other calls to learning and you may find yourself once again being called to embark on a hero's journey. Like other pilgrims who have gained skill and confidence from answering the call, you will never be starting at ground zero again. Now that you have experienced all the elements, you are better equipped for future exploration and learning. Some of these growth experiences will take days or months. Sometimes you will experience several mini quests in a day. Each time you explore, you will be called to open your heart, your mind, and your will, and experience Source in new ways so you can manifest your essence more fully. Now that you have had practice, like the White Queen in *Alice in Wonderland*, sometimes you will be able to believe as many as six impossible things before breakfast.

Each call to growth may also awaken some inner voices of despair and entropy. As you face the voice of judgement, the voice of cynicism, and the voice of fear, you now know that these are not roadblocks but simply filters that challenge you to open to new levels of knowing and being. Rather than being trapped in old patterns of resistance and inertia, you are now equipped to open your mind, heart, and will to new ways of being and experiencing. Each time you let go of old ways of thinking and being, you courageously go through another metamorphosis allowing old baggage to be discarded and new ways of experiencing life to emerge. Each quest, large or small, shifts your inner and outer reality, preparing you to show up more fully and to live life with a greater sense of purpose.

The profound spiritual experiences of the quest have shifted your perspective. Like other pilgrims returning from a quest, there will be a time of feeling slightly off balance and moments of feeling like a stranger in your own world. This is the fertile territory of transition. Take time to settle in. Breathe deep and experience life from new levels of knowing. The transformation that has occurred during your quest has disrupted the status quo and shifted your internal world forever. You have broken free of old boundaries. You have experienced unconditional love for Self and others. During Steps 8 through 11 you have been integrating your learning. Step 12 is both an ending and another beginning. This new threshold, the nexus between your inner and outer life, becomes a dynamic opportunity to stay connected to your authentic Self while being fully engaged in the world from a place of deep inner knowing. Awakened to the possibilities within and without you now can live with a new more expansive and aligned sense of purpose.

Develop a Gratitude Habit

Write down at least one thing you are grateful for at the end of each day. Your journal is an accountability partner. Developing a habit of noticing the small mercies and serendipities of life over time will increase your awareness and help you become more aware and more mindful, even more grateful.

You can also collect mementos of special events that fill your heart with gratitude. Get a colourful storage box and use it as a memory box. Toss in theatre tickets, a race number from your 10K, a picture from a vacation, a card, a note of appreciation, a note from a child. Having a record will be a comfort when you go through a dark time and need to be reminded that the "sun will come out tomorrow."

Choose Happiness

As a Difference Maker much of your effectiveness with Self and others will be determined by your state of happiness. Happiness is not the belief that everything is great; instead happiness is the belief that change is possible. Shawn Achor, researcher and author of *Before Happiness*, defines happiness as "the joy one feels striving for one's potential." Studies show that choosing a positive mindset results in 23 per cent greater energy in the midst of stress and 31 per cent higher productivity.[165] By choosing to focus on the positive you can greatly increase your energy and your effectiveness.

Herb Kelleher, Chairman of Southwest Airlines who led Southwest through forty years of continuous growth and profitability stated he never had a worst day at work because the worse things were the better he felt about it because he felt useful helping things get back on track. Herb said, "If you enjoy the responsibility, if you enjoy the challenge, if that's the kind of thing that makes you passionate, you don't have bad days."[166] Herb Kelleher is a savvy business leader but he is probably most famous for the unique transformational culture he created at Southwest, where employees are not only encouraged to help control costs, but to have fun. And he walks the walk, often showing up at a gate at three in the morning to hand out donuts and help clean a plane, or unloading baggage to help turn the plane around quickly.

Groucho Marx said, "I, not events, have the power to make me happy or unhappy today. I can choose which it shall be. Yesterday is dead, tomorrow hasn't arrived yet. I have just one day, today, and I'm going to be happy in it."[167] When you choose happiness you accept the responsibility and the challenge of showing up fully every day and choosing deep inner happiness even when life is difficult. Your inner life and your outer life are meant to be experienced as more than a solemn march. Laughter really is the best medicine and you can choose to be happy if you want to.

Daily Review

If it isn't working, it isn't working. Self-leadership is about living with more joy, more vitality, and better relationships. It is important at the end of each day to assess your learning and your progress. Meditation and setting intentions each morning shapes your day. A compassionate review each evening allows for course corrections.

This compassionate listening to the small gratitudes and graces that have flitted through your busy day will increase your awareness and enrich your life. Too often we miss the best things in life because they are small. Often it is the smile in passing or the judgement you had the wisdom not to express that needs to be noted. Stillness and good questions will allow you to pause for a few moments to experience the life that is flowing through you and to open yourself to more of what brings you joy.

Anne Frank wrote, "How noble and good everyone could be if, every evening before falling asleep, they were to recall to their minds the events of the whole day and consider exactly what has been good and bad. Then without realizing it, you try to improve yourself at the start of each new day."[168]

With that in mind each evening, spend five to ten minutes reviewing your day. Ask yourself questions to prompt your reflections. Make a note of the things that you can do better or differently, so that when a similar situation happens again on another day you will be able to respond with love and awareness.

Connectedness

With the constant flow of information in social media it would seem that there have never been so many opportunities for connectedness, yet many leaders seeking to lead from a fresh perspective lack the emotional and psychic support to maintain their evolving vision for the future. Mihaly Csikszentmihalyi states the challenge this way,

> It is very difficult for a person acting alone to keep intact the vision of a goal that is by necessity always changing and impossible to pin down. It is for this reason

that to have a sustained impact on the direction of evolution one needs to create larger social systems that share the goal and help implement it in concrete, manageable steps.[169]

The good news is that those larger social systems are taking shape. These are not just typical business gatherings where people exchange pleasantries and business cards. These are modern mastermind groups where Self-leaders are coming together to challenge, encourage and inspire each other. These holistic future oriented leadership groups will give Difference Makers, like you, the critical mass of creativity, optimism, energy, safety, accountability, and support to explore possibilities and innovate.

If you cannot find such a group, start your own Mastermind Group with your life partner, a friend, a colleague or mentor and use formal meeting times to explore what is trying to happen in your work and lives and serve as accountability partners. Use Stephen R. Covey's first habit as a guide to keep you from wasting time awfulizing. 'Habit One' reminds us, "Proactive people focus their efforts on their Circle of Influence. They work on the things they can do something about: health, children, problems at work. Reactive people focus their efforts in the Circle of Concern—things over which they have little or no control: the national debt, terrorism, the weather. Gaining an awareness of the areas in which we expend our energies is a giant step in becoming proactive."[170]

In your group, as you meet with open minds, open hearts and open wills, you will create a safe space where each of you will be able to draw upon the inner wisdom and psychic energies of the group to explore the field of possibilities and to confidently begin to prototype new ways of thinking and being. Keep your group small and intentional. As you focus on leading from within and making a positive difference for Self and others, you will attract other like-minded evolutionaries and deep connections will lead to inspiration and empowerment for each of you.

> If you choose to bring a group together to study our book, go to www.12stepsofselfleadership.com to request a complimentary copy of our Facilitator's Guide.

Course Correction

Choosing to lead Self and others with openness and creativity is not a straight path. Winston Churchill once defined leadership as "going from failure to failure without losing enthusiasm." As you move from the domain of ideas to the domain of action the feedback will help you make course corrections.

In many ways, coming to the end of *12 Steps of Self-Leadership* is only the end of the beginning. This book has been mostly about letting go of old ways of thinking and doing, and shifting your awareness to being more powerfully connected to your inner possibilities. With a renewed sense of purpose you now have a much more accurate and responsive compass, but creating meaningful processes to live out your purpose will be a path of ongoing learning and discovery. Giving yourself to transcendent values and something larger than yourself while allowing your inner destiny to emerge will provide the information you need for the next steps.

As long as you are true to your best Self and in the right relationship with the people in your Circle of Influence your future will evolve. You do not have to have all the answers. Trust your awareness and take action. "Effective prototyping requires the capacity to stay connected and grounded in your deepest source of inspiration and larger will while simultaneously learning to listen to all the feedback your actions elicit."[171]

When your daily review reveals that your attitudes or behaviours have been hurtful or unproductive, promptly admit it and take corrective action. See each day as an adventure in authentic living. As an evolving learner it will always be win-win. Paulo Coelho wrote, "When you find your path, you must not be afraid. You need to have sufficient courage to make mistakes. Disappointment, defeat, and despair are the tools God uses to show us the way."[172] When your plans and actions don't produce the results you envisioned breathe deep, reassess, do what needs doing, and keep your enthusiasm.

Weekly Review

Author and teacher Stephen R. Covey spoke of regularly setting aside time for sharpening the saw. Sharpening the saw means preserving and enhancing your most important asset—you. Each week he suggested you set aside a time to review your past few days and to envision the path ahead. To stay fresh you need to have a balanced program of renewal in the four areas of your life: physical, social/emotional, mental, and spiritual.

Covey wrote,

> As you renew yourself in each of the four areas, you create growth and change in your life. 'Sharpen the Saw' keeps you fresh so you can continue to practice the other six habits. You increase your capacity to produce and handle the challenges around you. Without this renewal, the body becomes weak, the mind mechanical, the emotions raw, the spirit insensitive, and the person selfish.[173]

As with daily practices, these weekly reviews do not need to be formal sessions that become onerous and abandoned because of a busy life. You can do a weekly review in many ways—in your office as part of your end of week practice, in your mind as you walk or run, in a meeting with your life partner, or through weekly journaling.

The important thing is to make assessment and reflection a regular part of each week and an integral part of your regular pauses. By frequently checking with your best Self, your heart's desire, your purpose, and your progress, you will flow through your days with a deep sense of integrity. Leaning into the future you need to use every experience as information as you open yourself up to what is trying to happen in and through your life.

Stay Open

The path of Self-leadership is challenging and exciting. As a transformational leader you are learning to allow life to flow through you, and increasingly, you feel vibrantly alive and your thoughts are clear and efficient. In order to continue to move forward on your path you need to keep your mind and heart open. Be aware when you move to judgement of Self or others. Observe the thought but do not dwell on it. Just notice and keep your mind open and curious. Be aware of your feelings. Notice your energy with people, ideas, and experiences. Notice when you are open and fully alive. Notice when anger, fear, disappointment, or other emotions sneak in and begin to shift your energy. Your goal in Step 12 is to create ongoing practices that will keep you open to life in the moment so that your mental, physical, spiritual, and emotional energy flows from your intentions and awareness, in alignment with your highest future potential. Realizing when you start to close down or drift away is an important skill in learning to show up fully in life, work, and relationships.

Notice when you leave the conversations in your life, and acknowledge that you have been absent. Soon you will recognize when you are exiting and be able to stay present and stay open more consistently. When you start to see the conversation as sacred ground you will realize that conversations have their own agendas as well, and there are times when the conversation is too important to be jammed into five minutes at a coffee shop or on a bus ride. There is nothing more powerful with a colleague, friend, or family member than to recognize an important conversation as it emerges and then to say, "Wow. I really want to hear these thoughts. When can we sit for an hour to give this conversation the attention it deserves?"

> By staying open and aware and dealing with the issues you discover, you will increase your ability to be present.

Part of staying open involves inner housekeeping. Nothing in your life can shut you down more quickly than incomplete grief. In a world filled with sickness, death, war, and conflict, loss and grief are a constant reality. For this reason, acceptance and forgiveness and letting go is not a one-time thing. Ongoing awareness and compassion are essential practices to allow your energy to continue to stay in flow. The practice of forgiveness has been shown to reduce anger, hurt, depression, and stress, and lead to greater feelings of hope, peace, compassion, and Self-confidence. Keep a short list. When you experience grief or loss take time to attend to it. As old hurts, failures, and disappointments stir within allow them to rise into consciousness. As the morning news triggers your emotions, pay attention. If an issue requires action, do what needs to be done. Don't push your emotions down or allow resentment or incomplete grief to linger. Avoid emotional indigestion. You are an energetic being. Emotions are vibrational energy. By staying open and aware and dealing with the issues you discover you will increase your ability to be present.

As you experience life with a new sense of purpose, forgiveness and recalibration will become an ongoing aspect of your Self-led life. As you deal with anything that gets in the way of being vibrant, in the moment, energetic, fresh, and totally alive, your thoughts, brain patterns, and actions will become more and more natural. Transformational Self-leadership will no longer be about 'doing' the thing right it will be about 'being' the right thing—the energetic, loving, forgiving, authentic you.

Keep Learning

You have come so far on your quest. Although you continue to learn and grow you know what is needed to keep your focus and to live a Self-authored life. You know there is no finish line. The journey is the destination, and each day is an opportunity to shift your perspective a little higher. As you 'Keep It Fresh' it isn't about winning or losing, it is about staying open to what is trying to happen in your life and leadership. You have made a decision to live with purpose and passion and mindfully engage in life, work, and relationships.

Make it a habit to read every day. Whether that is an e-book, a magazine, poetry, a newspaper, a novel or a non-fiction book, reading opens and expands your thoughts. No matter how busy you are, reading gets you out of yourself and into the larger world. Through reading you can live a thousand lives. You can travel the world. You can explore. You can challenge and expand your potential. As little as ten minutes a day will make a difference. Build a library of some of the leadership classics we have mentioned in the previous Steps and make them part of your regular reading habit.

The coaching exercises and additional materials at the end of the chapters are not meant to be digested all at once. Ruminate on the ideas. Discuss them with others. Revisit them from time to time. As Rainer Marie Rilke wrote to his mentee,

> Be patient toward all that is unsolved in your heart and try to love the questions themselves, like locked rooms and like books that are now written in a very foreign tongue. Do not now seek the answers, which cannot be given you because you would not be able to live them. And the point is, to live everything. Live the questions now. Perhaps you will then gradually, without noticing it, live along some distant day into the answer.[174]

Be Hopeful

> "... to live now as we think human beings should live, in defiance of all that is bad around us, is itself a marvelous victory." ~ Howard Zinn

Hope is an act of courage in the face of the sometimes harsh realities of life. Hope is not some fluffy concept for poets and people who have not experienced hardship or pain.

In fact, the very nature of hope is just the opposite. Hope is believing in love, creativity, and courage when all the evidence denies any positive outcome. Choosing to be hopeful is a commitment to be fully alive.

Howard Zinn, an American historian, author, playwright, and social activist, wrote,

> To be hopeful in bad times is not just foolishly romantic. It is based on the fact that human history is a history not only of cruelty, but also of compassion, sacrifice, courage, and kindness. What we choose to emphasize in this complex history will determine our lives. If we see only the worst, it destroys our capacity to do something. If we remember those times and places—and there are so many—where people have behaved magnificently, this gives us the energy to act, and at least the possibility of sending this spinning top of a world in a different direction. And if we do act, in however small a way, we don't have to wait for some grand utopian future. The future is an infinite succession of presents, and to live *now* as we think human beings should live, in defiance of all that is bad around us, is itself a marvelous victory.[175]

C. S. Snyder, author of *The Psychology of Hope*, defined hope as a "motivational construct" that allows one to believe in positive outcomes, conceive of goals, develop strategies, and muster the motivation to implement them. "Low hope" individuals, he found, have ambiguous goals and work toward them one at a time, whereas "high hope" individuals often pursue five or six clear goals simultaneously. Hopeful people had preferred routes to achievement and alternate pathways in case of obstacles. Low scorers didn't.[176]

Recent research by Anthony Scioli, a professor of psychology and author of *The Power of Hope*, shows that hope is a skill you can acquire. It is self-perpetuating—hopeful people tend to be more resilient, more trusting, more open, and more motivated than those less hopeful, so they are likely to receive more from the world, which in turn makes them more hopeful. Hope sustains our intimate bonds, gives life purpose and meaning, and determines our prospects for survival and health. Scioli's research found that a high level of hope was the most powerful predictor of well-being—a finding that surprised even him.[177]

You are the leader of your inner and outer life. Keep your hope fresh. Start each day with a hopeful attitude. Be that non-anxious presence. Learn to hear the inner bird that Emily Dickinson described as "the thing with feathers that perches in the soul, and sings the tune without the words, and never stops at all."[178]

Evolving with Synergy

As you choose to live from a place of inner life and increased vulnerability you will be taking risks as you bring your authentic Self into life, work, and relationships. Since you are always learning and growing there will be uncomfortable moments. There will be disappointments and failures. Sometimes the people you live and work with will not embrace your new attitudes and perspectives. Sometimes you will allow anger or fear to dominate and you will not manifest the energy and wisdom you know lies within. This ongoing unfolding is an important part of the work of Step 12. It involves trust in all the other Steps and the path you have followed. You have changed. You have learned. You will continue to change and learn. Lean in. Keep moving forward.

To stay fresh you will need to make continuous subtle shifts. Even with practice, old response patterns and attitudes can still activate fear and anger and lead to resistance and win-lose thinking. It is important in your ongoing evolution that you maintain a learner's mind. As long as you love yourself, respect others, and continue to be a learner, good things will happen. Engaged Buddhist, Thich Nhat Hanh, teaches that both our negative and positive feelings are organic and belong to the same reality. So there is no need to fight; we only need to embrace and take care. He writes,

> You may think you have to combat evil and chase it out of your heart and mind. But that is wrong. The practice is to transform yourself. If you don't have garbage, you have nothing to use in order to make compost. And if you have no compost, you have nothing to nourish the flower in you. You need the suffering, the afflictions in you. Since they are organic, you know that you can transform them and make good use of them.[179]

Mindfulness practices that help you to continuously observe and embrace your inner condition will transform your interactions with others. When you are angry or out of esteem you will learn to be silent and do your inner work before speaking or taking action. As you continue to accept and honour your best Self you will create safe places for others to show up fully with their negative attitudes and immature thinking. As you become safe in your private moments, you will become safe in your public interactions. As you become aware of the inner and outer emotional weather you will be able to read the emotional field and live with the passion that John Amodeo speaks of in *Dancing with Fire*, "navigating through the joys and sorrows of relationships with presence, awareness, and kindness."[180]

As you commit to ongoing practices to keep it fresh in Step 12, it is not a process of shedding all your fears and ignoring all the challenges. It is a process of accepting life as it is and believing that the Universe is working in your favour. There will be times of assessment and recalibration. There will be moments of declaration. There will be days of just putting one foot in front of the other. As you continue to live from an inner place of vision and passion you will have a calm knowing of what comes next and you will be able to forward the agenda with confidence and positive energy.

Here are the **values** and the **guiding principles** of the *12 Steps of Self-Leadership*. We encourage you to refer to these often and keep developing them through your ongoing inner and outer work. When you need to refocus or enhance one of these use the *12 Steps* as a Guide to Living and Leading on Purpose.

• **Awareness** — Intuitive awareness awakens potential. (Step 1)

- **Openness** — Anticipatory openness expands possibilities. (Step 2)

- **Commitment** — Intentional commitment attracts support. (Step 3)

- **Curiosity** — Courageous curiosity discovers hidden treasures. (Step 4)

- **Responsibility** — Appropriate responsibility leads to integrity. (Step 5)

- **Authenticity** — Courageous authenticity leads to confidence. (Step 6)

- **Stillness** — Focused stillness facilitates clarity. (Step 7)

- **Service** — Compassionate service engages the best of Self and others. (Step 8)

- **Purpose** — Recognized purpose gives meaning to life and leadership. (Step 9)

- **Processes** — Planned processes generate meaningful outcomes. (Step 10)

- **Leadership** — Transformational leadership inspires and engages others. (Step 11)

- **Renewal** — Regular renewal creates synergistic flow. (Step 12)

By focusing on these values and guiding principles in conjunction with your own Self, Inc. core values and guiding principles, you will continue to be a transformational Difference Maker.

The End of the Beginning

The Self-leadership quest is a lifelong commitment to regular ongoing practices that keep you spiritually, emotionally, intellectually, and physically alive and well. As you develop your daily, weekly, and seasonal routines, trust the process. Let the rhythm of exploration and renewal become a part of your natural flow through life.

Continue weaving a fabric of life that has strong vertical and horizontal elements that create balance and strength. The vertical energy comes from a calm contented mind, a growing awareness of an integrated Self that is creative, resourceful, and whole, with a vibrant continuous connection with the Energy of Life that flows in, around, and through you. The horizontal energy comes from a well-nourished and active body, the support of friends and family through meaningful relationships, important work, and a continuous co-creative connection with community.

May you continue to learn and grow as you explore the incredible potential and Difference Making Quotient that is contained in and through your FISC empowered Self. We invite you to become part of the Difference Making Movement by inspiring, engaging and transforming Self and others on a lifelong leadership quest.

Moving along the Path with STEP 12...

I intentionally Self-lead in ways that inspire, engage, and transform my evolving effectiveness as a Difference Maker.

STEPPING STONES

- Memorize Thich Nhat Hanh's poem "I Have Arrived" and use it often as a walking meditation.

- List the spiritual practices will you commit to in order to keep Self refreshed, connected to a power greater than yourself, and actively contributing the best of your FISC in making a difference in life, work, and relationships?

- What processes or tools will you use to remember and benefit from the serendipitous insights, intuitive feelings, and creative business ideas that flit through your consciousness?

- If you start to feel that you're off course from your Self, Inc. purpose and processes, take a break. If you only have a moment, take a micro pause. As soon as possible, go for a walk, or take a half day or longer if needed to renew, refresh, and recalibrate.

- When you lose your focus, use the values and guiding principles of the *12 Steps of Self-Leadership* to identify the areas where you need to focus and regain your confidence and vision as CEO of Self, Inc.

TRAVEL TIPS

1. In the midst of the action never shortchange yourself on rest and recreation. They are essential to maintaining your DMQ.

2. Commit to an attitude of gratitude.

3. Continuous engagement creates synergistic flow. Pay it forward.

The Journey Continues...

The *12 Steps of Self-Leadership* is just a part of an ongoing Difference Makers journey. It is your invitation to a different way of living and leading. We invite you to join us in making a positive difference in our world, to be part of a growing movement of Self-leaders who make a difference by living and leading on purpose in service to Self, others, and the greater good.

Through Eagle Tree Leadership we invite you connect to the synergy and creativity that is emerging at home and around the world. Regardless of your title, your age or stage, we want to support you as you respond to your vocation to embrace the Difference Making potential and purpose in your life, work, and relationships. Through speaking, coaching, workshops, and retreats we look forward to working with you and your organization or business.

12 Steps of Self-Leadership Book Study Groups

If you're interested in starting up a *12 Steps of Self-Leadership* Book Study Group to enhance your learning and support others on the journey of working through the book, we encourage you to go to www.12stepsofselfleadership.com to request a free copy of our *12 Steps of Self-Leadership Book Study Group Facilitator's Guide*. This Guide will give you a framework and best practices for creating an effective and safe space for sharing and learning, ensuring that everyone benefits from your time together.

Share Your Difference Making Stories

As you do the work of *12 Steps of Self-Leadership* and increase your Difference Making Quotient™ you will experience deep insights, wonderful serendipities, increased awareness about Self and others, more vibrant relationships, and new skills. You will recognize the important part you play in making a difference in our world. To read about other Difference Makers, and/or share your story or insights with us, go to www.difference-makerscircle.com.

Support for your Journey

To support you along your Self-leadership journey, we offer a number of coaching and development services that will help you develop your inner awareness and outer effectiveness.

You will learn how to...

Discover untapped inner resources and manage 'hindrances' to effectiveness	So that you can ...*skillfully do more with 'less' and achieve even greater outcomes.*
Listen better to both Self and others	So that you can ...*improve decision-making discussions and outcomes— individually and collectively.*
Leverage your unique strengths and manage your 'weaknesses'	So that you can ...*improve your leadership performance and increase your 'promote-ability'.*
Recalibrate more quickly when your Self-confidence drops	So that you can ...*lead from an inner place of confidence and strength.*
Live and lead on Purpose	So that you can ...*optimize your contribution as a Difference Maker.*

To learn more about how you can increase your skills and step more fully into your potential in life, work, and relationships, go to www.eagletreeleadership.ca.

Permissions

Special thanks to the writers and poets who have granted permission for our use of their poems and larger quotes. Readers, please note that it is a violation of copyright for you to use these works without contacting those writers or their agents directly for permissions.

"How to Climb a Mountain" and "old and new" by Maya Stein. Used with permission from Maya Stein. All rights reserved.

"The Call" by Charlotte Mew from *Collected Poems and Prose of Charlotte Mew* edited by Val Warner. Imprint FyfieldBooks November 1997. Used with permission from Carcanet Press. All rights reserved.

"Potential" by Ricky Thakrar. Used with permission from Ricky Thakrar. All rights reserved.

"There is a Grace Approaching" by Stephen and Ondrea Levine. Used with permission from Stephen and Ondrea Levine. All rights reserved.

"Where I'm From" by George Ella Lyon appeared in WHERE I'M FROM, WHERE POEMS COME FROM (Absey & Co., 1999) and is reprinted with the poet's permission. For more information and to hear Lyon read the poem visit www. georgeellalyon.com

"My Misery" by Herman Hesse ..."Das ist mein Leid" (My Misery) from Hermann Hesse, Sämtliche Werke in 20 Bänden. Herausgegeben von Volker Michels. Band 10: Die Gedichte. © Suhrkamp Verlag Frankfurt am Main 2002. All rights reserved by and controlled through Suhrkamp Verlag Berlin.

"Unconditional" by Jennifer Paine Welwood. Used with permission from Jennifer Paine Welwood. All rights reserved.

"I Will Not Die an Unlived Life" by Dawna Markova, PhD (Berkeley: Conari Press, 2000). Used with permission from Dawna Markova. All rights reserved.

"Don't Go Back to Sleep" by Rumi from *The Essential Rumi*. Translated by Coleman Barks with John Moyne (New York: Harper Collins, 1995). Used with permission from Coleman Barks. All rights reserved.

"Inter-Relationship" and "I Have Arrived" by Thich Nhat Hanh. Reprinted from *Call Me By My True Names* by Thich Nhat Hanh. © Parallax Press, 1999. Used with permission from Parallax Press. All rights reserved.

"2015 Coaching Survey." Sherpa Executive Coaching. http://www.sherpacoaching.com. Referenced with permission. All rights reserved.

Suggested Further Reading

Kornfield, Jack. *After the Ecstasy, the Laundry.* New York: Bantam Books, 2001.

May, Gerald. *Addiction & Grace.* New York: HarperCollins, 1988.

Mindell, Amy. *Metaskills: The Spiritual Art of Therapy.* Oakland: Lao Tse Press, 2003.

Narofsky, Thomas. *F(X) Leadership Unleashed.* Papillon: Narofsky Publishing Group, 2013.

Peterson, Eugene H. *Under the Unpredictable Plant.* Grand Rapids: Eerdmans Publishing, 1994.

Redfield, James. *The Celestine Prophecy.* New York: Warner Book, 1993.

Scott-Maxwell, Florida. *The Measure of My Days.* New York: Penguin, 1968.

Shepherd, Philip. *New Self New World.* Berkeley: North Atlantic Books, 2010.

Singer, Michael A. The Untethered Soul: The Journey beyond Yourself. Oakland: Harbinger, 2007.

Tessina, Tina B. *The Real 13th Step.* Franklin Lakes: Career Press, 2001.

Bibliography

Albom, Mitch. *Tuesdays with Morrie*. New York: Random House, 1997.

Alcoholics Anonymous. *The Big Book*. New York: Alcoholics Anonymous World Service, 1976.

Amodeo, John. *Dancing with Fire: A Mindful Way to Loving Relationships*. Wheaton: Theosophical Publishing, 2013.

Angelou, Maya. *I Know Why the Caged Bird Sings*. New York: Ballantine, 1997.

—*Letter to My Daughter*. New York: Random House, 2008.

Barnett, Kristine. *The Spark*. Toronto: Vintage Canada, 2013.

Beck, Martha. *Finding Your Own North Star: Claiming the Life You were Meant to Live*. New York: MJF Books, 2001.

—*Leaving the Saints: How I Lost the Mormons and Found My Faith*. New York: Three Rivers Press, 2006.

—*The Joy Diet: 10 Daily Practices for a Happier Life*. New York: Harmony, 2003.

Berne, Eric. *Games People Play*. New York: Ballantine, 1964.

Bridges, William. *Transitions*. Reading: Addison-Wesley, 1980.

Brown, Brené. *Daring Greatly*. New York: Gotham Books, 2012.

Burns, David D. *The Feeling Good Handbook*. New York: Penguin, 1999.

Cameron, Julia. *The Artist's Way*. New York: Jeremey P. Tarcher/Putnam, 1992.

—*The Vein of Gold*. New York: Jeremey P. Tarcher/Putnam, 1996.

Campbell, Joseph. *The Hero with a Thousand Faces*. New York: Princeton/Bollingen, 1973.

Carroll, Lewis. *Alice in Wonderland*. New York: Bantam Classics, 1984.

Carter-Scott, Cherie. *If Life is a Game, These are the Rules: Ten Rules for Being Human.* New York: Harmony, 1998.

Chopra, Deepak. *The Spontaneous Fulfillment of Desire: Harnessing the Infinite Power of Coincidence.* New York: Harmony, 2004.

Coelho, Paulo. *The Alchemist.* New York: HarperOne, 2006.

Cohen, Andrew. *Evolutionary Enlightenment: A New Path to Spiritual Awakening.* New York: SelectBooks Inc., 2011.

Covey, Stephen R. *The 7 Habits of Highly Effective People.* New York: Simon & Schuster, 1989.

—*The 3rd Alternative: Solving Life's Most Difficult Problems.* New York: Simon & Schuster, 2011.

Csikszentmihalyi, Mihaly. *The Evolving Self.* New York: Harper Perennial, 1994.

Debashis, Chatterjee. *Leading Consciously.* New York: Butterworth-Heinemann, 2011.

Dinesen, Isak. *Out of Africa.* New York: Random House, 2011

Emerald, David. *The Power of TED: The Empowerment Dynamic.* Bainbridge Island: Polaris, 2006.

Ford, Debbie. *The Secret of the Shadow.* New York: HarperCollins, 2002.

Fox, Matthew. *The Reinvention of Work.* New York: HarperCollins, 1995.

Frank, Anne. *Diary of a Young Girl.* New York: Doubleday, 1995.

Frankl, Viktor. *Man's Search for Meaning.* New York: Washington Square Press, 1985.

Frattaroli, Elio. *Healing the Soul in the Age of the Brain.* New York: Penguin, 2002.

Gerlach, Peter. *Who's Really Running Your Life?* Bloomington: Xlibris, 2011.

Gibran, Kahlil. *The Prophet.* New York: Knopf, 2003.

Glasser, William. *Choice Theory.* New York: HarperCollins, 1998.

—*Take Charge of Your Life.* Bloomington: iUniverse Books, 2011

Gottman, John. *The Seven Principles for Making Marriage Work.* New York: Three Rivers Press, 1999.

—*The Relationship Cure.* New York: Three Rivers Press, 2001.

Hanh, Thich Nhat. *Anger: Wisdom for Cooling the Flames.* New York: Riverhead Books, 2001.

—*Call Me By My True Names*. Berkeley, California: Parallax Press, 1999.

—*Happiness: Essential Mindfulness Practices*. Berkeley, Parallax Press, 2009.

Harrington, H. James and Frank Voehl. *The Organizational Master Plan Handbook*. Boca Raton: CRC Press, 2012.

Hesse, Hermann. *The Seasons of the Soul*. Berkeley: North Atlantic Books, 2011.

Hill, Napoleon. *Think and Grow Rich*. New York: Fawcett Books, 1963.

Hurston, Zora Neale. *Their Eyes Were Watching God*. New York: Harper Perennial, 2006.

James, John W. and Russell Friedman. *The Grief Recovery Handbook*. New York: Collins, 2009.

Kieves, Tama. *This Time I Dance*. New York: Jeremey P. Tarcher/Putnam, 2003.

—*Inspired & Unstoppable*. New York: Tarcher/Penguin, 2012.

Lappé, Frances Moore. *Getting a Grip*. Cambridge: Small Planet Media, 2007.

Lindbergh, Anne Morrow. *Gift from the Sea*. New York: Vintage Books, 1991.

Lyon, George Ella. *Where I'm from: where poems come from (Writers' & Young Writers' series, Book 2)* Spring: Absey & Co., 1999.

Mackey, John, and Raj Sousa. *Conscious Capitalism*. Boston: Harvard Press, 2014.

Markova, Dawna. *I Will Not Die an Unlived Life*. Berkeley: Conari Press, 2000.

Myss, Caroline M. *Anatomy of the Spirit*. New York: Simon & Schuster, 2004.

Nani, Christel. *Sacred Choices: Thinking outside the Tribe to Heal Your Spirit*. New York: Harmony House, 2006.

Noer, David M, *Breaking Free*. San Francisco: Jossey-Bass, 1997.

Palmer, Parker J. *A Hidden Wholeness: The Journey Toward an Undivided Life*. San Francisco: Jossey-Bass, 2009.

—*Let Your Life Speak: Listening for the Voice of Vocation*. San Francisco: Jossey-Bass, 1999.

Peck, M.Scott. *The Road Less Traveled*. New York: Touchstone, 1980.

—*The Different Drum: Community Making and Peace*. New York: Touchstone, 1987.

Pickavance, Norman. *The Reconnected Leader*. Philadelphia: Kogan Page, 2015.

Pink, Daniel H. *A Whole New Mind: Why Right-Brainers Will Rule the Future*. New York, Riverhead, 2005

Reynolds, David K. *A Handbook for Constructive Living*. Honolulu: University of Hawaii Press, 2002.

Rilke, Rainer Maria. *Letters to a Young Poet*. Seaside: Merchant Books, 2012.

Ruiz, Don Miguel. *The Four Agreements*. San Rafael: Amber-Allen, 2012.

Rumi, Jalal al-Din. *The Essential Rumi*. Trans. by Coleman Barks with John Moyne. New York: HarperCollins, 1995.

Schaar, John H. *Legitimacy in the Modern State*. New Brunswick: Transaction Publishers, 1989.

Scharmer, C. Otto. *Theory U: Leading From the Future as it Emerges*. San Francisco: Berrett-Koehler, 2007.

Scharmer, Otto and Katrin Kaeufer. *Leading from the Emerging Future: From Ego-System to Eco-System*. San Francisco: Berrett-Koehler, 2013.

Schatz, Halé Sofia. *If the Buddha Came for Dinner*. New York: Hyperion, 2004.

Scott, Susan. *Fierce Conversations*. New York: Berkley Publishing, 2004.

Scrivener, Leslie. *Terry Fox: His Story*. Toronto: McClelland & Stewart, 2010.

Senge, Peter, Otto Scharmer, Joseph Jaworski, Betty Sue Flowers. *Presence: Human Potential and the Field of the Future*. New York: Crown Publishing, 2004.

Strayed, Cheryl. *Wild: From Lost to Found on the Pacific Crest Trail*. New York: Knopf, 2012.

Thoreau, Henry David. *Walden and Other Writings*. New York: Barnes & Noble Books, 1993.

Tindell, Kip. *Uncontainable*. New York: Grand Central Publishing, 2014.

Tolkien, J.R. *The Fellowship of the Ring*. New York: Del Rey, 2012.

—*The Hobbit or There and Back Again*. Orlando: Houghton Mifflin Harcourt, 1977.

Vanier, Jean. *Becoming Human*. Toronto: Anansi Press, 1998.

Voskamp, Ann. *One Thousand Gifts: A Dare To Live Fully Right Where You Are*. Grand Rapids: Zondervan, 2000.

Walsch, Neale Donald. *Conversations with God*. New York: Hampton Roads Publishing, 1995.

Warner, Val, ed. *Collected Poems and Prose of Charlotte Mew*. Manchester: Carcanet Press, 2003.

Watts, Alan. *Does it Matter? Essays on Man's Relation to Materiality*. Novato: New World Library, 1971.

Werke, Sämtliche, trans. "Das ist mein Leid" (My Misery) in *Hermann Hesse: Complete works in 20 volumes*. Edited by Volker Michels. Berlin: Suhrkamp Verlag, 2007.

Whitney, Diana and Amanda Trosten-Bloom. *The Power of Appreciative Inquiry: A Practical Guide to Positive Change*. San Francisco: Berrett-Koehler Publishers Inc., 2003.

Wigglesworth, Cindy. *SQ21: The Twenty-One Skills of Spiritual Intelligence*. New York: SelectBooks Inc., 2014.

Wilber, Ken. *Integral Spirituality*. Boston: Shambhala Publications, 2006.

Williamson, Marianne. *A Return to Love*. New York: HarperCollins, 1992.

Zinn, Howard. *You Can't Be Neutral on a Moving Train*. Boston: Beacon Press, 2002.

About the Authors

Doug Lester has been studying and teaching leadership skills for nearly 50 years. As an educator, counsellor, coach, and mentor, Doug has helped people of all ages increase their Difference Making Quotient. Doug's Self-leadership quest has led to degrees in Psychology, Curriculum Development, and studies in Theology, Therapy, Addictions, Grief Recovery, and Coaching.

Doug's passion for reading and researching is evident whether it's the stack of books he's reading or his reputation for connecting others to books, articles, and resources that are relevant to their current personal or professional quests. As a mentor-coach, Doug introduces others to the great teachers of our time and helps people develop the inner awareness to become conscious leaders.

As Doug wrote *12 Steps of Self-Leadership*, Cheryl played a key role as a visionary, thought partner, influencer, challenger, and encourager.

When Doug's not working, or leading workshops, he enjoys reading, running, traveling, art galleries, music festivals, bookstores, ball games, long walks, and fierce conversations.

Cheryl Lester is a respected leadership development coach who over the last two decades has provided mentor-coaching and strategic support to leaders in over 50 countries.

Through working with leaders from diverse backgrounds, Cheryl has gained a rich understanding of the inner and outer challenges and opportunities leaders face in dynamic environments complexified by geographic, religious, generational, and cultural issues.

As a Difference Maker, Cheryl helps leaders step more fully into their purpose and potential through focusing on both their Self-leadership performance as CEO of Self, Inc. and their performance as a leader of others. Cheryl's creative thinking, wisdom, vision, and intuitive sense of possibilities and potential have all played a key role in the writing of *12 Steps of Self-Leadership*.

When Cheryl's not coaching or leading workshops, she enjoys theatre, black and white movies, musical events, traveling, museums, long walks, and conversations with family, friends, and colleagues.

Endnotes

Introduction

1. Doug Lester, "Open Your Eyes", 2015.

2. Peter Senge, Otto Scharmer, Joseph Jaworski, Betty Sue Flowers, Presence: Human Potential and the Field of the Future (New York: Crown Publishing, 2004), 5.

3. Otto Scharmer and Katrin Kaufer, Leading from the Emerging Future (Oakland: Berrett-Koehler, 2013), 18.

4. E. E. Cummings, accessed July 2, 2015, http://www.brainyquote.com/quotes/quotes/e/eecummin161592.html.

5. Henry David Thoreau, Walden and Other Writings (New York: Barnes & Noble Books, 1993), 7.

6. William Hutchison Murray, "The Scottish Himalayan Expedition, 1951," accessed July 2, 2015, http://www.goodreads.com/quotes/128689-until-one-is-committed-there-is-hesitancy-the-chance-to.

Foundations

7. Maya Stein, How to Climb a Mountain, accessed July 14, 2015, https://thealchemyofpilgrimage.wordpress.com/2009/08/22/how-to-climb-a-mountain/.

8. Scharmer, Leading from the Emerging Future, 23.

9. Steve Jobs, Stanford University Commencement, 2005.

10. Jalal al-Din Rumi, The Essential Rumi, trans. Coleman Barks with John Moyne, (New York: Harper Collins, 1995), 36.

11. Richard Schwartz, Evolution of the Internal Family Systems Model (Oak Park: The Center for Self Leadership), accessed July 14, 2015, http://www.selfleadership.org/about-internal-family-systems.html.

12. Cindy Wigglesworth, SQ21: The Twenty-One Skills of Spiritual Intelligence (New York: SelectBooks Inc., 2014), 65.

13. Schwartz, accessed July 15, 2015, http://www.selfleadership.org/about-richard-schwartz.html.

14. Ken Wilber, Integral Spirituality (Boston: Shambhala Publications, 2006), 32.

15. Thoreau, Walden and Other Writings, 267.

16. Quinn, Robert E., Deep Change: Discovering the Leader Within (San Francisco, Jossey-Bass, 1995), 45.

Step 1 — The Birth of Awareness

17. Charlotte Mew, "The Call" in Collected Poems and Prose of Charlotte Mew, ed. Val Warner (Manchester: Carcanet Press, 1997), 55.

18. Ann Voskamp, One Thousand Gifts: A Dare To Live Fully Right Where You Are. (Grand Rapids: Zondervan, 2000), 45.

19. Gwen Moran, "5 Ways Leaders Think Differently than the Rest of Us," accessed July 16, 2015, http://www.fastcompany.com/3040069/5-ways-leaders-think-differently-than-the-rest-of-us.

20. Ibid.

21. Cohen, Evolutionary Enlightenment, 41.

22. R. Buckminster Fuller, "Thoughts of Buckminster Fuller," Whole Earth Catalog, Winter 1998, accessed July 16, 2015, http://www.wholeearth.com/issue/1340/article/191/thoughts.of.buckminster.fuller.

23. Parker J. Palmer, Let Your Life Speak: Listening for the Voice of Vocation (San Francisco: Jossey-Bass, 1999), 16.

24. Tama Kieves, "Freedom Means Going Rogue. Burn up the Pictures of Where You Think You Should Be," accessed July 16, 2015, http://www.tamakieves.com/freedom-means-going-rogue-burn-up-the-pictures-of-where-you-think-you-should-be/.

25. Nelson Mandela, accessed July 16, 2015, http://www.nelsonmandelaonline.net/#quotes.

26. Alan Watts, Does it Matter? Essays on Man's Relation to Materiality. (Novato: New World Library, 1971), 32.

Step 2 — Doorway to Possibility

27. Ricky Thakrar, "Potential," accessed July 16, 2015, http://hellopoetry.com/poem/160637/potential/.

28. Albert Einstein, accessed July 16, 2015, http://heartquotes.com/Einstein.html.

29. Julia Cameron, The Vein of Gold (New York: Jeremey P. Tarcher/Putnam, 1992), 7.

30. Thoreau, Walden and Other Writings, 267.

31. Murray, "The Scottish Himalayan Expedition."

32. Marilyn Ferguson, "Quotable Quote," accessed July 16, 2015, https://www.goodreads.com/author/quotes/207146.Marilyn_Ferguson.

33. Kristine Barnett, The Spark (Toronto: Vintage Canada, 2013), 249.

34. Cherie Carter-Scott, "Quotable Quote," accessed July 16, 2015, https://www.goodreads.com/author/quotes/209683.Cherie_Carter_Scott.

35. Williamson, Marianne, A Return to Love (New York: HarperCollins, 1992), 188.

36. Francis of Assisi, "Quotable Quote," accessed July 16, 2015, http://www.goodreads.com/author/quotes/149151.Francis_of_Assisi.

37. Ray Zahab, "Running the Sahara," accessed July 16, 2015, http://www.runningthesahara.com/science.html.

38. John H. Scharr, Legitimacy in the Modern State (New Brunswick: Transaction Publishers, 1989), 321.

39. Christel Nani, Sacred Choices: Thinking Outside the Tribe to Heal Your Spirit (New York: Harmony Books, 2006), 1.

40. Katie Byron, "Quotable Quote," accessed July 16, 2015, http://www.goodreads.com/author/quotes/6374.Byron_Katie.

41. M. Scott Peck, The Road Less Traveled (New York: Touchstone, 1980), 15.

42. Viktor Frankl, Man's Search for Meaning (New York: Washington Square Press, 1985), 86.

43. Martha Beck, "Insight from Martha," Blog, November 10, 2013, accessed July 16, 2015, http://marthabeck.com/2013/11/taming-wild-mustangs/.

44. Deepak Chopra, The Spontaneous Fulfillment of Desire: Harnessing the Infinite Power of Coincidence (New York: Harmony, 2004), 136.

45. Halé Sofia Schatz, If the Buddha Came for Dinner (New York: Hyperion, 2004), 58.

Step 3 — Crossing the Threshold

46. Stephen Levine and Ondrea Levine, "There is a grace approaching," accessed July 17, 2015, http://heartsteps.org/2014/grace-approaching/.

47. Elio Frattaroli, Healing the Soul in the Age of the Brain (New York: Penguin, 2002), 110.

48. John Mackey and Raj Sousa, Conscious Capitalism (Boston: Harvard Press, 2014), 266.

49. Brett Steenbarger, "Self-Leadership and Success," accessed July 17, 2015, http://www.forbes.com/sites/brettsteenbarger/2015/05/15/self-leadership-and-success/.

50. J. R. R. Tolkien, The Fellowship of the Ring (New York: Del Rey, 2012), 72.

51. Nelson Mandela, "In his own words: The inspiring speeches of Nelson Mandela," accessed July 17, 2015, http://www.express.co.uk/news/world/447158/In-his-own-words-The-inspiring-speeches-of-Nelson-Mandela.

52. Jean Vanier, Becoming Human (Toronto: Anansi Press, 1998), 12.

53. Joseph Campbell, The Hero with A Thousand Faces (New York: Princeton/Bollingen, 1973), 77.

54. Leslie Scrivener, Terry Fox: His Story (Toronto: McClelland & Stewart, 2010), 63.

55. Terry Fox Humanitarian Award Program, accessed July 17, 2015, http://terryfoxawards.ca/our-story/.

56. George Bernard Shaw, "The True Joy in Life," accessed July 17, 2015, http://creativeleadership.com/2011/06/06/the-true-joy-in-life/.

57. Susan Boyle, "I Dreamed a Dream," video accessed July 17, 2015, http://youtu.be/wnmbJzH93NU.

Step 4 — Discovering Treasures Within

58. "Where I'm From" by George Ella Lyon appeared in Where I'm from, Where Poems Come From (Absey & Co., 1999) and is reprinted with the poet's permission. For more information and to hear Lyon read the poem visit www.georgeellalyon.com.

59. Maya Angelou, Letter to My Daughter (New York: Random House, 2008), 10.

60. Palmer, A Hidden Wholeness, 33.

61. "Das ist mein Leid" (My Misery), from: Hermann Hesse, Sämtliche Werke in 20 Bänden. Herausgegeben von Volker Michels. Band 10: Die Gedichte. © Suhrkamp Verlag Frankfurt am Main 2002. All rights reserved by and controlled through Suhrkamp Verlag Berlin.

62. Peter Gerlach, Who's Really Running Your Life? (Bloomington: Xlibris, 2011), 39.

63. Richard Schwartz, "The Larger Self," accessed July 20, 2015, http://www.selfleadership.org/the-larger-self.html.

64. Gerlach, Who's Really Running Your Life?, 41.

65. Ibid, 19.

66. Schwartz, "Internal Family Systems."

67. Steven Covey, "Nothing Fails Like Success," accessed July 17, 2015, http://www.stephencovey.com/blog/?p=38.

68. Aristotle, "Quotable Quote," accessed September 30, 2015, https://www.goodreads.com/quotes/20103-the-whole-is-greater-than-the-sum-of-its-parts.

Step 5 — Impact Assessment

69. Hesse, "Das ist mein Leid."

70. Carl Rogers, "Quotable Quote," accessed August 3, 2015, http://www.goodreads.com/quotes/50836-the-curious-paradox-is-that-when-i-accept-myself-just.

71. Kip Tindell, Uncontainable (New York: Grand Central Publishing, 2014), 9.

72. Arnold Joseph Toynbee, "Quotable Quote," accessed August 3, 2015, http://www.goodreads.com/quotes/774055-society-is-the-total-network-of-relations-between-human-beings.

73. Stephen R. Covey, The 7 Habits of Highly Successful People (New York: Simon & Schuster, 1989), 81.

74. Martha Beck, Finding Your Own North Star: Claiming the Life You were Meant to Live (New York: MJF Books, 2001), 151.

75. Cameron, The Vein of Gold, 7.

Step 6 — Divided No More

76. Jennifer Paine Welwood, "Unconditional," accessed July 21, 2015, http://jenniferwelwood.com/poetry/.

77. Elio Frattaroli, Healing the Soul in the Age of the Brain (New York: Penguin, 2002), 113.

78. Palmer, A Hidden Wholeness, 5.

79. Palmer, Let Your Life Speak, 12.

80. Don Miguel Ruiz, The Four Agreements (San Rafael: Amber-Allen, 2012), 117.

81. Joe Dispenza, "The Art of Change," accessed July 21, 2015, http://www.drjoedispenza.com/index.php?page_id=The-Art-of-Change.

Step 7 — Integral Pause

82. Maya Stein, "old and new," accessed July 21, 2015, http://www.mayastein.com/10-line-tuesday/2011/10/18/october-11-2011.html.

83. Thich Nhat Hanh, Anger: Wisdom for Cooling the Flames (New York: Riverhead Books, 2001), 41.

84. Martha Beck, Leaving the Saints (New York: Three Rivers Press, 2006), 260.

85. Rainer Maria Rilke, Letters to a Young Poet (Seaside: Merchant Books, 2012), 30.

86. Marianne Williamson, A Return to Love, (New York: HarperCollins, 1992), 188.

87. Diana Whitney and Amanda Trosten-Bloom, The Power of Appreciative Inquiry: A Practical Guide to Positive Change (San Francisco: Berrett-Koehler, 2003), 54.

88. Ibid, 6.

Step 8 — Call to Conscious Leadership

89. Dawna Markova, I Will Not Die an Unlived Life (Berkeley: Conari Press, 2000), 1.

90. Mackey, Conscious Capitalism, 29.

91. Neurotracker, "6 NeuroTracker Performance Concepts," accessed August 3, 2015, http://neurotracker.net/performance/4585042503.

92. Mitch Albom, Tuesdays with Morrie (New York: Random House, 1997), 137.

93. Debashis Chatterjee, Leading Consciously (New York: Butterworth-Heinemann, 2011), 159.

94. John Gottman, The Seven Principles for Making Marriage Work (New York: Three Rivers Press, 1999), 29.

95. Fierce, "fierce tip of the week: come out from behind yourself, into the conversation and make it real," accessed August 3, 2015, http://www.fierceinc.com/blog/fierce-conversations/fierce-tip-of-the-week-come-out-from-behind-yourself-into-the-conversation-and-make-it-real.

96. William Glasser, Choice Theory (New York: HarperCollins, 1998), 21.

97. Susan Scott, Fierce Conversations (New York: Berkley Publishing, 2004), 6.

98. Ibid, 11.

99. M. Scott Peck, "M. Scott Peck quotes," accessed August 3, 2015, http://thinkexist.com/quotation/there_can_be_no_vulnerability_without_risk-there/339057.html.

100. Epoch Inspired, "One More Reason to Admire Malala — Winning the Nobel Peace Prize," accessed August 3, 2015. http://www.theepochtimes.com/n3/inspired/1134765-nobel-peace-prize-2014-winners-malala-yousafzai-kailash-satyarthi/.

101. Eleanor Goldberg, "Unpaid Cook and Janitor Cared for Assisted Living Residents after State Abandoned Them," accessed August 3, 2015, http://www.huffingtonpost.com/2014/12/01/valley-springs-manor-closes_n_6223160.html.

102. Tindell, Uncontainable, 4.

103. Daniel J. DeNoon, "7 Rules for Eating," accessed August 3, 2015, http://www.webmd.com/food-recipes/news/20090323/7-rules-for-eating.

104. Thich Nhat Hanh, "Quotable Quote," accessed August 3, 2015, http://www.goodreads.com/author/quotes/9074.Th_ch_Nh_t_H_nh.

105. Ibid, "Quotable Quote," accessed August 3, 2015, https://kirankukar.wordpress.com/tag/thich-nhat-hanh/.

106. Christopher Reeve, Still Me, accessed August 3, 2015, http://www.chrisreeve-homepage.com/stillme.html.

107. David M. Noer, Breaking Free (San Francisco: Jossey-Bass, 1997), 10.

108. Caroline M. Myss, Anatomy of the Spirit (New York: Simon & Schuster, 2004), 184.

109. Martha Beck, The Joy Diet: 10 Daily Practices for a Happier Life. (New York: Harmony, 2003), 8.

Step 9 — Purposeful Leading

110. Doug Lester, "Don't Settle," 2015.

111. Frankl, Man's Search, 130.

112. Ibid, 131.

113. Martha Graham, "Quotable Quotes," accessed July 21, 2015, http://www.goodreads.com/author/quotes/47790.Martha_Graham.

114. Rachel Reman, "The Healer's Art," accessed July 21, 2015, http://www.rachelremen.com/learn/medical-education-work/the-healers-art/.

115. Elizabeth McKenzie, "Are You Getting Your Purpose and Your Process Mixed Up?" accessed July 21, 2015, http://www.huffingtonpost.com/elizabeth-mckenzie/are-you-getting-your-purp_b_5625275.html.

116. George Bernard Shaw, "Quotable Quote," accessed July 21, 2015, http://www.goodreads.com/quotes/456466-i-am-of-the-opinion-that-my-life-belongs-to.

117. Palmer, Let Your Life Speak, 3.

118. Ibid, 4.

119. Norman Pickavance, The Reconnected Leader (Philadelphia: Kogan Page, 2015), 256.

120. David. J. Powell, "The Three Marriages: Work, Relationships, Self," accessed July 21, 2015, http://www.recoverytoday.net/articles/362-the-three-marriages-work-relationships-self.

121. McKenzie, "Your Purpose."

122. Frances Moore Lappé, Getting a Grip (Cambridge: Small Planet Media, 2007), 113.

123. Mihaly Csikszentmihalyi, The Evolving Self (New York: Harper Perennial, 1994), 149.

124. Mackey, Conscious Capitalism, 57.

125. Frankl, Man's Search, 133.

126. Albert Schweitzer, "Quotable Quote," accessed July 21, 2015, http://www.goodreads.com/quotes/186768-the-purpose-of-human-life-is-to-serve-and-to.

Step 10 — Putting it All Together

127. Rumi, The Essential Rumi, 36.

128. Rebecca Solnit, "The Faraway Nearby," CBC Sunday Edition interview, Sept. 29, 2013, accessed July 22, 2015, http://www.cbc.ca/radio/thesundayedition/retired-opp-officer-public-pensions-rebecca-solnit-and-living-like-a-monk-1.2904812.

129. David Brooks, "The Rush to Therapy," New York Times, Nov. 9, 2009, accessed July 22, 2015, http://www.nytimes.com/2009/11/10/opinion/10brooks.html?_r=0.

130. Chopra, Spontaneous Fulfillment of Desire, 90.

131. Stephen R. Covey, The 3rd Alternative: Solving Life's Most Difficult Problems. (New York: Simon & Schuster, 2011), 31.

132. Tama Kieves, "Facebook page," accessed July 22, 2015, https://www.facebook.com/TamaKieves?fref=nf.

133. C. Otto Scharmer, Theory U: Leading from the Future as it Emerges (San Francisco: Berrett-Koehler, 2007), 27.

134. C. Otto Scharmer, "Addressing the Blind Spot of our Time," accessed July 22, 2015, https://www.presencing.com/sites/default/files/page-files/Theory_U_Exec_Summary.pdf.

135. Maya Angelou, "On leadership, courage and the creative process," accessed July 22, 2015, http://www.washingtonpost.com/blogs/on-leadership/wp/2014/05/28/maya-angelou-on-leadership-courage-and-the-creative-process/.

136. Charles de Lint, "Quotable Quote," accessed July 22, 2015, http://www.goodreads.com/quotes/273984-it-s-all-a-matter-of-paying-attention-being-awake-in.

137. David K. Reynolds, A Handbook for Constructive Living (Honolulu: University of Hawai'i Press, 2002), 124.

138. Scharmer, Leading from the Emerging Future, 216.

139. Ibid, 216.

140. Ghandi, "Quotable Quote," accessed July 22, 2015, http://www.goodreads.com/quotes/2253-live-as-if-you-were-to-die-tomorrow-learn-as .

141. Thoreau, Walden, 267.

142. Bob Chapman, "What is Truly Human Leadership?," accessed August 26, 2015, http://www.trulyhumanleadership.com/.

143. Barry-Wehmiller, "We're Building a Better World," accessed July 22, 2015, http://www.barrywehmiller.com/.

144. "Conscious culture," accessed July 22, 2015, http://www.consciouscapitalism. org/culture.

145. Scharmer, Leading from the Emerging Future, 4.

146. H. James Harrington and Frank Voehl, quoting Lester R. Bittel, The Organizational Master Plan Handbook (Boca Raton: CRC Press, 2012), 34.

147. Tama Kieves, "The Genius Code: How One Step Creates Everything," accessed July 22, 2015, http://www.tamakieves.com/ezine/ezine.041311.html.

Step 11 — Transformational Leadership

148. Thich Nhat Hanh, Reprinted from Call Me By My True Names (1999) by Thich Nhat Hanh with permission of Parallax Press, Berkeley, California.

149. Theodore Roosevelt, "The Man in the Arena," accessed July 22, 2015, http:// www.theodore-roosevelt.com/trsorbonnespeech.html.

150. Brené Brown, Daring Greatly (New York: Gotham Books, 2012), 2.

151. Ibid, 2.

152. James MacGregor Burns, Leadership (New York: Harper, 1979), 20.

153. Kendra Cherry, "What is Transformational Leadership?" accessed July 22, 2015, http://psychology.about.com/od/leadership/a/transformational.htm.

154. Navi Radjou, Jaideep Prabhu, and Simone Ahuja, "How SAP Labs India Became an Innovation Dynamo," Harvard Business Review, April 2013, accessed July 22, 2015, https://hbr.org/2013/04/ how-sap-labs-india-became-an-i.

155. Bernard M. Boss and Ronald E. Riggio, Transformational Leadership (Mahway: Lawrence Erlbaum Associates Inc, 2006), 3.

156. Susan Adams, "Disconnected from your job? So are two thirds of your fellow workers," Forbes, Dec. 2013, accessed July 22, 2015, http://www.forbes.com/sites/susanadams/2013/06/12/ disconnected-from-your-job-so-are-two-thirds-of-your-fellow-workers/.

157. Sherpa Executive Coaching, "2015 Coaching Survey," accessed July 22, 2015, http://www.sherpacoaching.com.

158. Noer, Breaking Free, 185.

159. Eagle's Flight, "About Eagle's Flight," accessed July 22, 2015, http://www.eaglesflight.com/company.

160. Simon Sinek, "Leaders Eat Last: Why some teams pull together and others don't," accessed July 22, 2015, http://www.success.com/mobilenodeview/22331.

161. W. Timothy Gallwey, The Inner Game of Work (New York: Random House, 2001), 8.

Step 12 — Keeping It Fresh

162. Thich Nhat Hanh, Reprinted from Happiness: Essential Mindfulness Practices (Berkeley: Parallax Press, 2009).

163. Anne Morrow Lindbergh, Gift from the Sea (New York: Vintage Books, 1991), 108.

164. T. S. Eliot, "Little Gidding," accessed July 21, 2015, http://www.columbia.edu/itc/history/winter/w3206/edit/tseliotlittlegidding.html.

165. Dan Schawbel, "Shawn Achor: What You Need To Do Before Experiencing Happiness," accessed July 21, 2015, http://www.forbes.com/sites/danschawbel/2013/09/10/shawn-achor-what-you-need-to-do-before-experiencing-happiness/.

166. Herb Kelleher, "Managing in Good Times and Bad," accessed July 21, 2015, https://www.youtube.com/watch?v=wxyC3Ywb9yc.

167. Groucho Marx, accessed July 26, 2015, http://www.goodreads.com/quotes/80713-i-not-events-have-the-power-to-make-me-happy.

168. Anne Frank, Diary of a Young Girl (New York: Doubleday, 1995), 107.

169. Csikszentmihalyi, The Evolving Self, 293.

170. Stephen R. Covey, accessed August 26, 2015, https://www.stephencovey.com/7habits/7habits-habit1.php.

171. Senge, Presence, 148.

172. Paolo Coelho, quote from "Brida," accessed July 21, 2015, http://www.goodreads.com/work/quotes/3252430-brida.

173. Covey, The 7 Habits, 287.

174. Rilke, Letters to a Young Poet, 30.

175. Howard Zinn, You Can't Be Neutral on a Moving Train (Boston: Beacon Press, 2002), 208.

176. Louise Palmer, "Growing Hope," accessed July 21, 2015, http://spirituality-health.com/articles/growing-hope.

177. Ibid.

178. Emily Dickinson, "'Hope' is the thing with feathers," accessed July 21, 2015, http://www.poetryfoundation.org/poem/171619.

179. Thich Nhat Hanh, Anger (New York: Riverhead Books, 2001), 69.

180. John Amodeo, Dancing with Fire (Wheaton: Theosophical Publishing, 2013), 11.

CPSIA information can be obtained at www.ICGtesting.com
Printed in the USA
LVOW07*1153210116

471124LV00006B/30/P